PSYCHOSYNTHESIS

SUNY SERIES IN

TRANSPERSONAL AND HUMANISTIC PSYCHOLOGY

RICHARD D. MANN, EDITOR

PSYCHOSYNTHESIS

A Psychology of the Spirit

JOHN FIRMAN *and* ANN GILA

STATE UNIVERSITY OF NEW YORK PRESS

Published by
STATE UNIVERSITY OF NEW YORK PRESS
ALBANY

For information, address
State University of New York Press
90 State Street, Suite 700, Albany, NY 12207

Production, Laurie Searl
Marketing, Anne M. Valentine

Library of Congress Cataloging-in-Publication Data

Firman, John, 1945–
    Psychosynthesis : a psychology of the spirit / by John Firman and Ann Gila.
    p. cm. — (SUNY series in transpersonal and humanistic psychology)
    Includes bibliographical references and index.
    ISBN 0-7914-5533-5 (alk. paper) — ISBN 0-7914-5534-3 (pbk. : alk. paper)
    1. Transpersonal psychology. 2. Psychosynthesis. I. Gila, Ann. II. Title. III. Series.

BF204.7 .F575 2002
150.19'8—dc21
                                                                    2002017736

10   9   8   7   6   5   4   3   2   1

To those who worked, played, laughed, and cried with us in the Psychosynthesis Institute. We all learned a great deal the hard way.

CONTENTS

ACKNOWLEDGMENTS

First, we would like to express our deepest gratitude to our colleague and friend, Chris Meriam, for his generous support throughout the writing of this book. His authenticity, compassion, and knowledge of the path were immensely valuable to us. Chris not only encouraged and advised us at various points in this writing but was actively involved in providing feedback and editorial changes in the content of the book.

Many thanks also to Philip Brooks, who read the manuscript in its entirety and engaged in extended theoretical discussions with us. Philip's friendship, heartful presence, and clinical wisdom were significant in the writing of this book.

We would like as well to warmly acknowledge John Thatcher for his many insightful comments and helpful questions about the manuscript; David Klugman for reviewing our treatment of modern psychoanalysis and for sharing his personal story; Anne Ziff for allowing us to quote her own personal experience; and John White for his help and support in the publication of both of our books with State University of New York Press.

Our gratitude also goes to David "Pope" Firman, John's brother, who rendered all of the many illustrations for the book. Pope's patient care, artistic ability, and technical knowledge were invaluable in the production of this book.

Finally, since this text derives from our work with individuals and groups over the past thirty years, we would like to extend our gratitude to all of our students and clients over these years for sharing their personal journeys with us.

INTRODUCTION

Psychosynthesis presupposes psychoanalysis, or, rather, includes it as a first and necessary stage.

—Roberto Assagioli

I believe psychoanalytic method and theory is a necessary sub-structure for any such "higher" or growth psychology.

—Abraham Maslow

Roberto Assagioli was an Italian psychiatrist who, in 1910, rejected what he felt was the psychoanalytic overemphasis on analyzing the childhood dynamics underlying psychopathology. Accordingly, he conceived "psycho*synthesis*," emphasizing how the human being integrated or synthesized the many aspects of the personality into increasing wholeness. An early student of psychoanalysis, Assagioli respected and valued Freud's views but considered them "limited" (Assagioli 1965a). Here, Assagioli, in an interview with *Psychology Today*, describes his relationship to early psychoanalysis:

> I never met Freud personally but I corresponded with him and he wrote to Jung expressing the hope that I would further the cause of psychoanalysis in Italy. But I soon became a heretic. With Jung, I had a more cordial relationship. We met many times during the years and had delightful talks. Of all modern psychotherapists, Jung is the closest in theory and practice to psychosynthesis. (Keen 1974, 2)

As Jung would do after him, Assagioli became a psychoanalytic "heretic," refusing to accept Freud's reductionism and neglect of the positive dimensions of the human personality. Psychosynthesis thus became the first approach, born of psychoanalysis, which would include: the artistic, altruistic, and heroic potentials

1

of the human being; a validation of aesthetic, spiritual, and peak experiences; the insight that psychological symptoms can be triggered by spiritual dynamics (often now called *spiritual emergency*); and the understanding that experiences of meaning and purpose in life derive from a healthy relationship between the personal self and a deeper or higher Self in ongoing daily living, or what is called *Self-realization*. These concerns were later to place psychosynthesis within the developing fields of humanistic and transpersonal psychology.

By developing psychosynthesis, Assagioli sought, then, to address not only the resolution of early childhood issues—a focus on what he called the *lower unconscious*—but to give attention to the sphere of aesthetic experience, creative inspiration, and higher states of consciousness—which he called the *higher unconscious* or *superconscious*. He sought to give each of these central dimensions of human experience its proper due, avoiding any reduction of one to the other.

So although extending beyond psychoanalysis, Assagioli did not intend to leave Freud's system completely behind. In the first of his two major books, *Psychosynthesis* (1965a), Assagioli envisioned psychosynthesis as founded upon a psychoanalytic exploration of the lower unconscious:

> We have first to penetrate courageously into the pit of our lower uncon-
> scious in order to discover the dark forces that ensnare and menace us—the
> "phantasms," the ancestral or childish images that obsess or silently domi-
> nate us, the fears that paralyze us, the conflicts that waste our energies. It
> is possible to do this by the use of the methods of psychoanalysis. (21)

As this exploration of the unconscious proceeded—including the higher unconscious and *middle unconscious* as well—the individual was more free to develop a conscious relationship with a deeper or higher Self beyond the conscious personality or, in Assagioli's words, "widening the channel of communication with the higher Self" (27).

This relationship with Self could then guide a new synthesis of the personality embracing the fruits of the prior self-exploration and, more, it could become a source of direction and meaning in a person's life. This ongoing relationship with Self, emerging from prior exploration of the unconscious, is called Self-realization and is a fundamental principle of psychosynthesis.

For Assagioli, then, analytic work was an essential part of the personal exploration upon which the process of psychosynthesis was based. Assagioli seemed clear that both psychoanalysis and psychosynthesis were needed to work with the whole person.

THE PSYCHOANALYSIS-PSYCHOSYNTHESIS SPLIT

Over the years, however, psychosynthesis (at least within the English-language literature) drifted away from the developments taking place in psychoanalysis and from a focus on the lower unconscious. In the words of Will Friedman, cofounder of the Psychosynthesis Institute of New York, psychosynthesis "lost touch with its psychoanalytic roots" (Friedman 1984, 31). And psychologist Frank Haronian, former vice president of the Psychosynthesis Research Foundation, warned that psychosynthesis needed "to pay more attention to the lower unconscious," because it was overlooking "human weaknesses and limitation" (Haronian 1983, 31, 27).[1]

It seems that an important reason for this separation from psychoanalysis was that Assagioli and later psychosynthesis thinkers had basic philosophical differences with Freud. Assagioli's stance was in strong conflict with, for example, Freud's reductionistic drive theory, his contempt for spirituality and religion, and his insistence upon a disengaged attitude on the part of the analyst.

Assagioli could not include such principles in his system, because they were fundamentally at odds with his view of human nature. He saw personal selfhood, choice, and responsibility existing at a more essential level than the drives, validated the spiritual and religious dimensions of life on their own terms, and maintained that authenticity and empathic connection were central to psychotherapy. At a most basic level, Assagioli understood the human being not as an isolated individual to be observed but as a subject in continuous, active interaction with a larger relational field:

> Indeed, an isolated individual is a nonexistent abstraction. In reality each individual is interwoven into an intricate network of vital, psychological and spiritual relations, involving mutual exchange and interactions with many other individuals. (Assagioli 1965b, 5)

Given these basic differences, among many others, psychoanalysis and psychosynthesis were destined to follow two very separate courses of development.

THE SYSTEMS EVOLVE

As psychosynthesis developed, it tended to focus on personal growth, self-actualization, and the higher unconscious, while having less to say about early human development or the roots of psychological disturbances. It went on to become one of the early systems within the larger movements of existential/humanistic psychology and transpersonal psychology. These latter approaches too were moving beyond the Freudian focus on the lower unconscious and psychopathology in order to study what Abraham Maslow (1971) called "the farther reaches of human nature."

Assagioli, along with the likes of C. G. Jung, Abraham Maslow, and Carl Rogers, was considered an important figure in the "new pathways in psychology" and "the post–Freudian revolution" (Wilson 1972) and a major early thinker in transpersonal psychology (Boorstein 1980; Scotton, Chinen, and Battista 1996).

Indeed, psychosynthesis notions such as *Transpersonal Self* or *Higher Self,* *higher unconscious* or *superconscious, subpersonalities, identification, disidentification,* and the *observing self* or *"I"* have infused the thinking of many in contemporary psychological movements. Furthermore, many of these movements also utilize traditional psychosynthesis techniques such as guided imagery, creative use of visualization, dialoguing with parts of the personality, disidentification, exploring levels of identification, and relating to an inner symbol of wisdom.

Psychoanalysis, on the other hand, followed its own developmental line beyond Freud, and as it happened, toward some of Assagioli's earlier relational conceptions. As psychosynthesis before it, psychoanalysis too became part of the global paradigm shift toward viewing reality not as composed of isolated objects interacting in space but as a vast system in which all things—including the observer—are included and interrelated. From Einstein's earthshaking insights, Heisenberg's uncertainty principle, and Bertalanffy's general systems theory, to family systems theory, the women's movement, and nature-centered spiritualities, to the environmental agenda, the "global village," and religious ecumenism, existence itself was being revealed as fundamentally relational.

> This trend towards synthesis is already apparent and is spreading more and more; psychosynthesis is only bringing its own contribution to it.
>
> —Roberto Assagioli

As psychoanalysis moved in this relational direction, it increasingly perceived the person not as the isolated object of Newtonian mechanics but as an interactive part of a relational system or field. The notion of the isolated individual struggling with inner drives began to yield to a concept of the person as an integral part of a larger whole. This relational stance is represented in today's psychoanalysis by, for example, object relations theory, self psychology, and intersubjective psychology. Each of these, in its own way, attempts to focus on the interactive field, and each is a part of a major paradigm shift toward what has been called the *relational model* in psychoanalysis (Mitchell 1988).

TOWARD INCLUDING A
PSYCHOANALYTIC PERSPECTIVE

It would appear, then, that the time is ripe for psychosynthesis to move toward a deeper engagement with psychoanalytic insight and, further, to include current research into early childhood development as well. This is one of the tasks that we attempt to accomplish in this book.

However, it is important to understand that this increased inclusion of a psychoanalytic perspective does not mean a blending of all the formal concepts of psychoanalysis and psychosynthesis into a unified theory, nor does it necessarily forge any sort of elaborate theoretical common ground between practitioners of these systems. Rather, there is here simply an attempt to expand and deepen Assagioli's original conception so that it can more fully embrace the important dimensions of human experience traditionally left to depth and developmental psychologies—again, the inclusion of these dimensions seems to have been Assagioli's original intention.

In this approach, Assagioli's understanding of Self-realization can become the central organizing principle synthesizing three important areas in a psychology of the whole person: developmental theory, personality theory, and clinical theory. These three areas are revealed as intimately connected, illuminating and supporting Self-realization in all practical applications of psychosynthesis.

DEVELOPMENTAL THEORY

Here is elaborated a theory of human development that is not only founded upon core psychosynthesis thought but is at the same time coherent with modern psychoanalysis, intersubjective psychology, attachment theory, and current infant research. Following Assagioli's understanding of a relationship to Self, this relationship is seen as the essential bond or connection by which the human spirit flourishes throughout the life span. The supportive holding provided by this relationship allows us to negotiate developmental stages, harmonize our personalities, and find meaning and direction in our lives. A relationship with Self is present at any and all stages of development, manifesting within significant inner and outer environments, and so Self-realization itself is not considered a particular stage of human development.

PERSONALITY THEORY

From this developmental perspective arises a theory of personality in which an intact relationship with Self is seen to allow a creative engagement with the many diverse facets of the human personality—body, feelings, mind, intuition, imagination, drives, subpersonalities, and so on. This natural multiplicity may form an inner coherence or community within the inclusive empathic field of the person who is in turn held within the empathic field of Self. The higher and lower unconscious are not here seen as naturally occurring personality structures or levels of development; rather, these sectors of the unconscious are considered the result of wounding to the relationship with Self, and are found to underlie many psychological disturbances both mild and severe, personal and transpersonal. The view here is that both the higher and lower unconscious are sectors in need of ongoing exploration and integration.

CLINICAL THEORY

If an intact empathic relationship with Self allows for the emergence of the human spirit, a coherent expression of personality, and a sense of meaning in our lives, then it follows that a disruption in this empathic connection will cause disturbances in these areas. Furthermore, if an empathic disruption causes wounding, it can only be that an empathic connection can heal this wounding. Thus a profound empathic intersubjective resonance between the psychosynthesis practitioner and client becomes the healing center of all work in psychosynthesis. The functioning of an empathic field is perhaps the most important way that Self operates in psychosynthesis practice and, again, without this empathy there can be no true healing and transformation. While the breadth of psychosynthesis allows the use of many techniques and methods from widely different approaches, these are completely secondary to this empathic resonance.

Reviewing these three areas, it is clear that psychosynthesis can be of special help to those who work with the heights and depths of human experience, with psychological difficulties and spiritual practices, and with integrating the transcendent in daily life. On the one hand, we need not avoid psychological work, believing that this is a sidetracking of our spiritual path or an ensnarement in illusion; on the other hand, we need not consider religious experience a psychological symptom nor spiritual practice a defense mechanism.

Psychosynthesis instead addresses the common experience in which psychological difficulties, interpersonal challenges, personal self-actualization, and higher states of consciousness all exist side by side in the same personality—the situation, after all, of most of us. But even more important than this, psychosynthesis seeks to recognize and support the particular life journey of the person—the individual's own unique path of Self-realization.

THE PURPOSES OF THIS BOOK

We have written *Psychosynthesis: A Psychology of the Spirit* with several purposes in mind:

- The case examples and practical theory in this book are designed to support those seeking to understand and facilitate their own personal journey of Self-realization. While this does not take the place of walking this path with fellow travelers and/or experienced guides, here there is helpful information about much of the terrain that may be encountered during such a journey.

- As a foundational text, this work is useful for beginning and advanced psychosynthesis courses, professional training programs, or any course of study seeking a transpersonal integration of developmental, personality, and clinical theory. We here address the seven essential topics of psychosynthesis training outlined by Assagioli: disidentification, the personal self or "I," the will, the ideal model, synthesis, the superconscious or higher unconscious, and Self (1974).[2]

- It also is appropriate for general psychology courses, as it reveals some of the relationships between psychosynthesis and contemporary developmental research, object relations theory, self psychology, intersubjective psychology, trauma theory, the recovery movement, Jungian psychology, humanistic and transpersonal psychology, and common psychological diagnoses.

- Finally, educators, social workers, career counselors, personal coaches, therapists, spiritual directors, physicians, pastoral counselors, nurses, and parents will find herein a broad framework within which they can apply their particular expertise. Since psychosynthesis is not a technique but a broad integrative view of the human being, it can provide a useful context for a wide variety of applications.

THE CONTENTS OF THIS BOOK

While this book elaborates on much of the traditional material found in the psychosynthesis literature since the 1970s, it also integrates some current advances in psychosynthesis thought.

Many of these newer developments are further detailed in our book *The Primal Wound: A Transpersonal View of Trauma, Addiction, and Growth* (1997). This current volume may be considered a companion to that work, which in turn is supported by John Firman's earlier effort, *"I" and Self: Re-Visioning Psychosynthesis* (1991). Brief descriptions of the chapters follow.

Taken together, the Introduction and Chapter 1 outline a history of psychosynthesis. We describe Assagioli's involvement with early psychoanalysis and his apostasy from it, the evolution of psychoanalysis and psychosynthesis, and the later place of psychosynthesis within humanistic and transpersonal psychology.

Chapters 2 and 3 describe and extend two of the most fundamental aspects of psychosynthesis theory—the model of the person and the stages of psychosynthesis—initially outlined in the first chapter of Assagioli's seminal book, *Psychosynthesis: A Manual of Principles and Techniques* (1965a). New developments in both conceptions are elaborated.

Chapter 4 employs an extended case example to elaborate an important insight of psychosynthesis: that the normal personality can be seen to comprise different parts, or subpersonalities. We outline a view of subpersonality formation and the phases of harmonization.

Chapter 5 plumbs the depths of Assagioli's notion of personal identity, showing that the essence of this identity is formed within a relational matrix. Topics include empathy, disidentification, dissociation, consciousness and will, and transcendence-immanence.

Chapter 6 presents a uniquely psychosynthetic developmental theory founded in Assagioli's seminal ideas. Here psychosynthesis is shown to resonate strongly with aspects of object relations theory, self psychology, attachment theory, and modern infant research.

Chapter 7 deals with the levels of the unconscious and how they are formed by empathic misattunement from the environment. Using an adaptation of Assagioli's original model, an understanding of different psychological disorders is suggested.

Chapter 8 closes the book with a discussion of Self-realization, the subject toward which all other chapters have pointed in different ways. Self-realization is seen as an ongoing relationship with a deeper Self over the human life span, a relationship that gives meaning and direction to human life. Here, Self-realization is understood not as a destination but as a journey.

> I consider it [psychosynthesis] as a child—or at the most as an adolescent—with many aspects still incomplete; yet with a great and promising potential for growth.
>
> —Roberto Assagioli

In sum, we can say that psychosynthesis is a system that attempts to understand both analysis and synthesis, both wounding and healing, both personal and transpersonal growth, and both abyss and peak experiencing. Again, and above all, this is a perspective that allows an empathic connection to the unique human person, no matter what the stage of healing and growth, and draws upon techniques, methods, and practices only from within this empathic understanding.

ONE

THE LIFE AND WORK
OF ROBERTO ASSAGIOLI

He was very early. Who was there to hear such a large and balanced statement? Not many . . .

—from a eulogy for Roberto Assagioli, *Synthesis 2*

In 1909, C. G. Jung wrote to Sigmund Freud about a young Italian psychiatrist in training, Roberto Assagioli (1888–1974), who seemed to be a promising candidate to develop psychoanalysis in Italy. Jung wrote of Assagioli as

> a very pleasant and perhaps valuable acquaintance, our first Italian, a Dr. Assagioli from the psychiatric clinic in Florence. Prof. Tanzi assigned him our work for a dissertation. The young man is very intelligent, seems to be extremely knowledgeable and is an enthusiastic follower, who is entering the new territory with the proper *brio*. He wants to visit you next spring. (McGuire 1974, 241)

If one reads *The Freud/Jung Letters* (McGuire 1974), it is clear that Assagioli was indeed "an enthusiastic follower" deeply interested in the early psychoanalytic movement. He contributed the article "Freud's Theories in Italy" to the *Jahrbuch für Psychoanalytische und Psychopathologische Forschungen*, the psychoanalytic periodical conceived by Freud and edited by Jung; was published in the journal *Zentralblatt für Psychoanalyse*, listed with the likes of Karl Abraham, Ludwig Binswanger, A. A. Brill, and Jung (Berti 1988); was a member of the psychoanalytic group, formed by Jung in 1910, whose elected president was Ludwig Binswanger, later famous for *Daseinsanalyse* or *existential analysis*; and received psychiatric training under renowned psychiatrist Paul Eugen Bleuler—who coined the terms *schizophrenia, ambivalence,* and *autism* (Gay 1988)—at the Burghölzli Hospital of the University of Zürich, where Jung also had trained.

However, when Assagioli did complete his doctoral dissertation at the University of Florence, he had entitled it not "Psychoanalysis" but rather "Psychosynthesis" (*"La Psicosintesi"*). So even at this early date, Assagioli was beginning to move beyond Freud's psychoanalysis:

> A beginning of my conception of psychosynthesis was contained in my doctoral thesis on Psychoanalysis (1910), in which I pointed out what I considered to be some of the limitations of Freud's views. (Assagioli 1965a, 280)

In developing psychosynthesis, Assagioli sought not only to employ *analysis*—analytic insight into the human personality and its dysfunction—but *synthesis* as well, an understanding of how human growth moves toward increasing wholeness, both within the individual and in the individual's relationship to the world at large.

Assagioli agreed with Freud that healing childhood trauma and developing a healthy ego were necessary aims, but he held that human growth could not be limited to this alone; he sought an understanding of human growth as it proceeded beyond the norm of the well-functioning ego into the blossoming of human potential, which Abraham Maslow (1954, 1962, 1971) later termed *self-actualization*, and further still into the spiritual or transpersonal dimensions of human experience. A quotation from the *Textbook of Transpersonal Psychiatry and Psychology* follows:

> Whereas Maslow explored fundamental issues in transpersonal psychology, Roberto Assagioli pioneered the practical application of these concepts in psychotherapy. Assagioli proposed a transpersonal view of personality and discussed psychotherapy in terms of the synthesis of personality at both the personal and spiritual levels. He dealt with the issue of spiritual crises and introduced many active therapeutic techniques for the development of a transcendent center of personality. (Scotton, Chinen, and Battista 1996, 52)

In other words, Assagioli envisioned an approach to the human being that could address both the process of personal growth—of personal healing, integration of the personality, and self-actualization—as well as transpersonal development—that dimension glimpsed, for example, in *peak experiences* (Maslow) reported during inspired creativity, falling in love, communing with nature, scientific discovery, or spiritual and religious practice. Assagioli (1965a, 1973a) called these two dimensions of growth, respectively, *personal psychosynthesis* and *spiritual* or *transpersonal psychosynthesis*.

As we shall see, subsequent evolution of Assagioli's thought has understood the personal and transpersonal dimensions as distinct developmental lines within the larger process of what he called *Self-realization*. In his concept of Self-realization, Assagioli recognized a deeper *Self* operating supraordinate to the conscious personality. This Self not only provides direction and meaning for individual unfoldment—both personal and transpersonal—but operates as a source of *call* or *vocation* in life. Such call invites us to discover and follow our deepest truth, the most essential meaning and purpose in our lives, and to live this out in our relationships with ourselves, other people, nature, and the planet as a whole.

Psychosynthesis is, therefore, one of the earliest forerunners of humanistic psychology and transpersonal psychology—the third and fourth forces in the history of psychology—which emerged in the 1960s to join the first two forces, behaviorism and psychoanalysis (see Scotton, Chinen, and Battista 1996). Assagioli's conception of personal psychosynthesis has an affinity with humanistic psychology and other approaches (such as existential psychology) that attempt to understand the nature of the healthy personality and the actualization of unique, personal selfhood. Similarly, his conception of transpersonal psychosynthesis is related generally to the field of transpersonal psychology with its study of mystical, unitive, and peak experiences in which the individual moves beyond a sense of independent selfhood to experience a unitive and universal dimension of reality. Accordingly, Assagioli served on the board of editors for both the *Journal of Humanistic Psychology* and the *Journal of Transpersonal Psychology*.

> We accept the idea that spiritual drives or spiritual urges are as real, basic and fundamental as sexual and aggressive drives.
>
> —Roberto Assagioli

So what were the influences on this man who developed a system that so early foreshadowed these important movements in psychology?

ROBERTO ASSAGIOLI AND HIS INFLUENCES

Any discussion of influences on a person's life begins most naturally with personal history. However, Assagioli was notoriously reticent about discussing his life. He felt that it was a mistake to focus too much on his own personality rather than on the development of his work. He seemed concerned that such a focus on personality might lionize him, perhaps even encourage the view that he was a spiritual teacher or guru rather than the practicing clinician and psychological thinker he was. Such a distorted perception of himself might have, in turn, distorted the perception of psychosynthesis, leading people to mistake it for a spiritual teaching or a philosophical doctrine rather than the open-ended, evolving, psychological system he had created. In light of this, it makes sense, too, that Assagioli was not interested in leading some sort of movement or organization, and thus he staunchly refused any administrative control over the development of psychosynthesis as a whole.[1]

It was only toward the end of his life that Assagioli finally did—yielding to pressure from his colleagues—choose a biographer, the Boston psychotherapist, Eugene Smith. But Assagioli died shortly thereafter, and Smith was left with little direct information from Assagioli himself and thus remained largely dependent on Assagioli's friends and colleagues for biographical information (Rindge 1974). But even this biography has never seen the light of day, so it is no surprise to find that there exists little in the literature about Assagioli's life.

While we may lament this dearth of material—along with those who pressed him for a biography—this lack happily follows Assagioli's own personal wishes. He obviously believed that psychosynthesis should be evaluated on its own merits rather than on the pedigree or personality of its creator. Perhaps we can keep this in mind as we explore the biographical data we do have and move through this to examine psychosynthesis itself as the most valid field for uncovering the influences on Assagioli.

BIOGRAPHY

Roberto Assagioli was born Roberto Marco Grego in Venice, Italy, on February 27, 1888. He was the only child of Elena Kaula (1863–1925) and Leone Grego (?–1890). Leone died when Roberto was about two years old, and his mother then married Dr. Emanuele Assagioli.[2]

The Assagiolis were "a cultured upper-middle-class Jewish family" (Hardy 1987), and to this Judaism was added Elena's later interest in Theosophy. The family spoke Italian, French, and English at home, and during his life Roberto also was to study German, Latin, Greek, Russian, and Sanskrit. Clearly, richly diverse currents of philosophy, culture, and religion ran through Assagioli's life from his earliest years.

The family moved from Venice to Florence in 1904 so that Roberto could study medicine at the Istituto di Studi Superiori, and "from 1905 on his friends in Florence were the young philosophers, artists, and writers who were responsible for the cultural and literary review *Leonardo*" (Smith 1974). He trained with Bleuler in Switzerland, as noted above, studied psychoanalysis, made the acquaintance of C. G. Jung, and became especially interested in the work of William James and Henri Bergson. He received his medical degree from the University of Florence, with specializations in neurology and psychiatry. He wrote in 1910 the dissertation, "Psychosynthesis," which contained a critique of psychoanalysis.

> In 1911 I presented my view on the unconscious in a paper at the "International Congress of Philosophy" in Bologna.
>
> —Roberto Assagioli

Upon entering practice as a psychiatrist, he also in 1912 founded the bimonthly scientific periodical, *Psiche* (*Psyche*), editing and writing for this until it folded in 1915, due to World War I. This journal published "the first of Freud's writings in Italian, translated by Assagioli and approved and authorized by Freud himself" (Berti 1988, 25).

During World War I, Assagioli was a "lieutenant-doctor," and after the war he married Nella Ciapetti, a Roman Catholic and Theosophist. He and Nella were married for forty years and had one son, Ilario (1923–1951). Roberto's mother died in 1925, and a year later he founded what became the Istituto di Psicosintesi in Rome, "with the purpose of developing, applying and teaching the various techniques of psychotherapy and of psychological training" (Assagioli 1965a, 280). The following year, the Institute published the book, *A New Method of Treatment—Psychosynthesis*, in English.

In the 1930s, Assagioli produced perhaps two of the most seminal articles in psychosynthesis to this day. First written and published in Italian, they also were translated into English and appeared in the *Hibbert Journal*. These two articles eventually became the lead chapters in his later book, *Psychosynthesis* (1965a), under the titles "Dynamic Psychology and Psychosynthesis" and "Self-Realization and Psychological Disturbances." The first article outlines two fundamental constructs in psychosynthesis—the basic psychosynthesis model of the person and the stages of psychosynthesis—and will form the framework for the next two chapters of this book as well. The latter article concerns the tumultuous experiences that may attend a spiritual awakening, and it has been republished many times over the years, from a *Science of Mind* journal (Assagioli 1978), to a popular intellectual journal (Assagioli 1991a), to an important book in the field of spiritual emergency (Grof and Grof 1989) and, finally, to a compendium dealing with depression (Nelson and Nelson 1996).

World War II proved to be much more of a disruption in the life and work of Dr. Roberto Assagioli than was the first war. His institute in Rome was closed by the Fascist government, which was critical of his "Jewish background, his humanitarianism, and his internationalism" (Smith 1974). The government then accused him of being a pacifist, because he claimed that true peace could only be found within, and not by violent, political, or legal means—and consequently he was locked in solitary confinement for a full month. But Assagioli made use of his imprisonment by making it what he called a "spiritual retreat," focusing on meditation and his inner life, and he recorded the following transpersonal experience during this time:

> A sense of boundlessness, of no separation from all that is, a merging with the self of the whole. First an outgoing movement, but not towards any particular object or individual being—an overflowing or effusion in all directions, as the ways of an ever expanding sphere. A sense of universal love. (in Schaub and Schaub 1996, 20–21)

There are varying accounts of Assagioli's activities after his release from prison, one author writing that he joined the underground north of Rome

(Smith 1974), and another that he and his son, Ilario, were forced to hide in the Italian countryside, with Ilario possibly contracting tuberculosis from which he eventually died in the early 1950s (Hardy 1987).

After the war, Assagioli founded the Istituto di Psicosintesi at via San Dominico 16, in Florence, where he lived and worked for the rest of his life. He wrote, "from 1946 onwards courses of lectures on psychosynthesis . . . were given in Italy, Switzerland and England; and further articles and pamphlets were published in various languages" (Assagioli 1965a, 280). By the 1960s, psychosynthesis institutes had been founded in the United States, Greece, England, Argentina, and India, and several international conferences had been held.

> International Conventions on Psychosynthesis were held at Villeneuve near Montreux, Switzerland, in 1960 and 1961, and in Rome in 1967.
>
> —Roberto Assagioli

Assagioli always took spiritual matters seriously, both personally and professionally. He was known to practice hatha yoga, raja yoga, and various types of meditation, and he also was involved in Theosophy (discussed later). In both his own practice and his work, he placed particular emphasis on service, understanding this as the most natural expression of Self-realization. For example, in the 1950s, he founded the Italian Union for Progressive Judaism, which was "based on an attitude of openness, and of understanding and collaboration with other peoples and religions" (Berti 1988, 38).

Over the years, Assagioli's interest in different spiritual and philosophical traditions led to contact with such notables as Jewish philosopher Martin Buber, esotericists P. D. Ouspensky and Alice Bailey, sage Lama Govinda, Indian poet Rabindranath Tagore, astrologer Dane Rudhyar, Sufi mystic Inhayat Khan, Buddhist scholar D. T. Suzuki, logotherapy founder Viktor Frankl, and humanistic psychologist Abraham Maslow.

Assagioli died on August 23, 1974, at age eighty-six, in his villa in Capalona, Arezzo, which he had named after his beloved son Ilario. Shortly after his death, one eulogy pointed out with wonder how early Assagioli had conceived of psychosynthesis, and how long he had to wait before its more general acceptance:

> He was very early. Who was there to hear such a large and balanced state-ment? Not many people in the twenties, not in the thirties, not in the for-ties, not in the fifties, were ready. It was only in the late sixties that, with the suddenness born of deep and massive need, his books and other writ-ings were taken up by thousands. Almost sixty years needed to elapse, so far was he ahead of his time. (in Vargiu 1975)

By the time of the publication of the *International Psychosynthesis Directory 1994–1995* (Platts 1994), there were 107 institutes operating in thirty-two countries, and international conferences were being held on a regular basis.

INFLUENCES REVEALED IN ASSAGIOLI'S WORK

Assagioli seems to have written and edited his entire professional career, writing more than 150 articles and essays during his life, although many were reportedly lost when the Fascists ransacked and dynamited his home during the war (Smith 1974). There appear to be no complete unpublished manuscripts, although the institute he founded has a wall of boxes filled with small notes he made during his professional life. His two major English-language books still remain *Psychosynthesis* (1965a) and *The Act of Will* (1973a), although a posthumous collection of articles, *Transpersonal Development* (1991b), also was published.

In agreement with Assagioli himself, we believe that it is to his writings more than to his biography that we must turn to recognize the influences he brought into his work. His major books bristle with references to leaders of Western psychology, from Freud, Jung, Adler, and Rank to Maslow, William James, Richard Bucke, Viktor Frankl, and Rollo May. But he drew from disciplines beyond psychology as well, referring also to Bach, Mozart, and Beethoven; St. John of the Cross, St. Catherine of Sienna, and St. Dominic; Socrates, Plato, and Aristotle; Dante, Emerson, and Thoreau; Nietzsche, Teilhard de Chardin, and Evelyn Underhill; Patanjali, Radhakrishnan, and Vivekananda; Ghandi, Schweitzer, Buber, and Martin Luther King; and the Buddha and Christ. Further, Assagioli discusses experiential states from diverse traditions such as the dark night of the soul, samadhi, prajna, satori, and cosmic consciousness, as well as subjects such as yin and yang, Shiva-Shakti, and the Tao.

Clearly, Assagioli's psychological work, while remaining true to his psychiatric training and clinical experience, also embraced an appreciation for many diverse cultures and traditions. In our teaching at the Institute of Transpersonal Psychology, each year we realize anew the breadth of Assagioli's thought as graduate students respond to their introductory course in psychosynthesis. These are students keenly interested in the connection between psychology and spirituality, and they come from many different spiritual traditions. As they study psychosynthesis, they often recognize principles from their own tradition in aspects of psychosynthesis, and so they infer that their tradition has been an important influence on Assagioli.

For example, one student demanded to know why Assagioli did not reference Ramana Maharshi, since psychosynthesis obviously drew upon the thought of that Hindu sage. Another wrote in his term paper that psychosynthesis was so coherent with his meditation practice that Buddhism must have been a strong influence on Assagioli, while a Christian student wondered why psychosynthesis had not been taught in her seminary, since it so clearly was founded on Christian principles. A longtime practitioner of Jewish mysticism claimed that he could see the Kabbala in the models of psychosynthesis; a teacher within a shamanic tradition said that her tradition and psychosynthesis were viewing the same reality from different directions; and a Rosicrucian wrote that her attraction to psychosynthesis derived from its similarity to that system.

Such speculations about the possible influences on Assagioli are not reserved to those new to psychosynthesis. Some in the field apparently believe that psychosynthesis is the "exoteric expression" or a "stepped-down version" of Theosophy, particularly as developed by Alice Bailey, with whom Assagioli worked—even though psychosynthesis was conceived in 1910 or earlier, and Assagioli did not join Bailey's group until 1930 (Berti 1988, 33). Assagioli was indeed active within the Theosophical movement subsequent to his creation of psychosynthesis, but even then, he strove to keep what he called a "wall of silence" between these two spheres of his work, ever cautioning against confusing the two. He wrote clearly that psychosynthesis was to remain neutral toward religion and metaphysics, and that it should not be confused with them (more later on this).

IN CONCLUSION

What, then, may we conclude from this vast range of possible influences on Assagioli and psychosynthesis? Precisely this: Whether such influences made any direct explicit impact or not, Assagioli has succeeded in developing an approach that, while firmly rooted in Western psychology, is yet consistent with widely disparate traditions. Thus it is a psychology suitable for use within a broad range of different traditions.

Unlike Freud's psychoanalysis, for example, psychosynthesis does not adopt a reductionistic view of religious and spiritual experience but quite the reverse—it embodies a profound respect for the fundamental spiritual nature of the human being and a supportive attitude toward the development of this dimension of human experience. This is not to say that psychosynthesis is itself a spiritual path, a metaphysical philosophy, or a religion. Rather, its purpose is to remain a psychology, a "nondenominational" psychology, so to speak, and thus available to any and all spiritual paths. According to Assagioli:

> At this point the question may arise as to the relationship between this conception of the human being [psychosynthesis] on the one hand and religion and metaphysics on the other. The answer is that psychosynthesis does not attempt in any way to appropriate to itself the fields of religion and of philosophy. It is a scientific conception, and as such it is neutral towards the various religious forms and the various philosophical doctrines, excepting only those which are materialistic and therefore deny the existence of spiritual realities. Psychosynthesis does not aim nor attempt to give a metaphysical nor a theological explanation of the great Mystery—it leads to the door, but stops there. (1965a, 6–7)

Having surveyed this vast array of influences, it can yet be said that psychosynthesis, while doubtlessly born and developed among these influences, remains distinct from them all. It remains a psychological approach, "neutral towards the various religious forms and the various philosophical doctrines," which can therefore be employed with the utmost respect for the spirituality, philosophy, culture, ethnicity, and worldview of the unique, individual person. In short, it remains a profoundly empathic discipline that does not ignore or pathologize the central experiences and meanings of people's

> It is first and foremost a dynamic, even a dramatic conception of our psychological life . . .
>
> —Roberto Assagioli

lives but rather recognizes and values these. Psychosynthesis is not a doctrine or teaching in which to believe, nor a religion or spirituality to be practiced; it is an open, developing psychology that seeks to facilitate human growth within the context of a person's *own* deepest aspirations and life path.

The next two chapters elaborate two of the most fundamental constructs of psychosynthesis thought—the basic model of the human person and the stages of psychosynthesis—presented by Assagioli in the first of his two seminal articles, "Dynamic Psychology and Psychosynthesis," mentioned above.

TWO

THE PSYCHOSYNTHESIS MODEL
OF THE PERSON

Freud said, "I am interested only in the basement of the human being." Psychosynthesis is interested in the whole building.

—Roberto Assagioli

In 1931, Assagioli published the seminal pamphlet, *Psicoanalisi e Psicosintesi* (*Psychoanalysis and Psychosynthesis*), in which he presented the fundamental outline of psychosynthesis theory and practice. So key is this work that it was translated into English and published again in 1934, and it finally was revised to become the lead chapter of his first book, *Psychosynthesis* (1965a), under the title, "Dynamic Psychology and Psychosynthesis." This article begins by placing psychosynthesis historically within the development of Western psychology, beginning with Pierre Janet, moving through Freud, Adler, Rank, and Jung, and including Karl Abraham, Sandor Ferenczi, Wilhelm Stekel, Melanie Klein, Karen Horney, Erich Fromm, Ludwig Binswanger, and Viktor Frankl.

After setting this historical context, including some comments about broader cultural movements (e.g., psychosomatic medicine, the psychology of religion, interest in Eastern psychology, etc.), Assagioli presents the vital core of psychosynthesis theory, outlining (1) the basic psychosynthesis model of the person and (2) the stages in the process of psychosynthesis. He thereby presents both the structure or "anatomy" of the person as well as the growth and transformation—the "physiology"—that one encounters over the course of psychosynthesis. This chapter examines the basic psychosynthesis model of the person, and the next chapter presents the stages of psychosynthesis.

ASSAGIOLI'S DIAGRAM OF THE PERSON

Assagioli's basic model of the person has remained an integral part of psychosynthesis to the present time. Assagioli (1965a) said that this model was "far from perfect or final" (16), and that it was "of course, a crude and elementary picture that can give only a structural, static, almost 'anatomical' representation of our inner constitution" (17). In light of these words, we shall develop here an understanding of this model that brings it more into alignment with current thinking in psychoanalysis, developmental psychology, contemporary psychosynthesis, and the study of psychological disturbances and childhood wounding. A modified version of the original diagram is presented in Figure 2.1.

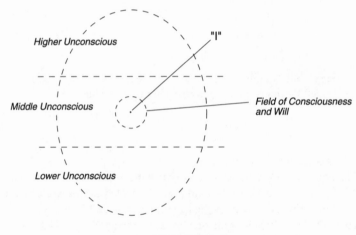

FIGURE 2.1

The major difference between this diagram and the original is that *Self* (or *Transpersonal Self*) is not depicted at the apex of the higher unconscious, half inside and half outside the oval. Instead, Self is not represented at all and should be imagined as pervading all of the areas of the diagram and beyond. The need for this change will be discussed at the end of the chapter.

One general comment about the diagram is that Assagioli understood the oval to be surrounded by what C. G. Jung called the *collective unconscious* (unlabeled), or "a common psychic substrate of a suprapersonal nature which is present in every one of us" (Jung 1969a, 4). This realm surrounds and underpins the personal unconscious and represents propensities or capacities for particular forms of experience and action common to us all. The collective is the deepest fount of our shared human potential, or as Assagioli wrote, "The collective unconscious is a vast world stretching from the biological to the spiritual level" (1967, 8).[1] In the words of Jung, the [collective] unconscious is not merely conditioned by history, but is the very source of the creative impulse. It is like Nature itself—prodigiously conservative, and yet transcending her own historical conditions in her acts of creation. (Jung 1960, 157)

A last general comment about Assagioli's diagram is that the different levels of the unconscious constitute a spectrum of potentially conscious experience. That is, these various strata are called "unconscious," simply because the material contained in them is not within the immediate field of awareness. But the dotted lines shown separating the sectors indicate that contents from these sectors may move through these boundaries—a "psychological osmosis" (Assagioli 1965a, 19, 68)—and thus may enter consciousness under different circumstances. The dotted lines also symbolize the fact that even when unconscious material remains unconscious, it nevertheless causes effects, sometimes powerful effects, in a person's conscious life (e.g., one may find an unconscious feeling of rage or fear wreaking havoc in interpersonal relationships, or one may be inspired to self-transformation by a pattern in the collective unconscious). Let us now examine this diagram in some detail, knowing that we will further explore most aspects of the diagram in later chapters as well.

THE MIDDLE UNCONSCIOUS

Assagioli wrote that the middle unconscious "is formed of psychological elements similar to those of our waking consciousness and easily accessible to it. In this inner region our various experiences are assimilated" (Assagioli 1965a, 17). Thus this is the area in which we integrate the experiences, learnings, gifts, and skills—guided by the patterns from the collective unconscious and in relationship to our particular environment—that form the foundation of our conscious personality. In order to understand the middle unconscious, then, it is necessary to discuss how we form our inherited endowments and life experiences into a coherent, personal expression of ourselves in the world.

> There is no hard and fast division between conscious and unconscious.
>
> —Roberto Assagioli

As many researchers have noted (e.g., Bowlby 1969; Piaget 1976; Stern 1985), from the earliest stages of life we form inner patterns that constitute maps or representations of our ongoing experience of self and other. Through these inner patterns—called variously *schema* (Piaget), *internal working models* (Bowlby), or *representations of interactions that have been generalized* (Stern)—we understand ourselves and our world, develop our personalities, and learn to express ourselves.

According to Jean Piaget, this mapping can begin with the most basic reflexes, such as sucking. Here forming a map or pattern (Piaget's *schema*) for sucking allows the infant to apprehend the sucking reflex and to incorporate it into a more elaborate pattern of volitional behavior: "After sucking his thumb during fortuitous contact, the baby will be able, first, to hold it between his lips, then to direct it systematically to his mouth for sucking between feeding" (66). So it seems that even our most basic preverbal senso-rimotor functions are mapped and then integrated into more elaborate structures of self-expression.[2]

This developmental achievement is, of course, conditioned by the pre-existing pattern within the collective unconscious: "The entire pattern—thumb-to-mouth—is an intrinsically motived, species-specific behavioral pattern" (Stern 1985, 59). This learning also takes place within a facilitating matrix of empathic nurture provided by caregivers; as has been said, archetypal patterns need to be triggered by a facilitating environment (Neumann 1989) or what we will call a *unifying center*.

This inner structuralization pertains to all dimensions of human experience, including physical, emotional, cognitive, intuitive, imaginal, and transpersonal. It appears that through interacting with the different aspects of our own psyche-soma, and with the environment, we gradually build up structures that synthesize various elements of our experience into meaningful modes of perception and expression.

Whether learning to walk, acquiring language skills, developing roles within family and society, or forming particular philosophical or religious beliefs, we go about this by synthesizing patterns of experience into increasingly complex structures—guided by the innate proclivities from the collective unconscious and our unique social environment. But what does this have to do with the middle unconscious?

THE ROLE OF UNCONSCIOUSNESS

It is important to recognize that while certain patterns are the building blocks for more elaborate structures, the individual building blocks themselves must remain largely unconscious for the structures to operate. The diverse elements that form the more complex expressions cannot remain in consciousness, or we would simply be unable to function beyond the most basic level; our awareness would be so filled with the many individual elements, that a focus on broader, more complex patterns of expression would be impossible.

The following statement by Piaget illustrates the importance of individual elements remaining out of awareness: "Hence we can quickly walk down a flight of steps without representing to ourselves every leg and foot movement; if we do, we run the risk of compromising this successful action" (41). That is, if the many elements of the movement were not somewhat unconscious, our awareness would be filled with them (their "representations"), thereby impairing the larger movement. Assagioli also writes about this natural role of the unconscious:

... there occurs a gradual shifting from a conscious focusing of the full attention on the task to an increasing delegation of responsibility to the unconscious, without the direct intervention of the conscious "I." This process is apparent in the work of acquiring some such technical accomplishment as learning to play a musical instrument. At first, full attention and conscious direction of the execution are demanded. Then, little by little, there comes the formation of what might be called the mechanisms of action, i.e., new neuromuscular patterns. The pianist, for example, now reaches the point at which he no longer needs to pay conscious attention to the mechanics of execution, that is, to directing his fingers to the desired places. He can now give his whole conscious attention to the *quality* of the execution, to the expression of the emotional and aesthetic content of the music that he is performing. (Assagioli 1973a, 191)

In other words, if we must be aware of the many discrete patterns involved in walking down a stairway, playing the piano, speaking a language, or performing a social role, we will be unable to perform these actions at all. We will instead be overwhelmed by the array of diverse elements making up the action. But by remaining *unconscious* of these many elements, we can enjoy a smooth, volitional movement. This is a function of the middle unconscious: to store many individual elements outside of awareness so that they may be synthesized into novel, more complex modes of expression. They become what John Bowlby (1980) called *automated systems* within the personality.

The concept of the middle unconscious thus indicates a sector of a person whose contents, although unconscious, nevertheless remain available to normal conscious expression. The middle unconscious demonstrates the wondrous gift of human unconscious functioning, "that plastic part of our unconscious which lies at our disposal, empowering us with an unlimited capacity to learn and to create" (Assagioli 1965a, 22). This "plastic" or pliable quality describes the capacity to embed patterns of skills, behaviors, feelings, attitudes, and abilities outside of awareness, thereby forming the infrastructure of our conscious lives. This is why the middle unconscious is depicted as immediately surrounding the consciousness and will of "I," the essence of personal identity.[3]

SUBPERSONALITIES

Central among the structures of the middle unconscious are what Assagioli (1965a) called *subpersonalities*. These are semi-independent coherent patterns of experience and behavior that have been developed over time as different expressions of a person.

For example, continuing Assagioli's example of the man learning to play the piano, we might envision that person, over time, synthesizing many elements—technical skill, natural ability, knowledge of theory, love of music, a joy of performance—into a pianist identity, a pianist subpersonality. This he would have accomplished by drawing on patterns established by past musicians and by being held within a social milieu suitable to nurture this development.

This subpersonality has become a structure within the larger personality by which these learnings and gifts may be expressed. An identity system has been born, a subpersonality, from which the person may experience and act in the world as a pianist. Of course, this will be only one of his subpersonalities, and this subpersonality will have to relate to other subpersonalities that he has developed in expressing other aspects of himself.

While subpersonalities are not limited to the middle unconscious, they often are the most striking psyche-somatic structures to move in and out of awareness on a daily basis. Subpersonalities are common even in psychologically healthy people, and while their conflicts can be the source of pain, they should not be seen as pathological. They are simply discrete patterns of feeling, thought, and behavior that often operate out of awareness—in the middle unconscious—and emerge into awareness when drawn upon by different life situations. Again, their formation has followed the same process that we saw earlier in more basic structuralizations of the personality (e.g., the thumb-to-mouth behavior).

A common way to become aware of subpersonalities is to notice that we seem to become "different people" in different life situations. For example, we may be dynamic and assertive at work but may find ourselves passive and shy in relationships; or we may find our self-confidence suddenly collapsing into anxiety and even panic in the face of an authority figure; or we may surprise others when our easygoing disposition turns to ferocious competitiveness when playing a sport. These are not momentary moods but consistent, abiding patterns—subpersonalities—moving into and out of consciousness from the middle unconscious.

> The organization of the sub-personalities is very revealing and sometimes surprising, baffling or even frightening.
>
> —Roberto Assagioli

Subpersonalities can be harmonized into a more coherent expression of the whole person through a variety of different techniques. Such work may or may not involve integrating them into a larger whole, but it will tend toward a situation in which each part can make its unique contribution to the life of the person. Although we devote Chapter 4 to subpersonalities, let us take a brief look at working with a subpersonality.

THE CASE OF LAURA

A woman we shall call Laura[4] entered counseling because she found herself acting like a helpless child when relating to her parents and other perceived authority figures. She would become childlike and passive with such people and then finally become angry when she was ignored. This had been causing difficulties in all of her adult relationships, and especially now with her current boyfriend.

Over the course of counseling, Laura realized that this younger part of herself was a subpersonality—she called it "Little One"—with particular feelings of anxiety, shame, and anger. She began relating to this subpersonality instead of attempting to get rid of it, and she became increasingly familiar with how it responded to other people and how it influenced her daily behavior. In listening to the subpersonality, Laura gradually became aware of Little One's deeper needs for acceptance, affection, and safety, and she began to intentionally make more room in her life for these valid human needs.

This work involved Laura in some brief, lower unconscious exploration as well. She uncovered the childhood roots of her negative feelings and had the painful realization that her parents, although nurturing in many ways, had been emotionally unavailable at a very basic level. She also came to see that her inward rejection of Little One replicated her parents' rejection of her.

As Laura formed an ongoing, empathic relationship with the subpersonality, there was a marked decrease in the feelings of anxiety, shame, and anger, and she found herself less and less overcome by these problematic feelings in her relationships. Furthermore, the positive qualities of Little One—creativity, playfulness, and spontaneity—became more available to her as well, enriching her relationships as never before.

Laura was involved primarily with the middle unconscious, in that she sought to develop an ongoing, conscious relationship with a subpersonality that moved easily into and out of awareness. Although she also did some lower unconscious investigation (uncovering the childhood conditioning of the subpersonality) and had some contact with the higher unconscious (unlocking the positive potential of the subpersonality), she remained focused upon work with the middle unconscious.

PROFUNDITY, DEPTH, AND CREATIVITY

The function of the middle unconscious can be seen in all spheres of human development, from learning to walk and talk, to acquiring a new language, to mastering a trade or profession, to developing social roles. All such elaborate syntheses of thought, feeling, and behavior are built on the learning and abilities that must eventually operate unconsciously. It is important to remember that the individual elements of these structures are not extinguished but merely operate in the unconscious—thus they often can be made conscious again if need be.

There also is a mysterious profundity of the middle unconscious that can be seen in the creative process. Here we may have been working toward a creative solution to a problem, become frustrated, and finally let go of consciously working on it, only to suddenly have an "Aha!" in which the solution appears to our consciousness fully formed. This type of experience is common in human creativity (see Vargiu 1977), in flashes of intuitive insight, and in the wisdom of nocturnal dreaming. Such experiences make sense in light of the middle unconscious, an active, organizing area operating outside of consciousness that can draw together many disparate elements into new patterns, wholes, or syntheses that can then become available to conscious functioning. As Assagioli wrote, in the middle unconscious "our ordinary mental and imaginative activities are elaborated and developed in a sort of psychological gestation before their birth into the light of consciousness" (Assagioli 1965a, 17).

The depth of the middle unconscious has further been revealed by biofeedback research. Here autonomic processes formerly thought to be beyond voluntary control—such as brain waves, heart rate, and blood pressure—have been brought under the influence of consciousness and will through various feedback devices. Similarly, the study of the mind-body connection in medicine has shown that conscious beliefs, attitudes, and images can influence physical health and disease. All of this research illustrates the interplay between consciousness and the deepest levels of psyche-soma organization in the middle unconscious, that supportive, unconscious substrate of our conscious lives.

> Paradoxically, paying conscious attention to, or being emotionally preoccupied with, creative processes disturbs them.
>
> —Roberto Assagioli

Last, the middle unconscious is that area in which we integrate material from the repressed sectors of the unconscious. As we shall discuss shortly, sectors of the personality have been rendered unconscious not in service of self-expression but in order to manage psychological wounding. After discovering and reowning repressed material, whether the heights of transpersonal experience or the depths of childhood wounding, we eventually can integrate these into expressive patterns that support our lives rather than disrupt them.

So the gift of unconsciousness is clear. It is that ability by which aspects of the personality remain outside of consciousness and yet make an active contribution to conscious expression. Here is a potential for developing increasingly creative modes of self-expression, allowing us to bring the widest range of our human potential to our lives. If we had to remain continuously conscious of all of the minute, individual components of our inner and outer expressions, we would function with only a very small percentage of our potential.

As we saw earlier in the case of Laura, it also may be that some of these structures in the middle unconscious are disruptive of our conscious functioning due to early wounding. In these cases, the process of structuralization will involve accessing and healing the wounded pattern, thereby allowing that aspect of ourselves to come into harmony with the personality as a whole. We shall discuss this process more fully in Chapter 4.

Having said all of this about the gift of unconsciousness, we must now say that this gift also is pressed into service of a much more desperate purpose—to survive within a traumatizing environment. Because such an environment is hostile to certain aspects of our experience, these aspects are simply too dangerous and disruptive to be a part of our day-to-day functioning. We therefore seek, in effect, to push these aspects of experience well beyond consciousness, well beyond the middle unconscious, and thereby to form areas of the unconscious that are not simply unconscious but repressed as well—the *higher unconscious* and *lower unconscious*. Unlike the middle unconscious, these realms of the unconscious are not in close communion with conscious functioning but are areas that we attempt to insulate completely from consciousness.

Before examining the lower unconscious and higher unconscious, let us first briefly discuss the wounding that we believe creates them, what we have called *primal wounding* (Firman and Gila 1997).

PRIMAL WOUNDING

As Freud (1965) recognized, there is not only an unrepressed unconscious available to conscious functioning but a repressed unconscious, an area of the personality forcefully kept beyond the reach of consciousness and will (Freud's *unconscious*). Repression is simply an extreme use of the "plastic" or malleable quality of the unconscious, of our ability to keep areas of our personalities out of awareness. But in repression we do not use unconsciousness to empower consciousness through a supportive, deep structure. We instead attempt to defend consciousness by permanently separating aspects of ourselves from consciousness. From what are we defending ourselves by these extreme measures? We defend against primal wounding.

Primal wounding results from violations of a person's sense of self, as seen most vividly in physical mistreatment, sexual molestation, and emotional battering. Wounding also may occur from intentional or unintentional neglect by those in the environment, as in physical or emotional abandonment; from an inability of significant others to respond empathically to the person (or to aspects of the person); or from a general unresponsiveness in the surrounding social milieu. Furthermore, wounding is inflicted by "the best of families"— some of what we thought was acceptable and normal in child rearing is now found to be harmful (Miller 1981, 1984a, 1984b).

In sum, it seems that no one among us has escaped some amount of debilitating primal wounding in our lives. All such wounding involves a breaking of the empathic relationships by which we know ourselves as human beings; it creates an experience in which we know ourselves not as intrinsically valuable human persons but instead as nonpersons or objects. In these moments, we feel ourselves to be "It"s rather than "Thou"s, to use Martin Buber's (1958) terms. Primal wounding thus produces various experiences associated with facing our own potential nonexistence or nonbeing: isolation and abandonment, disintegration and loss of identity, humiliation and low self-worth, toxic shame and guilt, feelings of being overwhelmed and trapped, or anxiety and depression/despair.

When we undergo primal wounding, we repress the experience in an attempt to prevent it from affecting our ongoing functioning. By forcing the wounding from consciousness, we seek to protect ourselves from its impact and create some semblance of safety within the traumatizing environment.

However, we not only repress the pain and trauma but also those valuable aspects of ourselves that were threatened in the wounding. True, we banish the pain so that our consciousness and will are not overwhelmed, and we can continue to function. But we also cleverly seek to protect and preserve the aspects of ourselves vulnerable to wounding by submerging them in the unconscious.

So, for example, if we expressed our creativity as a child, and this was rejected and shamed by others, we would quickly learn that it was dangerous to be creative, and that we must instead learn the rules and abide by them. In order to survive in such an environment, we strive to form ourselves into a more constricted, controlled personality, a mode of being in which creativity is not felt or expressed.

But in order to form such a personality, we have to somehow rid ourselves of creative impulses as well as the painful experiences of shame. We accomplish this by *splitting* (Fairbairn 1986; Freud 1981; Klein 1975) the shame experience from the experience of creativity within us. In this way we inwardly preserve the creativity safe from the shame. Then we repress both the shame and the creativity so that we can function oblivious of these dangerous experiences. This splitting and repression allow us to survive in an environment in which there is a rejection of our creative potential, because now the environment appears safe—there is now, seemingly, no shaming and no creativity in this world, thus there is no danger. We have survived the wounding.

Staying with the example of the repression of creativity, we can imagine that later in life we find that our days are beginning to seem endless and dreary, that something essential is missing. In exploring the roots of this crisis, we may uncover a powerful need to break the bounds of our rigid life, to be spontaneous, to express creativity. However, simultaneously we may feel extremely anxious, as if our very identity were threatened by this (seemingly) new potential. Phrases such as "You'd better do this perfectly or not at all" or "Watch out or you'll show how inept and worthless you are" might ring in our minds. These critical and shaming messages are precisely the other side of the creativity-shame split in us that we created long ago in the early nonempathic environment. Now, in reowning the creativity, we need to face the early shame as well. Both sides of the original split may now emerge to be owned, healed, and integrated.

> But whatever is repressed returns later, and often in disguise, to claim its due.
>
> —Roberto Assagioli

Over the course of our lives, there have been many wounding events and environments that have necessitated this type of splitting and repression, and all of us function with some amount of this. Thus the repressed area of the unconscious may be quite extensive and can be seen as having two distinct sectors. The sector in which are hidden the rich human potentials threatened by wounding—perhaps our ability to love, create, express joy, commune with nature, or sense a unity with the Divine—is called the *higher unconscious*. Similarly, the sector that hides the pain of the wounding—whether from covert or overt neglect and abuse—is called the *lower unconscious*. The lower unconscious and higher unconscious are the other two major levels of the unconscious represented in the oval diagram (Figure 2.1). We now will examine each of these areas in turn.[5]

THE LOWER UNCONSCIOUS

The lower unconscious is that realm of ourselves to which we relegate the experience of overwhelming woundings that we have suffered in our lives. Since a repressed unconscious is, by definition, inaccessible to consciousness, its presence must be inferred; this inference is drawn from moments in which highly charged material emerges into consciousness, which in retrospect had been present all along outside of awareness. (We will, for simplicity's sake, employ usages such as "lower unconscious experience" and "higher unconscious experience" when referring to experiences of material originating in each sector.) The emergence of lower unconscious material can be seen in the words of a man in psychotherapy:

> I always thought I'd had a great childhood. My parents seemed like they were always there for me, and all my friends used to say they wished they had my parents instead of theirs. But hitting my 40s, after my divorce, I began to have all this depression, feeling really bad about myself, and feeling abandoned by everyone, even my friends. It was very confusing and scary at first.
>
> But then I began to examine those feelings and see they were coming from a child part of me who had felt totally abandoned by my parents. Looking back, I could see that I had always felt this way at some level. And then I finally began to get that my parents were chronic functional alcoholics. They never missed a day's work or forgot one of our birthdays, but alcohol was always there acting as a barrier between them and us kids.

If we look back into this man's life, it is clear that he functioned up until his forties with no awareness of this experience of abandonment by his parents. He had become a successful, skilled professional, learning to express himself in productive ways that made full use of his middle unconscious. Yet a fundamental aspect of his life experience—his abandonment, depression, and low self-esteem—was never allowed into consciousness. Triggered by the divorce, this abandonment depression emerged from the lower unconscious into the middle unconscious and began to enter into his awareness until he was impelled to address this in therapy.

As this level of himself began to become conscious, it was at first "very confusing and scary." Why? Because the existence of such feelings went counter to the identity by which he had survived, that identity which was based upon the affirmation, "My parents were great." But this smoothly functioning and successful identity, under the stress of his divorce, began to be disrupted, and this deeper layer of his unconscious began to reveal itself. Here was a stunning challenge to the view he had of himself and others throughout his whole life.

Obviously, then, the lower unconscious exists in the present and affects our daily lives. In fact, this splitting of our experience also makes us blind to the current violation and neglect of ourselves by other people and by society in general. We may be relatively unaware of how we are personally affected by the tremendous level of violence pervading modern life, and indeed, we may be unaware of this even when we are the direct victims or perpetrators of this violence. This repression of the traumatic thus can support a variety of dramatic departures from authentic being and our sense of self, including naive optimism, otherworldly spirituality, and chronic patterns of abuse.

> The lower unconscious contains . . . many complexes, charged with intense emotion.
>
> —Roberto Assagioli

So note well: The lower unconscious does not simply comprise experiences we have had in the past and then repressed; it is our lost ability to experience the tragic dimension of existence.

SURPRISED BY PAIN

When material from the lower unconscious suddenly breaks through to consciousness, we may be "surprised by pain," as were Robert and Rachel. Robert entered therapy because his wife Rachel was complaining of his chronic demeaning attitude toward her, and she had threatened divorce if he did not correct this. Initially, Robert simply saw his behavior as "just joking around" and Rachel as being "too sensitive." But gradually he became aware of his rage underlying his behavior, and beneath that rage, the feelings of shame and worthlessness from childhood. As he got in touch with this childhood wounding, he recognized the abuse entrenched in his family of origin and so became sensitive to the hidden abuse in his own behavior.

As Robert began to change his demeaning attitude, Rachel found it necessary to work on her own attitude of contempt and on her need to control, which often triggered Robert's worthlessness and rage. Rachel also found herself exploring her own early wounding as she struggled to change. As they worked through their wounding and the reactions to this, Robert and Rachel gradually were able to create a safe, healing environment that could support their own growth and that of their children.

Robert and Rachel were "surprised by pain"—they experienced a disrupting emergence of lower unconscious material into their marriage. These feelings and attitudes had always been present, though operating outside of their awareness, and healing here led to a more trusting, intimate relationship.

Thus healing in the lower unconscious is not simply a healing of the past but a healing of the present. In such personal transformation, our here-and-now perception of self and world becomes increasingly clear and accurate; there is a developing freedom from compulsivity and rigidity; and we begin to find a sense of authentic personal identity and power from which to embrace life.

But the lower unconscious is not the only realm of human experience lost to normal, everyday awareness; we may split off not only the dimension of traumatic wounding but the positive dimensions of life as well. This splitting is a way we seek to protect our capacities for wonder, joy, creativity, and spiritual experience from an unreceptive, invalidating environment. This repression of our higher human potential has been discussed as the *repression of the sublime* (Desoille) by psychosynthesis psychotherapist Frank Haronian (1974), and it forms what is called the *higher unconscious*—a realm of ourselves that, like the lower unconscious, exists now, affects us in the present, and is cut off from normal, everyday awareness.

THE HIGHER UNCONSCIOUS

Recall the case of the man above who in his forties became aware of his abandonment depression and began psychotherapy. As he worked with his depression, he began having an inflow of a new kind of positive energy as well. He had a number of experiences in which, at the depths of the pain of his wounding, he felt a new appreciation for himself, his parents, and the world. At one point he had an important peak experience in which he felt connected to all of humanity and to a sense that all things were held by an even deeper presence that he could only call God. Here was a healing of the split from his early years, a reowning of a repressed "lens" through which he could appreciate the mystery and depth of life—an inflow from the higher unconscious.

The higher unconscious (or *superconscious)* denotes "our higher potentialities which seek to express themselves, but which we often repel and repress" (Assagioli 1965a, 22). As with the lower unconscious, this area is, by definition, not available to consciousness, so its existence is inferred from moments in which contents from that level affect consciousness.

Higher unconscious experiences are those moments—often difficult to put into words—in which we sense deeper meaning in life, a profound serenity and peace, a universality within the particulars of existence, or perhaps a unity between ourselves and the cosmos. This level of the unconscious represents an area of the personality that contains the "heights" overarching the "depths" of the lower unconscious. Assagioli says of the higher unconscious:

> From this region we receive our higher intuitions and inspirations—
> artistic, philosophical or scientific, ethic "imperatives" and urges to

humanitarian and heroic action. It is the source of the higher feelings, such as altruistic love; of genius and of the states of contemplation, illumination, and ecstasy. In this realm are latent the higher psychic functions and spiritual energies. (Assagioli 1965a, 17–18)

Note, however, that the higher unconscious does not indicate some realm of pure qualities or essences separated from the world. The characteristics of love, joy, unity, or beauty found in higher unconscious experiences are not independent higher qualities drifting down to the world from some heavenly realm; they describe empirical modes of sensation, feeling, and cognition in which we experience certain aspects of this world in particular ways. Higher unconscious experience is not so much an encounter with another higher world as it is a deeper, an expanded, or a more unitive view of *this* world.

Just as the lower unconscious prevents us from perceiving our own pain and the pain of others, so the higher unconscious is our lost ability to perceive the more sublime or spiritual aspects of the world. Splitting and repression have caused us to become blind to the profound mystery of the world, our unique place within it, and our fundamental relationship to it, to other people, and to the Divine.

Higher unconscious experience has long been studied by Western psychology, and here we will mention some of the thinkers that Assagioli himself regarded as addressing this area. As early as 1901, Canadian psychiatrist Richard Bucke (1967) published his study of higher unconscious experiences in his book, *Cosmic Consciousness*, making him one of the first transpersonal psychiatrists. Around the same time as Bucke's work, psychologist William James (1961) published his classic work on spiritual experience, *The Varieties of Religious Experience*. And adopting a term used by Rudolf Otto, C. G. Jung (1969b) affirmed higher unconscious contents as *numinosum*, which he said could cause an "alteration of consciousness" and pointed to the universality of such experiences.

> The superconscious is only a section of the general unconscious, but which has some added qualities that are specific.
>
> —Roberto Assagioli

Assagioli also believed that Viktor Frankl, in his system of logotherapy, referred to the higher unconscious in speaking of the *noetic* or *noological dimension* and of *height psychology* (Assagioli 1965a, 195, 197). Lastly, Abraham Maslow's study of peak experiences was, in Assagioli's view, dealing directly with the higher unconscious. In Maslow's words:

The term peak experiences is a generalization for the best moments of the human being, for the happiest moments of life, for experiences of ecstasy, rapture, bliss, and the greatest joy. (Maslow 1971, 105)

This quotation is a clear description of higher unconscious experience. As mentioned earlier, Maslow's groundbreaking work was instrumental in the birth of the fields of humanistic and transpersonal psychology. Many others, too numerous to name, have made higher unconscious experience the subject of serious psychological study.

SURPRISED BY JOY

As with the lower unconscious, splitting and repression keep the higher unconscious aspects largely out of awareness—the repression of the sublime. A strong repression of this spectrum of human experience eventually leads toward an uninspired life, a life from which all deeper love, wonder, and greater meaning have been excluded. Here we inhabit only one small dimension of the rich, multidimensional cosmos, adopting an attitude that is matter-of-fact, materialistic, and perhaps jaded or cynical. Unaware, we are cut off from the compassionate touch of the infinite and the eternal, and we come to assume that the deadness of our lives is a deadness of life itself. Again, the split in ourselves is not simply a split in the past but a split in the present; it affects how we experience ourselves and the world on a day-to-day basis.

However, as is the case with the lower unconscious, we can be surprised by the higher unconscious breaking into awareness—this is often what a peak experience is. Here C. S. Lewis' (1955) phrase, "surprised by joy," is very apt, as a seemingly new realm of human experience is revealed before our disbelieving eyes. A vast array of people from many different traditions and cultures throughout history have reported such experiences and have witnessed the power of these moments to transform human life.

But as Assagioli (1965a) pointed out, these higher experiences may surface lower unconscious material as well; we may feel our wounding, our fear, anger, and depression, in the face of this sublime aspect of reality. As the repression barrier is breached, the original reason for the repression—the earlier wounding—also may be brought to light. It is as if our organismic striving for wholeness attempts to bridge this original split between higher and lower, so that an emergence of either sector quite often entails the emergence of the other.[6]

MIDDLE UNCONSCIOUS EXPANSION

The higher unconscious and the lower unconscious become of practical importance, and perhaps a matter for psychosynthesis therapy, as we encounter these areas of potential experience and seek to include them in our lives. As we shall see, the integration of both the higher and lower unconscious is tantamount to an expansion of the middle unconscious; that is, our daily experiential range—the spectrum of reality that we potentially may be aware of and respond to—expands to include more of the heights and depths of human existence.

We shall discuss this type of work more fully later, but let us say here that this integrative expansion of our experiential range allows us to engage the world in a more whole way. The heights and depths of existence are not so much "surprises" but become more a part of our ongoing daily living: we can feel the joy of a sunset and then be touched by a sadness at the transience of life; we can feel the grief of childhood losses and then feel gratitude for the gifts that we have gained; we can fall in love and then be touched by the struggles of our beloved; or we can enjoy the richness and beauty of a forest and then become suddenly pained by humankind's abuse of nature. This wide dynamic range of experience, often repressed and unconscious, becomes more available to us on a daily basis as we integrate the higher and lower unconscious.

Note again that the higher unconscious and the lower unconscious do not simply comprise experiences that we have had and that are now repressed. Rather, they represent a splitting of our experiential range in the moment, and as such, they affect any new experiences that we have. They are not simply areas in which we store past experiences but are broken and missing "lenses" whose loss renders us blind to the heights and depths of existence. Following Bowlby (1980), we can say that "defensive exclusion" cannot only exclude from consciousness information already stored in long-term memory but also information arriving through sensory input in the present moment (i.e., "perceptual blocking").

Having discussed these three levels of the unconscious, we now can turn our attention to the last element of the oval diagram: the "who" who lives and moves among these levels—the human spirit or "I" who possesses the functions of awareness and will. "I" is represented by the point at the center of the oval diagram (Figure 2.1) and also is called *personal self* (written with a lowercase "s" to distinguish personal self from *Self*, written with an uppercase "S").

"I," CONSCIOUSNESS, AND WILL

Recall the case of Laura, described in the earlier section on the middle unconscious. Laura recognized a child subpersonality whose behavior was disrupting her adult relationships, and she was able to facilitate its harmonious inclusion in her life.

Implicit in Laura's transformation was her realization that she was not simply a childish person but that she had a child *part* of herself. This realization gave her the freedom to come into a relationship with this child subpersonality, to take responsibility for working with her, and to learn to nurture her as her parents had been unable to do. In other words, she discovered that her deeper identity was distinct—though not completely separate—from this subpersonality. Here is a movement from the stance "I am a child" to "I have a child." This ability to *identify* with, or *disidentify* from, different aspects of the personality reveals the profound nature of "I."

"I" is the essential being of the person, distinct but not separate from all contents of experience, a characteristic that we call *transcendence-immanence* (Firman 1991; Firman and Gila 1997). That is, Laura realized that she was distinct from—transcendent of—her child subpersonality, and from this disidentification, she found that she could be present to the child and include her—that is, she could be immanent, engaged, with the child. "I" is transcendent, in that "I" cannot be equated to any content, yet "I" is immanent, meaning "I" can be with, embrace, and experience all content. This profound transcendence-immanence is why "I" can be thought of as human spirit and not as a structure, a complex, or an organization of content.

"I" further possesses the two functions of *consciousness* (or awareness) and *will* (or *personal will*) whose field of operation is represented by the concentric circle around "I" in the oval diagram. "I" is placed at the center of the field of awareness and will to indicate that "I" is the one with consciousness and will. "I" is aware of the psyche-soma contents as they pass in and out of awareness; the contents come and go, while "I" may remain present to each experience as it arises. But "I" is dynamic as well as receptive: "I" has the ability to affect the contents of awareness, and can even affect awareness itself, by choosing to focus awareness, expand it, or contract it. Let us first briefly examine consciousness and then will, using Laura's work as an example.

CONSCIOUSNESS

As "I" disidentified from the child subpersonality, Laura's consciousness or awareness was no longer simply that of a child who was feeling completely overwhelmed by anxiety, shame, and anger. Instead, her awareness became open to more adult aspects of her personality from which she could then act in relationship to both the subpersonality and the outer environment. Note that in disidentification, her consciousness did not become dissociated from the feelings of the child, but rather her consciousness expanded to include the adult perspective *as well as* the feelings of the child. This clarification or expansion of awareness takes place as "I" disidentifies from a particular limited identification, and "I" is thereby able to include other perspectives as well—again, the principle of transcendence-immanence.

WILL

This ability to disidentify and become aware of different perspectives demonstrates not only the nature of consciousness but the nature of personal will. As Laura shifted her identification from "I am a child" to "I have a child part of me," she experienced the freedom to make choices that were not totally controlled by the child. She could choose, for example, to relate to the child, to explore her feelings and, finally, to make decisions in her life that were not limited to the perspective of this single part of herself. Laura's freedom clearly illustrates what Assagioli means by the term *will*.

Note that the will of "I" is not, then, the repressive force commonly referred to as "willpower." Willpower usually denotes the domination of one part of the personality by another, as Laura might have done had she attempted to push the child out of her life completely. Quite the contrary, will is that gentle inner freedom to act from a place that is not completely conditioned by any single part of ourselves. Will allows "I" to disidentify from any single perspective, and thereby to be open to *all* of the varied aspects of the personality.

> . . . the central place given in psychosynthesis to the will as an essential function of the self . . .
>
> —Roberto Assagioli

Through these functions of consciousness and will, transcendent-immanent "I" is the focus for engaging all the rich multiplicity of our personalities. Since "I" is that "who" who is able to identify with, and disidentify from, all of the many changing parts of the personality, "I" has the potential of being in communion with all of the parts, of knowing and acting from our wholeness.

THE RELATIONSHIP OF CONSCIOUSNESS AND WILL

The field of consciousness and will is illustrated as a single circle in the oval diagram (Figure 2.1). However, we may think of that circle as representing, in fact, two interpenetrating fields, one of will and one of consciousness. The field of consciousness and the field of will are in constant flux, with one or the other becoming larger and more operational often from one moment to the next.

For example, consciousness may overshadow will: imagine that you are relaxed and enjoying a sunset or a piece of music, allowing your mind to drift. You are not choosing to focus on anything in particular, not limiting your awareness in any way, but instead you are receptive to all of the myriad feelings, thoughts, and images that might arise. In this case, your consciousness is in the foreground, while your will remains in the background. You might even find it difficult to make a decision in this state, being aware of so many possibilities that you are hard put to choose anything at all. You might even know people who tend to be habitually imbalanced toward the awareness pole, who seem to have a broad consciousness but a limited ability to choose, to act.

On the other hand, will may overshadow consciousness: imagine that you are highly focused on riding a bicycle through heavy city traffic. In this experience, you will keep your awareness focused on the traffic, the road conditions, and the position of your bicycle. Instead of allowing yourself to be receptive to any and all content, you choose here to limit your awareness to task-related content only. In this way, your awareness strictly serves the many continual choices needed to ride safely through the traffic. Your will is in the foreground in this situation, with consciousness playing a more secondary or supportive role. There also are people whose will function habitually outbalances their consciousness function—they can be highly effective, making quick choices with ease and competence, but they may, perhaps, have little awareness of how their behavior affects themselves or others.

THE NATURE OF "I"

The nature of "I" is explored in psychotherapy when there is a focus on facilitating (1) the ability to become aware (consciousness) of various aspects of the personality or behavior, and (2) the ability to make choices (will) in relationship to these. This focus is in fact quite common among otherwise very dissimilar psychotherapies. For example, psychoanalysis encourages *free association*, a choice to focus upon the flow of thoughts, feelings, and images within us; humanistic/existential psychology encourages us to explore the reality of our direct experience and to take responsibility for this experience; cognitive-behavioral psychology directs our attention to the thought processes underlying particular moods and allows us to intervene in these; and transpersonal psychology might facilitate an awareness of higher states of consciousness and assist us in expressing these insights in our lives.

The nature of "I" also is revealed in spiritual practices such as vipassana and Zen meditation in the East and contemplative and centering prayer in the West. An aspect of these types of practice is to allow psyche-soma contents to come and go in awareness without becoming caught up in them. The principle is that we can learn to simply sit in silence, being present and mindful to the moment, while allowing sensations and feelings and thoughts and images to pass unhindered through awareness. What is sometimes overlooked is that this is not simply a state of "pure consciousness" but is actually a very intentional state—*we choose or will to remain in this receptive state*. In fact, we may frequently need to choose to bring back consciousness when it is caught up in distracting sensations, thoughts, and feelings.[7]

All such practices, whether psychotherapeutic or meditative, demonstrate that "I" is distinct, though not separate, from all of these contents of experience, in other words, "I" is transcendent-immanent within contents of experience, otherwise it would be impossible to observe such contents continuously coming and going, with our point of view remaining ever-present to each succeeding content. There must be someone who is distinct but not separate from the contents, remaining an observer/experiencer of the contents,

> . . . the direct experience of the self, of pure self-awareness—independent of any "content" of the field of consciousness.
>
> —Roberto Assagioli

and who can choose to affect them. "I" is this transcendent-immanent "who" who is in, but not of, the changing flow of experience and therefore can be present to any and all contents of experience.

This distinction between "I" and the content of experience is implicit in these spiritual practices, but it also is characteristic of any disidentification experience. For example, this distinction is central to Laura's realization that she was not the child subpersonality, that she need not be dominated by it, and that she could learn to care for this younger part of herself. Whereas a person in meditation might observe contents of experience passing into and out of awareness, Laura could observe her child subpersonality coming and going in her awareness. *Here she was not only noticing her sensations, feelings, and thoughts but was conscious of the deeper structure that organized her sensations, feelings, and thoughts.* She thus could realize that she was distinct from (transcendent of) this larger pattern and begin to work with it and include it (become immanent, engaged with the pattern).

Experiences such as these indicate that "I" is not a content or an object of experience but the *subject* of experience. Although "I" may indeed be caught up in strong feelings, obsessive thoughts, or habitual patterns of behavior, "I" is ever the experiencer, distinct but not separate from any of these. As we shall explore later, "I" also can be referred to as no-self or no-thing, because "I" is beyond anything that we can grasp and hold, beyond any content, process, or structure by which we might define ourselves. We shall take up the nature of "I" at length in Chapter 5.

SELF

Pervading all of the areas mapped by the oval-shaped diagram, distinct but not separate from all of them, is *Self*, which also has been called *Higher Self* or *Transpersonal Self*. The concept of Self points toward a deeper source of wisdom and guidance, a source that operates beyond the control of the conscious personality.[8]

Both Assagioli and Jung called this source *Self* and believed that this manifested as a deeper direction in an individual's life. One might experience Self as a movement toward increasing psychological wholeness, toward a growing "fidelity to the law of one's own being" (Jung 1954, 173), or perhaps toward a sense of purpose and meaning in life. Both thinkers also believed that many psychological disturbances were a result of finding oneself out of harmony with the deeper direction indicated by Self.

Jung deemed the experience of this direction of Self *vocation*, an invitation from the "voice of the inner man [or woman]" to undertake the way of individuation. Assagioli spoke of this deeper direction as the will of Self, or *transpersonal will*, and he saw the potential for a meaningful interaction between transpersonal will and *personal will*, or the will of "I." What follows is one example that Assagioli uses to illustrate this relationship of personal will and transpersonal will, the relationship of "I" and Self:

> Accounts of religious experiences often speak of a "call" from God, or a "pull" from some Higher Power; this sometimes starts a "dialogue" between the man [or woman] and this "higher Source." (Assagioli 1973a, 114)

Of course, neither Jung nor Assagioli limited the I-Self relationship to those dramatic experiences of call seen in the lives of great women and men throughout history. Rather, the deeper invitations of Self are potential to every person at all times. As will be discussed later, this deeper direction may be assumed to be present implicitly in every moment of every day, and in every phase of life, even when we do not recognize this. Whether within our private inner life of feelings and thoughts or within our relationships with other people and the wider world, the call of Self may be discerned and answered.

"I" AS AN IMAGE OF SELF

Among all of the elements depicted in the oval diagram, "I" has the most direct and profound relationship with Self. In earlier versions of the diagram, this relationship was illustrated well by a straight dotted line connecting "I" and Self (although the latter was placed at the apex of the higher unconscious). Assagioli spoke of the I-Self connection in the following way:

> ... the personal conscious self or "I," which should be considered merely as the reflection of the spiritual Self, its projection, in the field of the personality. (Assagioli 1965a, 37)

That is, "I" is not a differentiation of Self, not one aspect of Self, not an emanation of some supposed "substance" of Self, but a direct reflection or image of Self. The metaphor here is perhaps a candle flame whose image is reflected in a mirror, or the sun's image reflected on the surface of water. "I," essential human identity, is not an independent, self-sustaining entity but is directly and immediately held in existence by deeper Self.

To approach the metaphor from another angle, we might say that "I" is as indissolubly united to Self as a mirror image is indissolubly united to that which it reflects. Of this profound level of union, Assagioli says, "There are not really two selves, two independent and separate entities. The Self is one" (Assagioli 1965a, 20). There are, indeed, many experiences, known within both religious and nonreligious contexts, which seem to indicate this fundamental human dependency on, and hence unity with, a deeper source of being.

While Assagioli affirms this essential unity of "I" and Self, he also is extremely careful to emphasize the importance of maintaining the distinction between them. As profound as the I-Self unity is, this unity does not imply that "I" is an illusion. To apply the mirror metaphor: the mirror image has a relative or contingent existence, because it is dependent on the source, but this does not mean that its existence is unreal.

Not maintaining this distinction between "I" and Self can lead to serious difficulties in a person's life. Assagioli, along with many others, consistently warns about the dangers of confusing the reflected image with the reflecting source, "I" with Self:

In cases where awareness of the difference between the spiritual Self and the personal "I" is lacking, the latter may attribute to itself the qualities and power of the former, with megalomania as the possible end product. (Assagioli 1976, 10; see also 1965a, 44–45; 1973a, 128)

Thus the notion of "I" as a reflected image of Self can be helpful in understanding the paradoxical unity of "I" and Self. The two selves are one, fundamentally united by Self's act of creation, yet they are two, the image ever remaining an image and not the source.

THE NATURE OF SELF

Assagioli's idea that "I" is a reflection of Self also suggests a way of understanding the nature of Self by analogy to "I." By such an analogy, the nature of "I," which is implicit in personal experience, can be extrapolated to Self, a deeper center not nearly so available to personal experience. Assagioli (1973a, 124–25) himself states that analogy is a method by which to approach an understanding of Self.

The first thing that becomes apparent by this analogy is that Self is living, conscious, willing, Being. That is, if individual I-amness is a reflection of Self, then Self must be deeper I-amness. Self is, therefore, not to be viewed as a blind, undifferentiated unity; nor as an energy field, however subtle and rarefied; nor as an organismic totality; nor as a collective pattern or image of some sort; nor as a higher level of organization; nor as some impersonal or inanimate energy source; rather, it is to be viewed as deeper Being with consciousness and will.

In other words, Self is not some*thing*, not an "it" but some*one*. Self is a "Thou" to whom we may meaningfully relate. It is true that a sense of this "Thou-ness" may be submerged in a powerful moment of experienced union with Self, when "I" and Self are known as one. But quite practically, the ongoing, intimate, empathic relationship of "I" and Self is an "I-Thou"—not an "I-It"—relationship. This view of Self can be seen in Assagioli's words, quoted earlier, in which he affirms the possibility of meaningful "dialogue" with the "higher Source"—an activity that would be nonsensical if dealing with some sort of blind, impersonal cosmic force or universal energy. Such dialoguing is applied in many effective and practical psychosynthesis techniques designed to support a conscious relationship with Self (e.g., see Assagioli 1965a 204–7; Miller 1975), and it also is found in the field of transpersonal psychology (see Vaughan 1985).

... his spiritual Self who already knows his problem, his crisis, his perplexity.

—Roberto Assagioli

Pursuing this analogy of "I" to Self, we come to a second important insight into the nature of Self. If, as stated above, "I" is distinct but not separate from contents of awareness—transcendent-immanent—then Self also may be understood as distinct but not separate from such contents—transcendent-immanent. We might speculate that since "I" is "in but not of" all of the passing sensations, feelings, and thoughts of daily experience, Self is "in but not of" all of the content of all of the levels represented in the oval diagram (and perhaps beyond, as we shall discuss in Chapter 8).

SELF AND THE OVAL DIAGRAM

This transcendent-immanent omnipresence of Self implies that Self may be met at any level of the oval-shaped diagram, but that Self should not be confused with any particular level. Whether encountering the bliss of peak experiences, the more mundane events of daily life, or the depths of early childhood trauma, we can assume that Self is present, active, and available to relationship.

As mentioned earlier, the original oval diagram portrayed Self at the apex of the higher unconscious (on the boundary with the collective), but such a representation tends to obscure just this profound omnipresence and immediacy of Self at all levels of experience. That earlier placement of Self can give the impression that Self is approachable through the higher unconscious only, a view that Assagioli himself appeared to support at times: "The superconscious [higher unconscious] *precedes* consciousness of the Self" (Assagioli 1965a, 198, emphasis added). In effect, the earlier diagram seemed to represent Self-realization as leading, at least initially, upward into higher states of consciousness.

But this belies the fact that our life journey—the following of our path of Self-realization—can lead us to engage any level of experience at any point on the path. What follows is just one of countless examples:

> This morning I sit in prayer, discouraged, angry, and confused. I do my usual intentional connecting with Self, nature, etc. I speak out my anger and hopelessness directly to Self. My situation has not changed. Nothing is happening in my life, no movement is occurring, no changes are imminent. My heart is closed. The events that seemed to portend an opening and a new beginning for me a few days ago are gone. Nothing positive seems to have come from them. It is clarifying for me to speak this way. I feel present and deeply connected to my pain and confusion. The awareness that comes up for me is that I feel very available to myself right now.
>
> As I sit more with this, I can also feel held and supported in my pain and despair—no movement, no inrush of happy feelings—just held. It strikes me that this is Self, the Empathic Therapist at work, engaging me as I attempt to build a bridge with my anger and frustration. I'm more congruent with my feelings now.
>
> I am reminded of how often I attempt to provide a validating, empathic atmosphere for clients as they wrestle with their own difficult feelings and experiences. Often we end a session and they are still with their pain. Their struggle is not resolved but they seem more able to cope

and they often tell me so. Right now I feel this way. More able to cope, not especially liking the experience, but definitely more present to a difficult cycle I am going through. (Meriam 1996, 21–22)

This experience of communion with Self involved little higher unconscious experience but rather a call to engage current feelings of pain and despair, an invitation to "be here now." If we are direct "reflections" of Self, we are held in being throughout the entire range of our experience, and we may be called to engage any point on this range, from the heights to the depths. Remaining faithful to our deepest sense of truth, following our callings or vocations in life, can take us most anywhere and draw upon many different aspects of ourselves. To alter Assagioli's phrase just quoted, it may be anything at all that precedes contact with Self.

Given this observed omnipresence of Self, we and some others in the field (see Brown 1993; Meriam 1996) choose not to represent Self at the apex of the higher unconscious, rendering no image of Self at all, while making it clear that Self is to be understood as active and present throughout all of the levels of the person. We feel that representing Self in the direction of the higher unconscious can give the impression that Self-realization necessarily involves an ascent into the higher unconscious.[9] Others in the field elect to preserve the earlier rendering of Self, although they too agree that the omnipresence of Self throughout all levels must nevertheless be made quite clear (Djukic 1997; Marabini and Marabini 1996).

> Man's [and woman's] spiritual development is a long and arduous journey, an adventure through strange lands full of surprises, difficulties and even dangers.
>
> —Roberto Assagioli

In understanding Self as pervading all levels of the person, we must avoid the mistake of then *equating* Self to the wholeness of the person—Self is not simply the entire oval. Self is not the "totality" of the person, as Jung stated at times (Jung 1969a, 304; 1969b, 502). Self would be distinct but not separate from such a totality, always transcendent of the totality, yet immanent within the totality. In much the same way that "I" can be simultaneously aware of several different feelings and thoughts at one time, so Self might be simultaneously aware of all of the processes of the entire organism (and beyond) at the same time.

In sum, it seems clear that approaching the nature of Self through an analogy to "I" leads to various useful insights, and to the same single conclusion: Whether envisaging a deeper I-amness as the abiding ground of individual I-amness, or envisaging a deeper transcendence-immanence as the source of individual transcendence-immanence, it seems clear that the I-Self relationship can exist throughout all life experiences, in all spheres of life, and in every stage of life. This profoundly intimate relationship is the fundamental axis of the journey called *Self-realization*, discussed in more specific terms later.

Thus we have explored Assagioli's "anatomical" and "static" model of the human person, but what about the psychological "physiology" of the person, the dynamic changes of healing and growth? Keeping the oval diagram in mind, we now turn to the other major framework of psychosynthesis thought and practice outlined by Assagioli: the stages of psychosynthesis.

THREE

THE STAGES OF PSYCHOSYNTHESIS

Let us examine whether and how it is possible to solve this . . . fundamental infirmity of man. Let us see how he may free himself from this enslavement and achieve an harmonious inner integration, true Self-realization, and right relationships with others.

—Roberto Assagioli

Once Assagioli (1965a) presents the model of the person outlined in the previous chapter, he immediately moves into an elaboration of the stage model of psychosynthesis. The first two stages outline the process whereby "I" emerges from various identifications to express the functions of consciousness and will; the second two stages describe how we may then become conscious of, and respond to, the deeper motivations and meanings in our lives, the source of which is termed *Self*.

Curiously enough, although other stage models have been offered within psychosynthesis in the intervening years (e.g., Brown 1983; Ferrucci 1982), Assagioli's original stages apparently have not been further developed in the English-language literature. We here seek to elaborate, update, and expand an understanding of Assagioli's basic stages of psychosynthesis. But before outlining the stages themselves, we would like to make two points that seem important to an understanding of the stages as a whole.

The first point is that the stages of psychosynthesis are not steps in some invariant, sequential process. Assagioli says of them:

But it should be made clear that all the various stages and methods mentioned above are closely interrelated and need not be followed in a strict succession of distinct periods or phases. A living human being is not a building, for which the foundations must be laid, then the walls erected and, finally, the roof added. (Assagioli 1965a, 29)

The stages do, of course, follow a logical progression in which early stages lead naturally to the later stages. However, any particular individual at any specific time may be experiencing the stages well outside of this sequence— we are not "buildings." At one point we may be conscious of stage four, then of stage one, then stage three, and so on. The stages are not hierarchical levels in which earlier stages are subsumed by the later ones; they are sides or facets of the process of psychosynthesis that reveal themselves at different times as our unique journey unfolds. Indeed, we can think of psychosynthesis as manifesting as a whole—all stages simultaneously—while our awareness continually shifts from one facet or stage of psychosynthesis to another.

Quite practically, this means that the stages cannot be used as some sort of yardstick to measure our progress in psychospiritual development. They are not a ladder up which we climb; they are integral aspects of a single process, aspects that will each continue to expand and deepen as the process itself continues to expand and deepen. We never leave any stage behind, but rather we find each one continually becoming foreground and then background as our journey proceeds.

The second thing to be said of the stages as a whole is that Assagioli did not present them as *natural* stages in human development. For example, they do not represent a development sequence unfolding from birth to old age and, in fact, in theory all of the stages of psychosynthesis can be present at any age along the human life span.[1]

Rather than a natural pattern of growth, the stages respond to what Assagioli called "the fundamental infirmity of man [and woman]." In other words, they are a response to a dis-ease, a malady, a brokenness within the human condition. His powerful description of that fundamental infirmity deserves to be quoted in full (he is using "man" in the generic sense, of course):

> In our ordinary life we are limited and bound in a thousand ways—the prey of illusions and phantasms, the slaves of unrecognized complexes, tossed hither and thither by external influences, blinded and hypnotized by deceiving appearances. No wonder then that man, in such a state, is often discontented, insecure and changeable in his moods, thoughts and actions. Feeling intuitively that he is "one," and yet finding that he is "divided unto himself," he is bewildered and fails to understand either himself or others. No wonder that he, not knowing or understanding himself, has no self-control and is continually involved in his own mistakes and weaknesses; that so many lives are failures, or are at least limited and saddened by diseases of mind and body, or tormented by doubt, discouragement and despair. No wonder that man, in his blind passionate search for liberty and satisfaction, rebels violently at times, and at times tries to still his inner torment by throwing himself headlong into a life of feverish activity, constant excitement, tempestuous emotion, and reckless adventure. (Assagioli 1965a, 20–21)

While the above is an accurate, empathic description of the *normal* human condition, it is not for Assagioli a description of the *natural* human condition. He here describes a basic brokenness in the natural condition and, accordingly, his four stages outline a process by which "to heal this fundamental infirmity of man" (21).

As we turn to the stages of psychosynthesis, then, it seems important to understand something about this fundamental infirmity that the stages address. What is the source of this infirmity, and what, precisely, are its effects? The need for answering this question has led to our developing Assagioli's concept of infirmity into a stage that precedes the original four. This stage, stage zero, can be called the stage of *survival of wounding* or the *survival stage*. It describes the state for which the process of psychosynthesis offers a response. Our exploration of the stages of psychosynthesis will therefore begin with a discussion of this survival stage.

STAGE ZERO: SURVIVAL OF WOUNDING

If we look carefully at the fundamental infirmity described by Assagioli above, we see a state characterized by:

1. trance ("the prey of illusions and phantasms," "blinded and hypnotized by deceiving appearances");

2. splitting or fragmentation ("divided unto himself");

3. lack of empathy for self and other ("fails to understand either himself or others"); and

4. compulsions and addictions ("the slaves of unrecognized complexes" and "tries to still his inner torment by throwing himself headlong into a life of feverish activity, constant excitement, tempestuous emotion, and reckless adventure").

As has been described at length elsewhere (Firman and Gila 1997), all of the above are characteristic effects of what we have called primal wounding, that wounding caused when we are not seen as who we truly are:

> In this violation, we are treated not as individual, unique human beings, but as objects; our supportive milieu—whether early caregivers, peers, institutions, or society at large—does not see us as we truly are, and instead forces us to become the objects of its own purposes. (1)

In the previous chapter, we saw that these empathic failures in our lives create experiences such as shame, helplessness, fragmentation, abandonment, isolation, and anxiety, which we then separate from our consciousness to form the lower unconscious. We also separate the positive aspects of our experience such as love, joy, creativity, humor, trust, and connection to the Divine, aspects that were threatened by the wounding, forming the higher unconscious.

By hiding the fact that we are being wounded by the environment, and hiding as well the gifts threatened by it, we are able to manage the wounding and adapt to the nonempathic environment. No longer aware of these areas of experience that are rejected by the environment, we are free to shape our personality into a way of being that allows us to survive in spite of primal wounding.

In other words, we form a personality that is not an expression of our natural, authentic sense of self—not what we have termed *authentic personality* (Firman and Gila 1997)—but rather form a personality that is designed to survive the primal wounding, a formation called *survival personality* (Firman and Gila 1997). Survival personality exists to the extent that our personality is conditioned by survival mechanisms or so-called *defense mechanisms*, oriented to surviving within a nonempathic environment.[2]

SURVIVAL PERSONALITY AND SURVIVAL UNIFYING CENTER

Survival personality may take a wide variety of different forms depending on the individual and the environment, from a habitually withdrawn and passive personality to an extroverted, high-functioning personality. In fact, most any type of personal expression may be authentic or survival, depending on whether or not it is controlled by primal wounding. Furthermore, given that we have all suffered some amount of primal wounding, we all express some amount of survival personality. It is most accurate to think of authentic and survival personality as describing conditions of the personality that manifest in different and fluctuating amounts within us all.

An essential aspect of survival personality is an actual alteration in our experience of reality, as if we are now habitually and unconsciously wearing eyeglasses that filter out certain heights and depths of our true experience. Identified with survival personality, we are in a trance—we do not experience the inner and outer worlds in all of their richness but only in a truncated way, only from the point of view of surviving our primal wounding. Instead of living from the reality of our own unfolding experience, we live from an experience dictated by the demands of the early wounding environment.

> In our ordinary life we are . . . blinded and hypnotized by deceiving appearances.
>
> —Roberto Assagioli

This nonempathic environment and, later, its internalized pattern within us function as a *survival unifying center* (Firman and Gila 1997). That is, our experience of self and other is unified around the learnings, injunctions, and myths by which we survive within the wounding environment, for example, "Don't feel," "Don't voice your needs," and "Be perfect." Conditioned by the survival unifying center, we are largely out of touch with ourselves, other people, and Self. (Authentic personality and survival personality, and their respective unifying centers, are discussed more fully in Chapter 6.)

Through our experience with nonempathic environments, we gradually develop survival personality into an addiction. That is, we become addicted to, or identified with, this mode of functioning, and we seem to forget completely any other possible way of being. We cling to survival personality to not feel the wounding that underpins it.

It is then understandable that the maintenance of survival personality often gives rise to compulsions, attachments, and addictions that serve to maintain this constricted way of functioning. Addictions to behaviors, people, places, and substances are all ways of altering our experience in such a way that our consciousness is insulated from the pain of our wounding. For example, if you imagine that you are about to indulge a strong compulsion of your own, and then imagine that you do *not* so indulge, you may begin to feel the edge of the underlying primal wounding—you might perhaps feel uncomfortable, lost, alone, anxious, depressed, or worthless.[3]

In seeking this escape from our painful wounds, we may become addicted to food, sex, alcohol, drugs, relationships, power, money, work, service, higher states of consciousness, spiritual practices—virtually anything that will prevent the underlying wounding from emerging. Any failure in these survival strategies will touch the hidden tip of the primal wound "ice berg," and feelings such as anxiety, shame, and abandonment will begin to emerge.

Survival personality is fundamentally a broken empathy with ourselves, a truncation of our authentic experience of ourselves, the world, and the Divine. This broken self-empathy, caused by empathic failures in the environment, is the source of the fundamental infirmity addressed by Assagioli's stages, and the core of the survival stage.

This concept of the survival stage is quite similar to and, in part, inspired by Charles Whitfield's notion of what he calls Stage Zero:

> Stage Zero is manifested by the presence of an active illness or disorder, such as an addiction, compulsion or another disorder. This active illness may be acute, recurring or chronic. Without recovery, it may continue indefinitely. At Stage Zero, recovery has not yet started. (Whitfield 1991, 37)

Whitfield sees human being as originally in union with "Source" ("Higher Power, God/Goddess, All-That-Is"—quite similar to the psychosynthesis "Self"), but this state is broken by a wounding environment. For Whitfield, this wounding forces the True Self into hiding and plunges the person into Stage Zero, which may lead to the following conditions:

- stress
- addictions
- compulsions
- eating disorders

- mental disorders
- blocked grief (depression)
- fear (anxiety, panic)
- relationship addiction (advanced codependence)
- physical illness

But what can lead a person out of the survival stage? What can disrupt survival personality and begin to reveal the heights and depths surrounding our normal, everyday lives? Often this occurs through what we call a *crisis of transformation*.

CRISES OF TRANSFORMATION

Ellen grew up to be self-effacing, avoidant of conflict, and driven to please and produce. She had been brought up in a family in which to assert herself or her own needs was unacceptable. The family carried an injunction along the lines of: "It is selfish and self-centered to have your own needs. Good girls aren't concerned with themselves but with others." For her to express herself, to claim her own needs and passions, she had to face guilt, shame, and the threat of isolation and abandonment by the family—primal wounding.

As an adult, Ellen was moderately happy with her life and gained respect at work for her willingness to put in long, conscientious hours. Although she functioned very well at her job, showing talent and skill as well, she also was continually taken for granted and endured tremendous pressures and a crushing workload. She also habitually chose romantic partners who turned out to be emotionally abusive.

However, a transformation began when she was passed over for promotion. Shortly thereafter she found herself making uncharacteristically rude and cynical remarks to her coworkers, and she found her work suffering from a certain lack of energy and commitment.

Then one day, after a tense meeting with her manager, she closed her office door, sat down at her desk, and was suddenly overwhelmed by a flood of tears. She was startled by this, but she let the feelings come. She felt hurt, helpless, and hopeless. Then, to her growing surprise, she began to feel violated, betrayed, and finally furious. To her alarm, she felt like smashing up her office and physically hitting her manager.

At first this flood of feelings was upsetting to Ellen, because this was completely opposed to her normal way of being, her well-functioning survival personality. As she said later, "It just wasn't me, like I was going crazy." She even spoke of this event as "my breakdown," and indeed it was in a way—this was the breakdown of her self-effacing, people-pleasing identification and an opening to more of her authentic experience.

This was the beginning of a crisis of transformation for Ellen, a disconcerting time in which all of her beliefs about herself and the world were called into question. She moved into a period in which she encountered a vast range of experiences well beyond the constraints of her survival personality, from grief at having lived her life for others, to feeling like her life was a lie, to continually doubting her motives, to feeling the loss and abandonment that were masked by her habitual identification.

Mental health professionals presented with crises of transformation may refer to them as psychological disorder, regression, or mental illness. However, attempting to treat this disturbance by bolstering up the old survival personality will work to derail the transformational process; it is like attempting to keep a cocoon intact when the butterfly is emerging. Although alarming, a crisis of transformation is neither a breakdown nor a regression in some pathological sense. It is merely the disruption of the chronic and limiting survival personality and an entry into a wider range of human experience; it is a deeper encounter with the truth of our lives—an encounter that will always shake up the status quo.

A crisis of transformation can happen in many ways. It may simply dawn on us one day that we are trapped in repetitive life patterns, chronically addicted to self-destructive or self-distancing behaviors. Or we may suffer the loss of a loved one, a career, or a marriage, or face our own mortality in a serious illness or accident. Whatever the trigger, our old way of being begins to destabilize, and we may feel overwhelmed, helpless, lost, and abandoned—the surfacing of the wounding defended against since childhood. In the parlance of the chemical dependency field, we *hit bottom*.

On the other hand, we may *hit top* in the survival stage. That is, instead of being surprised by pain in contact with lower unconscious material, we may be surprised by joy as higher unconscious potentials break into our lives via peak experiences, creative inspiration, or spiritual awakening. We might suddenly become aware of a profound capacity for love, or we may be deeply touched by the beauty of the natural world or sense a connection with the Divine. Here we see the wondrous ways we might be in our lives. Just as in hitting bottom, here there is the realization that our normal, everyday lives are far from satisfactory, and that there must be a change in our way of living.

> Experiences of spontaneous illumination have been reported by many.
>
> —Roberto Assagioli

There also may be an interplay of higher and lower unconscious experience. Shaken by the death of a friend or a memory of childhood abuse, we may be plunged into a time of inconsolable despair, only to find in the depths of the pain a profound sense of a Divine presence holding all things. Or we may have a wondrous experience of union with the Universe, producing an ecstatic sense of the beauty, joy, and mystery of life, only to have this experience unaccountably fade, leaving feelings of isolation and worthlessness in its wake.

This type of interplay can be seen in less dramatic ways as well. Deciding to face our feelings of boredom and meaninglessness rather than distracting ourselves from them may lead to a gradual awakening to our authentic wants. Or feeling sad about a lost relationship might spark a renewed appreciation for and commitment to a current relationship. Or a movie with a heartwarming family ending might activate despair in us as we become aware, in contrast, of broken aspects of our own family.

Whether dramatic or subtle, these positive and negative aspects of our experience are just two sides of the same *primal split* in our being, so we need not be surprised if an emergence of one sector triggers the emergence of the other. They are, in effect, the two ends of our experiential range, split off by wounding.

It is important to remember here that we are not necessarily talking about a single experience, nor about only a single lifetime event. We may have many crises of transformation—dramatic and subtle, large and small—as we, at various points in our lives, outgrow forms that have become too constricting.

SURRENDER

Whether surprised by the lower unconscious, the higher unconscious, or both, these events demand that we recognize and accept a greater reality, that we realize that our lives, up until this point, have been very limited compared to what they might be. The realization dawns that we, other people, and life itself are far more wonderful and painful than we had ever imagined. We have entered a crisis of transformation, and if we can accept this expanded view and surrender to it, we will be led out of the survival stage.

In order for this surrender to take place, there needs to be a connection to a new context that can help us hold and integrate the newly discovered heights and depths of life—an *authentic unifying center* (Firman and Gila 1997). We need empathic others who are not threatened by this process, who understand it, and who can walk with us in it. Such a new unifying center(s) might be a self-help group, family and friends, counseling or therapy, spiritual direction, a religion, or even literature that maps out these uncharted regions and encourages their exploration. Whatever these unifying centers, they hold and nurture the seed of a more authentic life, one that transcends the limits of our wounding and opens the door leading out of the survival stage and into the next stage of psychosynthesis.

It is important for such a unifying center to be able to mirror not only our emerging wounding but our strengths as well. In a crisis of transformation, we might worry that we will simply become our wounds, fall into a "victim role," and completely lose the gifts and talents developed over the years. However, an authentic unifying center holds the whole person, wounds and gifts, weaknesses and strengths. Such an empathic connection is precisely what is needed as we attempt to hold both our brokenness and our wholeness without attaching to one and denying the other.

As the journey of transformation continues, we find that we do not lose our gifts; it is simply that they are no longer pressed into service in order to survive primal wounding, and become instead authentic expressions of our essential selves. For example, our love might be liberated from the survival need to control our partner, becoming more selfless and unconditional, or our creativity might be freed from a pattern of compulsive achievement, set up to avoid underlying feelings of worthlessness, to become the spontaneous expression of our true feelings and thoughts.

Furthermore, there are hitherto unknown gifts that may emerge as we reach to the wounded parts of ourselves. There are bright seeds of our potential, still viable and awaiting nurture, lying hidden in even the most bleak and despairing places within us. We might discover that as a repressed aspect of our adolescence is reclaimed, a sense of adventure and courage emerges that we have never experienced before; or, as we accept the wounds and dependence of a wounded child in us, we might discover that the child carries a profound wisdom born of a particularly close relationship with the Divine.

Journeying through a crisis of transformation, whether minor or cataclysmic, and held by empathic others in our lives, we can begin to find our way out of survival into the subsequent four stages of psychosynthesis. In stages one and two, we will recover that authentic expression of personal identity—"I"—lost to primal wounding, and in stages three and four we will discover our relationship to a deeper sense of meaning and purpose—Self.

STAGE ONE: EXPLORATION OF THE PERSONALITY

Again, a key factor in the movement into the *exploration of the personality* or the *exploration stage* is the breakdown of our old way of being and a shift toward more authentic relationships that can nurture the emergence of "I." Rather than relating to a context that says, in effect, "Don't trust your own experience but think, feel, and act only in these prescribed ways," we begin relating to contexts that say, "Trust your own experience, listen to it, heed it. There is far more to you than you have ever known, and you are free to explore this new terrain." Such authentic unifying centers—both external and later internal—encourage an empathic openness to the broad range of our natural experience, thus facilitating the emergence of the consciousness aspect of our authentic personal identity, of "I."

If Ellen had reached out in her crisis to her old conditioning—her survival unifying center—she would have received messages such as: "Stop your fuss! Get hold of yourself. You're a good girl, and good girls don't have feelings like this. You're not being yourself. Quit acting like a victim."

She did, of course, hear these messages within her, as the voices from her family system inwardly berated her, but her immediate environment can carry these messages too. The common denominator is a nonempathic response to her experience. For example, even the well-intentioned comments of a coworker, "Hey, buck up, you'll get over it, it's not the end of the world," would push her toward "getting over it" and reestablishing her old way of being, once again ignoring these depths within her. However, Ellen chose to explore what was happening to her by entering psychosynthesis therapy.

ELLEN IN EXPLORATION

As she began her exploration, Ellen discovered a deep rage that at first scared her. Going further, however, she discovered feelings hidden beneath the rage: feelings of helplessness and terror in the face of the mildest conflict with others. Here feelings that had been largely unconscious for many years were now more free to move into and out of her awareness.

Ellen chose to pay attention to these new feelings throughout her day. As she got to know them better, she explored many childhood moments in which she stood frozen with fear as her father, in an alcoholic rage, punished her older brother with a physical beating. Clearly it was dangerous to be anything but a self-effacing, quiet person in that environment, and her fear and anger needed to be repressed if she were to survive emotionally. This type of material is characteristic of the lower unconscious—here are the traumatic wounds, most deeply buried, which underpin her seemingly pleasant and sunny survival mode of being.

Then, too, higher unconscious material became evident in Ellen's exploration. As Ellen began taking responsibility for her authentic experience, she began to discover hitherto repressed higher unconscious qualities of self-confidence and personal power. Here was precisely the type of self-assertive energy that Ellen needed in her life. Furthermore, as she began to treat herself with empathy and compassion, she also began to contact higher unconscious qualities of sensitivity, wonder, and creativity—again, qualities largely absent in Ellen's life, but now finally being recovered from their safe hiding place.

At different points Ellen also encountered the larger, shared dimension of her themes of self-exploration. She saw and felt the insidious oppression of women in the workplace and her solidarity with the struggle against this; the historical acceptance of corporal punishment in her family, coming from her grandparents, great-grandparents, and from aspects of her cultural heritage itself; the denial of alcoholism in her family, again coming down through the generations and, again, supported by cultural myths; and, finally, she became very sensitive to the issue of child abuse and the growing societal awareness of this. In all of these insights she was moving beyond her own personal unconscious to see into the shared historical patterns of the collective unconscious.[4]

As we can see in Ellen's story, in the exploration stage our consciousness expands and allows both a disidentification from older, chronic ways of being and an empathic connection with the many split-off sectors of our personal universe. This includes an engagement with the higher and lower unconscious as well as aspects of the collective unconscious. As Assagioli points out, this stage can include an exploration of personal history, family of origin, intergenerational history, ethnic, class, and national background, and even "the present collective psyche of humanity as a whole" (Assagioli 1965a, 72).

It cannot be emphasized enough that this exploration is not simply an intrapsychic phenomenon but amounts to what poet William Blake would call a cleansing of the "doors of perception." The exploration of these dimensions of our experience amounts to an expansion of our experiential bandwidth; our doors of perception become more clear, and we become more aware of the joy and wonder, the pain and suffering, of human existence.

Stated most broadly, the exploration stage involves an increased openness to the middle, higher, and lower sectors of the unconscious, amounting to a far more lucid consciousness of ourselves, other people, and the world at large. This is a stage in which serious self-exploration takes place, as one addresses the question "Who am I?"

FRACTIONAL ANALYSIS

The expansion of consciousness in the exploration stage can be facilitated by any of the many growth methods now so widely available. The current culture is filled with techniques to alter consciousness, to get more in touch with feelings, to become aware of our bodies, to contact collective and archetypal material, to explore our family and cultural history, to gain more serenity and peace, to uncover the sublime states of consciousness in the higher unconscious, and to uncover the woundings from the past in the lower unconscious. So many are our options in this regard that it is frequently more difficult to choose among methods than it is to find them.

Given the ease with which we may today expand our consciousness in so many different directions, caution is in order. It is important to remember that this expansion is only the first stage in psychosynthesis and not an end in itself. That is, it is possible to become enthralled and distracted with discovering our heights and depths, seeking greater and greater insights, attaining higher states of consciousness, or exploring the vast array of growth methods available. What can then happen is that we forget the overall purpose of self-knowledge: to learn to respond well to the deeper meanings and directions in our lives.

> ... the exploration of the unconscious is carried out "by installments," so to speak.
> —Roberto Assagioli

So it is important to undertake exploration within this larger context, keeping in mind the subsequent stages of psychosynthesis as we go. Assagioli (1965a) referred to this principle as *fractional analysis*, by which the exploration of the unconscious is to take place only when needed, and then only in "installments," with plenty of time for the integration and expression of the material uncovered, all the while maintaining a broader perspective.

After developing some knowledge of our personality, there is a natural progression toward an increased experience of being distinct from all of these multiple dimensions of personhood. This new sense of self, of "I," is one from which we can take responsibility for and act in relationship to the knowledge gained in the exploration stage. This leads to stage two of psychosynthesis, *the emergence of "I."*

STAGE TWO: THE EMERGENCE OF "I"

Stage two is *the emergence of "I,"* or the *emergence stage.* Assagioli calls this stage "control of the various elements of the personality." Although the word "control" can be misunderstood, what he is pointing to here is that gentle and subtle second function of "I"—the will. As we have said, "I" does not only possess the function of consciousness but has a directive and guiding capacity as well, an ability to cause effects in both the inner and outer worlds. This directive function of "I" is will.

Further, since "I" is distinct-but-not-separate from the contents of the personality, the will of "I" can operate distinct-but-not-separate from any contents as well. Thus will is the source of our potential freedom, not to be controlled by but to interact with the many aspects of the personality. Assagioli's phrase "control of the various elements of the personality" can be understood in this light; it is the emergence of the human spirit, our true essence—"I"—with the functions of consciousness and will.

> The will . . . balances and constructively utilizes all the other activities and energies of the human being without repressing any of them.
>
> —Roberto Assagioli

While in the exploration stage we become conscious of the different levels of ourselves, in the emergence stage we realize that we are distinct from all of these levels and can take responsibility for them. We realize we can assist in the nurturance and growth of these different aspects, and finally that we can guide them into a more authentic expression of ourselves in the world. This fuller emergence of "I" involves, then, an active relationship with the material that has been uncovered in the exploration stage.

ELLEN IN EMERGENCE

Becoming increasingly open to her heights and depths, Ellen began relating to herself in an empathic, compassionate way. If she felt too stressed at work, she would take an extended lunch and go for a walk; if a man was hurtful, she would address that and/or remove herself; if she sensed that she needed time for herself in nature, she might take a trip to the beach.

This self-empathy and self-care went strongly against her family conditioning, from whom inwardly she heard the accusations, "You're being selfish. All you care about is yourself, old number one." These inner criticisms were echoed outwardly by subtle messages from the workplace: "You're not committed to your work, not pulling your weight. Who do you think you are?" But Ellen persevered in connecting to herself and making her life a place in which she could exist in an authentic way.

As she continued to make concrete decisions and carry out actions that were empathic toward herself, the seeds that had been buried and silent in her since childhood began to germinate. On the one hand, she began expressing integrity, strength, and personal power in standing up for herself; on the other hand, this self-care led to a flowering of her softer qualities of sensitivity, wonder, and creativity. Having broken the bounds of her old way of being, becoming open to her authentic pain, and empathically relating to the wounded parts of herself, she uncovered the treasure hidden there as well.

At work she was able to sit down and talk to her manager about the injustices and pressures that she had suffered. In this situation she actually could feel her burgeoning strength and clarity, although also aware of the nervousness emanating from her early wounds. This showed the power of her self-empathy—to hold both her strength and vulnerability.

But it was her relationships with men that produced some of the most striking results in this stage. Over time she found herself able to be sensitive and vulnerable as well as assertive and self-expressive. Respectful and caring men found this appealing, while the ones prone to domination and abuse seemed to stay away.

As we actively respond to ourselves empathically in this stage, we frequently will be at odds with our early, nonempathic conditioning, as Ellen's case demonstrates. If we persevere, however, we will find a healing of past wounds (lower unconscious) and a blossoming of hidden gifts (higher unconscious). We attain a stronger sense of personal essence and also find that we can contact and express transpersonal or universal qualities such as joy, wonder, creativity, and love; our essential I-amness, formerly bound in survival personality, begins to emerge.

As with the exploration stage, the emergence stage is supported by any number of authentic unifying centers, contexts and environments that mirror our authentic self-expression. For Ellen, this authentic mirroring was provided in her psychosynthesis therapy, but she also found empathic holding in her relationships with several good friends, a support group, her spiritual practice, and her reading in recovery literature.

BEYOND THE EMERGENCE OF "I"

This burgeoning of authenticity does not find its limit in the emergence stage. True, this stage often is rich with creativity and spontaneity, with self-expression over a wide dynamic range, and with an increasingly empowered way of being in the world. But there are other questions: "What is my life about?" "What am I here for?"

Such questions point beyond the exploration of the personality and the emergence of "I," beyond any integration of the lower unconscious and higher unconscious, and beyond personal psychosynthesis and transpersonal psychosynthesis (see Chapter 8). Here the issue becomes our lived relationship with our deepest values, meanings, and life direction—issues of Self-realization.

Clearly the earlier stages lead naturally toward the ability to hear the call or invitations of Self. Trapped in the thrall of survival personality, we were in no position to hear much of anything beyond the imperative of managing our wounding in any way we could; as we have seen, it is often only through crisis that we become open to hearing anything deeper.

Then, in the exploration stage, we most likely will have our hands full with the vast new territory of experience revealing itself to us; here it may be hard to distinguish the voice of Self while our consciousness is inundated with new insights and experiences.

With the emergence of "I," however, a more stable inner order begins to form as the newly discovered aspects of ourselves begin to find their places. A sense of self burgeons from which it is possible to enter into conscious communion with the very deepest in our lives. Of course, the deeper Self has been there all along, inviting us through even the earlier stages. It is simply that, often, to the extent that the earlier stages have been worked through, we can be more conscious and intentional in contacting and then responding to Self.

STAGE THREE: CONTACT WITH SELF

As we have an increasingly clear sense of the many levels of ourselves and assume the responsibility of actualizing these levels, we naturally are led to questions of direction. Now that we can express ourselves authentically, what is important to express? Now that we have the wherewithal to create, what is important to create? What seems to be my call in life, my path, my direction? In psychosynthesis terms, this is asking for a more intimate, conscious relationship with Self, or what is called *Self-realization*. Assagioli called this stage "Realization of One's True Self," and here we call this the stage of *contact with Self*, or the *contact stage*.

Again it seems clear that the prior progression from the stage of survival to exploration to emergence is a logical prelude to contact with deeper levels of our being. But this logical progression is not quite as neat and orderly as all that. The invitations from Self—the transpersonal will—can be discerned even in these earlier stages. As we have said, the I-Self relationship exists throughout all life experiences, in all spheres of life, and in every stage of life. Since "I" and Self are distinct-but-not-separate from all content and process, the I-Self relationship is ever-present, conscious or not.

In looking back, Ellen saw her "breakdown" as a moment of Self-realization. Not that Self caused the tense moment with her manager or even the upwelling of feelings, but in that moment she was invited to feel and accept unconscious aspects of herself that she had habitually cut out of her life. In this crisis of transformation was the opening of a path leading out of survival and into exploration. And, too, she followed that same sense of invitation as she chose to remain conscious of these depths of her soul, to plumb their depths and act upon what she found—the emergence of "I." All of this also is Self-realization, the I-Self relationship in manifestation; it is simply more in the background during these earlier stages and more in the foreground in the latter two stages. Again, as Assagioli said, we are not "buildings."

ELLEN IN CONTACT

> Ellen began her more formal or obvious transition to the contact stage as she encountered continuing difficulties at work. Formerly, in the stages of exploration and emergence, she had become much more of a force to be reckoned with in the workplace. She no longer could be easily ignored, was more vocal about the injustices she saw, and frequently found herself in conflict with the oppressive culture present there. So what to do now?
>
> Simply to revert to silent acquiescence felt like a betrayal of herself, so she began to entertain the idea of quitting her job. She longed to work with people who could see her potential, respect her as a person, and support her creativity.
>
> But then she began to struggle with her need for financial security, the fear and uncertainty of finding a new job, and a reluctance to leave the friends she had made in the company. Perhaps she was meant to stay in order to learn a difficult lesson, to work against the unjust system, and quitting was simply running away from this.
>
> Obviously there were no clear right or wrong answers to these questions—a completely logical case could be made for each and every choice she faced—and she agonized long over them. The questions demanded that she go deeper, to search for her own sense of truth, personal destiny, or call.

As in earlier stages, the transition to the contact stage involves finding authentic unifying centers that will support and encourage our need for a relationship with the Truth as we ourselves understand this. Since psychosynthesis therapy supports such an experiential relationship, Ellen found it helpful to continue with this. But she also joined a prayer group at her church, continued her daily meditation practice, sought out spiritual books, lectures, and workshops, and spent time talking with friends who could hear and support her.

> Then one night Ellen had a frightening dream. She dreamed that she woke up to the smell of smoke, heard shouting outside, and rushed to the window to see a massive fire rapidly approaching her house. Whipped by the wind, smoke was billowing through her house. She rushed frantically through the house in an attempt to gather up her most important belongings, but she realized that she would be risking her life if she did not get out immediately. After a moment of agonizing hesitation, she ran out of the house, turned, and watched helplessly as her home was engulfed in flames. She awoke quite shaken, feeling loss, grief, and loneliness.

This dream brought Ellen back into the stages of exploration and emergence. She did feel that this dream was a call to leave the security of the known in order to save her soul, but this also made her face her loss, grief, and loneliness that had been silently underpinning such a choice. In exploring these feelings, she connected to a younger part of herself that had been rejected and abandoned by her parents. This was confusing to her at first, because her parents had never physically rejected or abandoned her.

But in relating to the young one, she gradually realized that her parents' continual demeaning of her childhood efforts at self-expression meant that any time she moved to express herself she was emotionally abandoned; in other words, to be true to herself as a child meant placing herself beyond the security of parental concern, outside of the family, in nonexistence, abandoned, grieving, terrified—primal wounding.

Ellen saw that her self-effacing personality, secure job, and driven work ethic had been ways that she had been managing the feelings from this early wounding. As she connected empathically to this level of herself, she created a communion with this younger part that markedly reduced her desperation and anxiety around her career questions. Increasingly, she was able to sit more peacefully with these questions and to listen mindfully for answers.

> Over several months, Ellen experienced other events that seemed to speak to her. She was struck one Sunday by the Scripture reading "And why do you worry about clothing? Consider the lilies of the field, how they grow; they neither toil nor spin" (Matthew 6:28). She heard from several old friends who had successfully made major life transitions. In her reading she stumbled upon teachings about nonattachment and surrender as avenues to Spirit.
>
> But most compelling to her was reading and hearing of several unexpected deaths of people near her own age. This put her in a frame of mind to do what was most meaningful *now* and to not put things off.
>
> Through listening to all of these experiences, the conviction grew stronger and stronger that she absolutely had to quit her job, no matter what might happen. It was still scary for her to do this, but she felt that it would be "the death of my spirit" to stay.

Ellen's process of discernment is characteristic of the contact stage. Here there is a willingness to enter into a dialogue with whatever we feel to be the ultimate truth of our lives, an openness to hear from the most profound levels of our being.

Enacting this openness can take many forms, but invariably it will involve being in relationships with people, places, and things that support asking ultimate questions. These might include entering into a dialogue with different systems of morality and ethics; praying and meditating regularly; listening carefully to messages from nocturnal dreams; learning about different religions and theologies; frequenting places considered sacred; taking time in retreat and solitude; undertaking a vision quest or pilgrimage; and finding a mentor, an intimate friend, or a community who supports our relationship to Self. All such authentic unifying centers work to expand a sense of relationship to Self and to refine the ability to hear the call of Self.

OPENING TO CONTACT

As it did with Ellen, entering the contact stage can bring up many issues that again necessitate the stages of exploration and emergence. Here it is as if we "up the ante" in our psychospiritual growth; we become willing not to simply feel connected to or unified with the Divine but to make specific choices and perform concrete actions that we feel are in line with a larger direction in our lives. In psychosynthesis terms, it is the intention to align our personal will with the transpersonal will.

Ask yourself how you would feel if you were face-to-face with Ultimate Truth, the Divine, the Absolute, or whatever you think is an ultimate principle in your life. Then ask yourself how you would feel if you could hear from this Ultimate about the direction of your life in specific terms. In doing such an exercise, it is possible to sense the nature of the difficulties that may emerge in the contact stage. Here we might fear that something will be taken away from us, or that we will find out that we have been wasting our lives, or that we will no longer have any fun, or even that we will lose our identity. All of these reactions may have childhood antecedents that can be explored.

> Let the will of the Self guide and direct my life.
>
> —Roberto Assagioli

It also is common to encounter parts of ourselves that have become mixed up with our notion of the Ultimate. One man was scared of listening to God, because for him God was a punishing, vengeful deity. In working with this inner image, however, he discovered a critical part of himself in effect masquerading as God, a part of him conditioned by childhood religious abuse.

Many different types of uncomfortable reactions—often presenting as subpersonalities—can be triggered by the potential of facing the Ultimate. The point in this stage is to hear these parts of us, to empathically connect with them, to listen to the hopes and fears that they embody, to care for them, and to invite them into the larger community of the personality. As this occurs, we become more able to hear the call of Self.

STAGE FOUR: RESPONSE TO SELF

The last stage of psychosynthesis Assagioli represents as a period in which we are concretely responding to the invitations of Self and working with our psychospiritual development within this context. We call this stage *response to Self*, or simply, the *response stage*.

Many stories could be told to illustrate this stage. Perhaps we immediately think of famous people who throughout history responded to a powerful call and were led to great tasks. While such famous men and women are vivid examples of response to Self, there are far more examples from the lives of the less famous.

There are responses that lead to holy orders as a priest or shaman, to marriage and parenthood, to different forms of social activism, or to simply a more healthy way of being with ourselves and others. We have seen Laura (Chapter 2) and her growth via her work with a child subpersonality invited to expand her sense of self beyond that single part; and now we see Ellen called into a journey toward personal transformation, new relationships, and a new job. As Ellen learned, however, the response stage may involve yet another return to earlier stages.

> When Ellen finally made the decision to leave her job, she began sending out resumes, talking to friends in the business, and making contact with a professional job broker or "headhunter." She was aware of a profound sense of rightness about her direction now, and she felt the self-confidence and peace of mind that that had brought.
>
> But after a promising phone call with a prospective employer, she suddenly began to feel terrible. She was filled with doubt, fear, and a strong sense of being a bad person. Returning to the exploration stage, she followed these feelings and discovered a part of her that felt the job search was a betrayal of the company: "How could you leave, after all they've done for you? You're being ungrateful."
>
> Empathically connecting to this level within, Ellen found a younger part of her for whom leaving the job felt like a betrayal of her family, a betrayal for which the family would shame and reject her as a person. The threat of these feelings had kept her within her limiting role within the family: for her to in any way move beyond her limiting role meant betraying the family and facing shame and rejection.
>
> After awhile, Ellen found that her reaction was another level of the one in her who felt abandoned by the family, and who had emerged in the dream about the fire (above). These wounded feelings drove a desperate attachment to the status quo and her role within it, an attachment by which she sought never to suffer that abandonment again. This deeper level of wounding was being energized by the very concrete possibility of leaving the company.
>
> As before, Ellen established an ongoing relationship with this vulnerable part of herself, thereby in effect giving the part a new home. Ellen's feelings of doubt, anxiety, and shame did not simply disappear but were now held in compassion, and she was able to find a new job, quit her old one, and make the move to a new life.

Here we can see Ellen walking her path of Self-realization. She actively opened herself to whatever might be revealed by Self, responded to that sense of call, and then engaged the reaction that her response triggered. Self-realization is clearly not limited to only one moment or one experience, but rather it is an ongoing, lived relationship with our deepest sense of truth.

Thus psychosynthesis understands Self not simply as a passive presence but as continuously acting through the transpersonal will, to which we may respond with the freedom of our own personal will. Our contact and response to the invitations of Self may involve sweeping changes, as in discovering an overall life direction, or it may involve smaller changes, as in increased authenticity, deeper compassion, greater wholeness, and right relationships. Again, this ongoing interplay between "I" and Self is called Self-realization, and later we will devote an entire chapter to it.

Response as Dialogue

It is important to emphasize that this relationship with Self is indeed a true relationship, characterized by respect, empathy, dialogue, and mutual response. Assagioli wrote of this dynamic interplay between "I" and Self as "a 'dialogue' between the man [or woman] and his [or her] 'Higher Source,' in which each alternately invokes and evokes the other" (Assagioli 1973a, 114). This empathic relationship with Self can be seen in one of Ellen's psychosynthesis therapy sessions. She was working with the abandoned child who emerged after her dream but then moved into a relationship with an inner figure of wisdom:

Therapist: How is it to be with the little girl?

Ellen: It's okay, actually. She's letting me hold her. She doesn't feel so alone anymore. I feel very motherly towards her, but I worry.

T: About what?

E: Well, whether I can be a good mother to her. I'm afraid I'll forget to be with her. I'll probably screw this up like everything else.

T: Try something, Ellen. Imagine that with you now is a very wise person, a person who knows and loves you. (Pause.) Who do you see?

E: It's a wise old woman . . . looks like a crone . . . or Goddess even. She's hard to see clearly. She's got light around her. Just a presence.

T: How do you feel towards her?

E: I love her. She loves me. I just feel very peaceful with her.

T: Stay with that a bit. How is that? (Pause.)

E: Just very peaceful, like there's nothing to fear.

T: If you want, tell the wise woman about your worry about being a good mother.

E: She just laughs. In a nice way. She says not to worry, that she's here to help me. In fact, she's always been here.

T: How does that make you feel?

E: It makes me want to cry. I know she's speaking the truth. I've never really been alone.

This dialogue between Ellen and the wise woman is an example of the I-Self relationship emerging. Here there is a mutual love and respect, a shared sense of being heard and responded to, and even good-hearted humor. Also, as often may happen when this relationship becomes conscious, Ellen realized that this is an intimate relationship that has been present throughout her whole life, though not recognized. We can understand that even through the worst traumas in life, we were held and protected by a deeper Spirit.

So Self-realization is not simply a matter of hearing the call and then obediently carrying this out. The essence of the I-Self relationship is an empathic resonance, an intimate communion in which individuality and free will—"I"—are respected and supported. Indeed, individuality and free will *arise* from this relationship.

IN SUMMATION

In sum, then, the stages of psychosynthesis outline the various facets of a journey in which initially there emerges an expression of essential I-amness, which is then followed by a sense of relationship between "I" and a deeper source, Self. We have traced this journey from (0) being controlled by the addictive repression of higher and lower unconscious dynamics (survival stage); to (1) the discovery of, and empathic connection with, these levels (exploration stage); to (2) the expression of a more authentic sense of personal essence or "I" (emergence stage); to (3) making contact with a more profound sense of meaning and purpose (contact stage); and, finally, (4) to doing what is needed to respond to the specific call or vocation from this deeper sense of meaning and purpose (response stage).

Again, remember that while the linearity of this progression does make sense, these stages may not in fact be experienced in this sequence. Each stage may be in the foreground at different times, independent of the linear progression. Further, we never outgrow these stages; any one of them can be present at any time in our lives, no matter how long we have trod the way of Self-realization. In fact, it is safe to say that each of us at this very moment has a level of our experience in each of these five stages. So the stage model of psychosynthesis is not a ladder we climb rung by rung, nor one we climb once and for all time; the stages are different windows on a single process, windows whereby we participate in this process in different ways.

It has been clear in this outline of the stages of psychosynthesis, and in the earlier discussion of the model of the person, that we have many different aspects, levels, and dimensions within us. While our normal experience of ourselves may be that we are single, whole individuals, even cursory self-exploration will reveal that we are in fact inwardly complex, diverse, and multiple. We all fit the definition of the Renaissance person, "A person of many parts." As we have seen also, the process of human growth usually entails an encounter with this inner multiplicity and an ability to know, understand, and guide the various aspects of ourselves; this is a major theme in the journey of psychosynthesis.

One quite effective way to facilitate this growth is to work with subpersonalities, those semi-independent identities within us that act as virtual "people inside us" (Rowan 1990). Like Laura working with her child subpersonality, or Ellen with her childhood levels of experience, we can learn to recognize and work with this rich multiplicity within us. The next chapter will describe this type of work as an important tool in our Self-realization.

FOUR

MULTIPLICITY WITHIN
THE PERSONALITY

Have you ever noticed that you behave differently in your office, at home, in social interplay, in solitude, at church, or as a member of a political party?

—Roberto Assagioli

Part of me wants to be with him, but another part of me says, "No way." It's very confusing.

I'm always beating myself up. If I make one little mistake, I can hear the critic inside me yelling at me for being stupid—just like my father used to.

One minute I can be sailing along happy and carefree, and then suddenly, for no reason at all, I feel sad and scared. My girlfriend says I'm too moody.

I couldn't go to sleep because the committee was having a meeting in my head. All these arguments. It made me so upset I finally got out of bed.

As we begin to explore our ongoing inner experience in the first stages of psychosynthesis, it becomes obvious that there are many different parts operating within us. These different parts will be noticed emerging in response to the different life situations that we face daily. At work, we may recognize that we are intellectual and task oriented; with a lover, warm and intimate; with authority figures, anxiously passive or angrily rebellious; and when playing a favorite sport, perhaps ferociously competitive.

We may even refer to these aspects of ourselves in ordinary conversation: "That was my heart talking, not my head," or "My feelings got hurt," or "My artistic side needs to express itself." Other people also may notice our shifting parts: "This is a whole side of you I've never seen before," or "You don't seem yourself today," or "I like it when you let your playfulness out."

Each of these different parts of us is composed of various personality elements—particular skills, gifts, values, attitudes, worldviews—which are formed into an operating whole or synthesis through which we function in different environments. As mentioned in Chapter 2, these semi-autonomous subsystems within the personality are what Assagioli (1965a) called *subpersonalities*.

SUBPERSONALITIES ARE NORMAL

Before examining subpersonalities more closely, let us emphasize that multiplicity within the human personality is quite normal. Subpersonalities are an aspect of the gift of the middle unconscious (Chapter 2), an example of the structuralization process that begins with some of our most basic inborn reflexes. It is simply that in subpersonality formation this structuralization has proceeded to such an extent that an entire identity system has been created. From a range of different inborn abilities and learned skills, through interaction with the environment, a sophisticated expression of self has been formed. Further, as the various subpersonalities begin to relate in cooperative and synergistic ways, the same structuralization process may create even more sophisticated expressive patterns from the relationships among subpersonalities (discussed later).

It is quite true, of course, that there is a less common personality organization commonly known as *multiple personality disorder*, lately renamed *dissociative identity disorder*, or *DID* (First 1994). In personality structure, the subpersonalities or *alters* are so dramatically dissociated that there is little continuity of consciousness among them. For example, among other things, people with DID may have the experience of "losing time," in which they do not remember what occurred when another subpersonality was in charge. This personality organization can be seen as existing further along on a continuum of dissociation that we all share.

The difficulties that any of us experience with our multiplicity—inner conflict, ambivalence, anxiety, depression, and so on—are not a problem of multiplicity per se but of a *lack of cooperation* among the parts of the personality. The "cure" for our maladies here is not a matter of eliminating the multiplicity but of seeking better relationships among the multiple parts. Just as the United States is not a melting pot in which various ethnic and cultural groups are to be dissolved into one undifferentiated homogeneous mass, so the human personality is not a melting pot in which subpersonalities are to be fused into a seamless whole. The challenge—for both inner and outer societies—is to seek right relationships among diversities.

The normality of multiplicity within the personality has been recognized by many different psychological systems and cultural traditions, both past and present. The West historically has understood this diversity as the multiple abilities, faculties, and habits operating for good or ill within the human soul. In the East, there are *vasanas* and *samskaras*, terms that refer to tendencies, desires, and habits that may be in harmony or conflict within the person. And in a traditional African worldview, the normal human personality is "seen as a community in and of itself, including a plurality of selves" (Ogbonnaya 1994, 75).

In Western psychology, inner diversity has not only been widely recognized but has become the foundation for entire approaches to psychotherapy: from Freud's ego, superego, and id, Jung's complexes, William James' various types of selves, Melanie Klein's internal objects, Paul Federn's ego states, Fritz Perls' top dog and underdog, Virginia Satir's parts of the person, Erv Polster's population of selves, and Assagioli's subpersonalities, to the systems of transactional analysis (Berne 1961), gestalt therapy (Perls 1969; Polster 1995), ego therapy (Shapiro 1976), voice dialogue (Stone and Winkelman 1985), internal family systems therapy (Schwartz 1995), and ego state therapy (Watkins and Watkins 1997).

It also is safe to say that subpersonality theory is perhaps the most common topic of psychosynthesis literature (e.g., Brown 1983; Brown 1993; Carter-Haar 1975; Ferrucci 1982; Firman and Gila 1997; Firman and Russell 1993; Hardy 1987; Kramer 1995; Meriam 1994; Rueffler 1995a; Sliker 1992; Vargiu 1974b; Whitmore 1991). For an overview of a variety of approaches to subpersonalities, see John Rowan's *Subpersonalities* (1990).

Suffice it to say that numerous observers, both past and present, from diverse cultures and disparate disciplines have looked at the human being and seen the multiplicity of which we

> . . . the psychological multiplicity that exists in each of us.
>
> —Roberto Assagioli

are made. Again, and perhaps more to the point, this is easily demonstrated by anyone who is willing to undertake a careful examination of his or her lived experience over time.

Before moving into a discussion of subpersonality formation and harmonization, it should be noted that Assagioli himself wrote little about subpersonalities beyond affirming their existence and locating them within then-current psychological research (see Assagioli 1965a, 74–77). Like much of psychosynthesis thought and practice, it has been up to subsequent thinkers in the field to elaborate and extend Assagioli's initial concepts. What follows below is our own understanding of the genesis of subpersonalities, followed by a stage or phase theory modified from the work of Steven Kull, Betsie Carter-Haar, and James Vargiu (Vargiu 1974b) at the Palo Alto Psychosynthesis Institute, a theory that did have its origin in direct conversations with Assagioli.[1]

THE BIRTH OF A SUBPERSONALITY

George was generally satisfied with his career as a technical writer but was looking for something more in his life. One weekend he happened to attend a motorcycle rally with a friend and was intrigued by what he saw. He was attracted—one might even say "called"—by the beauty of the shiny motorcycles, the camaraderie among the riders, and the general atmosphere of freedom and adventure at the rally.

Note that the general culture of the motorcycle rally presented George with a *unifying center*, a center of meaning that began to evoke a deep response in him. His relationship to this unifying center offered him qualities such as beauty, camaraderie, freedom, and adventure (as we shall see, these qualities are called *transpersonal qualities* in psychosynthesis). He felt seen, held, and called by this environment; his spirit felt nurtured as a plant is nurtured by soil and sun, and he began to unfold a new branch of himself.

This relationship with the motorcycle world was the beginning of a process in which George gradually was to form a motorcyclist subpersonality. The motorcycle unifying center acted as a mirror, showing him hitherto unconscious potentials within himself that he could then work to actualize if he so chose. In Assagioli's words, "When the unifying center has been found or created, we are in a position to build around it a new personality—coherent, organized, and unified" (Assagioli 1965a, 26).

What George did not realize at the time was that he already had within him an adventuresome aspect of himself, a part that was feeling called by the motorcycle unifying center. As a boy, he had hitchhiked with his father and had grown up listening to his father's stories of his own youthful adventures hitchhiking and riding freight trains. As a young man, George too had hitchhiked, both through his own country and abroad, and he had always had a passion for travel, even working at various jobs that involved this passion. With the emergence of his professional career, however, this adventuresome spirit had languished until this awakening at the motorcycle rally.

THROUGH CHAOS TO ORDER

After some thought and planning, George finally bought a motorcycle and enrolled in a riding course—another important aspect of his newfound unifying center, which included his instructor, his fellow students, and the philosophy of the course. During the class he found that learning to ride involved mastering a number of different skills, including the use of the shifter, brake, clutch, and throttle, in addition to remaining aware of the road and other vehicles.

Early in the learning curve, he needed to focus intently upon these individual skills, seeking to master each of them in turn. But he found that when he gave his attention to shifting, he was not as aware of the road or the brakes, and when attending to the road and braking, that he could not use the clutch or shifter very well, and so on. He simply could not give every task the attention it needed to function as a smooth, stable, coordinated pattern.

Initially this process was extremely overwhelming and scary, but he felt sustained by his connection to the various elements of the motorcycle unifying center now working in his life; his respect for those centers, his desire to remain connected to them, and his determination to ride allowed him to persevere in his effort. Again, he felt called to motorcycling, even though he needed to move through significant amounts of anxiety, self-doubt, and pain to respond to that call.

However, over time, George gradually found that he did not have to focus so much on the mechanics of operating the motorcycle and that a new level of organization, a new synthesis, was emerging. The discrete behaviors that at first demanded so much attention began to function effortlessly and unconsciously—in the middle unconscious—leaving his consciousness free to enjoy the sights and sounds around him, and his will more free to choose how and where to ride.

Note that George's process of learning is dynamically the same as all other structuralizations that he has achieved throughout his life. Even as an infant, through this process he learned to stick his thumb in his mouth and suck on it: "The product of this development—a smoothly functioning thumb-to-mouth schema—may go unnoticed once formed [i.e., unconscious]. But the process of formation, itself, will be quite salient and the focus of heightened attention" (Stern 1985, 60).

Like the infant learning to suck a thumb, the child synthesizing a new role, or Assagioli's pianist moving from mastering technique to performing artistically (see Chapter 2), a structuralization of the middle unconscious began to support George's conscious expression of new aspects of himself.

TRANSPERSONAL QUALITIES AND ARCHETYPES

Throughout this process George also found new transpersonal qualities emerging as he related to his motorcycling unifying center (again, this unifying center includes things such as his instructor, his fellow students, the philosophy of riding, and the entire motorcycling world). Besides the original qualities that had attracted him, he also began feeling a certain joy, freedom, and courage that were new to him. It was as if his relationship with the motorcycling unifying center became an axis around which a pattern of innate aptitudes, instinctual drives, learned skills, and transpersonal qualities was coalescing that made up his ability to become a motorcyclist.

He further recognized that this developing pattern in himself resonated with an ancient pattern in the collective unconscious, a pattern called the Warrior. He felt connected to this archetype when he was riding his motorcycle, feeling like a courageous warrior in facing the dangers and adventure of the open road. This archetype functioned as still another unifying center, one that allowed him to feel a kinship with heroes and explorers throughout human history.

A SUBPERSONALITY IS CALLED INTO BEING

As George gained increasing experience with other motorcyclists and the motorcycle culture over time, this synthesis in him eventually developed into a discrete motorcyclist identity system. This new identify unified or synthesized the skills, gifts, drives, and qualities that he developed in riding, as well as particular beliefs and values concerning being a motorcyclist. The motorcyclist unifying center(s) in effect saw him as a motorcyclist and allowed him to see himself as a motorcyclist in turn, thereby supporting him in developing and unifying different elements into this unique expression of himself. The subpersonality arose from this relationship, with each side of the relationship playing its part. This process is illustrated in Figure 4.1.

From this new synthesis within him, he identified himself as a motorcyclist: he felt, thought, and viewed the world as a motorcyclist; he was alive to the sight and sound of any passing motorcycle; he viewed positive and negative comments about motorcycles in a personal way; and he even voted as a motorcyclist.

This new identity as a whole, then, came and went in his awareness—into and out of the middle unconscious—as appropriate. With nonmotorcyclist colleagues and friends, George's new identity did not enter consciousness at all, while in a motorcycle environment it emerged into consciousness and full expression.

Note too that the motorcyclist unifying center here has been to some extent internalized, becoming an *internal unifying center* (Firman and Gila 1997). The existence of the subpersonality no longer depends solely on the *external unifying center* (Assagioli 1965a) but has an internal structure supporting it, whether or not the external motorcycle environment is present. We will further explore internal and external unifying centers in subsequent chapters.

George's brief story reveals the birth of a subpersonality. Through a relationship with a unifying center(s), he felt called to develop a semi-indepen-

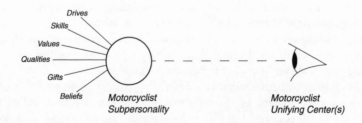

FIGURE 4.1

dent discrete identity, a coherent synthesis of more basic elements, which could then move into and out of expression as needed. In George's case, this subpersonality arose from an even earlier subpersonality that had emerged in relationship to his father, which he called the Adventurer. (In Figure 4.1, the Adventurer might be drawn within the Motorcyclist subpersonality.)

But whether a subpersonality develops early or late in life, we can imagine many different types of subpersonalities developing in much the same way as the Motorcyclist did. These different subpersonalities would arise in relationship to many different unifying centers—parents, siblings, school, profession, philosophical systems, religious environments, and the natural world (we will examine this developmental process more fully in Chapter 6).

Subpersonalities are called into being within our relationships to significant inner and outer environments that function as unifying centers for our experience. As we interact with these environments of meaning, we actively draw from the vast riches of our unique human potential, both learned and inherited, to form different unified, stable modes of expression. It is as if we are artists, our human potential is our palette, and subpersonalities are our creative expressions within particular environments (unifying centers). These creative expressions together, then, help form the larger system of the *personality*, that overall expression of ourselves in our lives as a whole.[2]

> ... each one of us has different selves—according to the relationships we have with other people, surroundings, groups, etc.
>
> —Roberto Assagioli

Clearly, subpersonality formation seems a natural and healthy structuralization process of the human personality, a gift of the middle unconscious, the subsystems that make up the larger system of the personality as a whole. So why should we be aware of them, much less learn to work with them? The answer is that few subpersonalities escape primal wounding, and so often will have difficulty finding their authentic expression within our inner and outer worlds. Indeed, we often first become aware of subpersonalities because they are disrupting our lives in some way.

Accordingly, the following phases of *personality harmonization* begin with a *survival phase*—quite like the survival stage in the larger process of psychosynthesis—in which subpersonalities operate as defensive structures rather than free expressions of our true selves. The phases of personality harmonization are: (0) *survival*, (1) *recognition*, (2) *acceptance*, (3) *inclusion*, and (4) *synthesis* (modified from Vargiu 1974b).

SUBPERSONALITIES IN SURVIVAL

To the extent that there has been an empathic responsiveness to us within our early environments—within early unifying centers—the subpersonalities and their relationships will be authentic expressions of who we truly are, together forming a larger personality that is authentic—in other words, authentic personality. But to the extent that empathic responsiveness is absent in our early environments, the subpersonalities and their relationships will embody strategies for surviving the primal wounding sustained in these environments, forming a personality devoted to this survival—in other words, survival personality.

For example, George's motorcyclist subpersonality might have developed as a result of being shamed and rejected by his father—primal wounding. Here the motorcyclist subpersonality might be based on an earlier Angry Teen subpersonality, developing eventually into an Outlaw Biker identity. This Outlaw Biker would be fueled by a rage and rebellion in reaction to these inner feelings of low self-worth. The subpersonality would now not be a free and natural expression of George's gifts and skills but a formation that manages primal wounding. This type of subpersonality might act out in a variety of ways, making it difficult to contact and heal the wounding.

Primal wounding can force any of our subpersonalities into a survival mode. Wounding might create, for example, not a parental subpersonality expressing our natural nurturing ability but a parental subpersonality who treats children as objects to fill a void of meaninglessness and loss. Or, instead of a lover subpersonality who expresses a gift for giving and receiving love, we might find a lover subpersonality who addictively uses relationships to stave off a sense of loneliness and isolation. Or, in place of a businessperson subpersonality expressing our highest values, instead there may be a subpersonality dominated by fear, greed, and self-centeredness.

Subpersonalities operating in survival mode are not natural expressions of our truest essential self or "I" but are dominated by the urgent necessity of managing primal wounding. Here our personality is rife with the rigidity, compulsions, and conflicts of the subpersonalities, and our consciousness and will are lost in these strong dynamics. In other words, we become chronically identified with, immersed within, the subpersonalities and so become unconscious of who we are. To the extent that this identification with subpersonalities occurs—and it seems to happen to each and every one of us to a greater or lesser degree—many different difficulties arise.

For one, subpersonalities in the survival phase place us at the mercy of the environment, because different situations will automatically trigger them in ways that may not serve us. Encountering an authority figure, we may unwillingly find ourselves becoming intensely hostile or overly passive—subpersonalities perhaps reacting to early abuses of parental authority. Or, as we begin to make an important speech, we may be filled with anxiety and have trouble even getting the words out—a young subpersonality still feeling the embarrassment and fear of childhood piano recitals. Or, facing the angry bullying of a partner, we may become frozen and unable to confront this emotional abuse—a helpless part of us going along in order to survive. Or, finally, attempting to become physically intimate with a lover, we may find ourselves inexplicably panicky or angry—a subpersonality reacting to early sexual wounding.

All such situations are ones in which the wounds of a subpersonality are impinged upon, automatically triggering learned survival reactions that may now be out of place and counterproductive in our lives. These reactions take place in spite of our will to do otherwise and in spite of our consciousness of a better way to respond. The subpersonalities are driven by primal wounding, and because of this powerful dynamic, they easily dominate and obscure our sense of "I."

Another thing that happens when subpersonalities are driven by wounding is that the relationships among them become highly charged and conflictual. For example:

> Beth reached out to her new friend with what she hoped was a humorous comment. But because she was fearful of rejection, the comment was forced and unnatural; the comment came out not humorous, but cynical and cutting, surprising and offending her friend. Alone later, Beth found herself in a terrible emotional state, feeling utterly ashamed and foolish. She angrily berated herself: "How could you have been so stupid? What a total idiot! Just keep your mouth shut next time." She felt hopeless, and her dark mood lifted only gradually over the next several days.

In Beth's case, she had a subpersonality who wanted to reach out to the new friend. But because of early experiences of rejection, the situation was profoundly clouded by an anxiety that caused a clash rather than a connection with the friend. Then a critical subpersonality took over, furious that the first subpersonality had made them vulnerable with the humorous comment. Further exploration revealed that the critical subpersonality also was afraid that being vulnerable in relationships would only lead to the hurts suffered in earlier relationships. In short, the wounding of the two subpersonalities caused a strong conflict within Beth, an interpersonal disconnection with her friend, and finally her depressed mood.

Much of our anxiety, depression, rage, and low self-worth often can be traced to such conflicts between subpersonalities, not to mention our everyday moods and ambivalences. For example, a risk-taking subpersonality may conflict with one who is seeking security; a relationship-oriented subpersonality might fight with a subpersonality who fears commitment; a subpersonality who wants to be liked may clash with one who wants to speak the truth; a student subpersonality's desire to study might collide with another's desire to go to the beach with friends; or a spiritual subpersonality may criticize the mundane practical concerns of a pragmatist subpersonality.

If there has been little or no wounding, we would expect minimal conflict among subpersonalities; conflicts such as those just listed, if they occurred at all, would be quite easily resolved as all of the various underlying needs were included in our lives as a whole. With wounding, however, such conflicts may become painful and even debilitating. Here subpersonalities operate from desperate, rigid positions, and mutual coexistence and cooperation are extremely difficult. Wounding creates a highly charged inner atmosphere that makes it difficult to have any sense of self from which to guide and express the parts in a coherent way.

Oddly enough, another problem with wounded subpersonalities occurs when they do *not* cause disruptions in our lives and instead operate smoothly to form survival personality. Here we move seamlessly among the subpersonalities over days, months, and years, never noticing that we are automatically adopting different and even dissonant patterns of thought and action in various situations. There is no thread of consciousness, no sense of "I," which is aware of the subpersonalities as they move into and out of expression. Thus the subpersonalities live our lives for us; we live on automatic pilot, in a trance.

Such a survival personality can be extremely high functioning and successful by all social standards. However, achievements and possessions will ultimately fail to fulfill; relationships will be superficial; compulsions, obsessions, and addictions will abound (though these often will be well hidden); the underlying despair, anxiety, and emptiness will haunt us; and the heights and depths of human existence will be beyond our grasp.

Whether wounded subpersonalities are reacting extremely to events, fighting among themselves, or forming a well-functioning survival personality, their need to manage the wounding can dominate our lives. Our essential I-amness is buried; we are identified with, immersed within, the tumult and trance of the subpersonalities. So too we are distracted from uncovering and expressing our highest values, our ultimate concerns, and our more profound life directions—treasures to be found in relating to deeper Self. This type of chronic identification with subpersonalities is characteristic of the survival stage of psychosynthesis, and as we will see shortly, working through the phases of personality harmonization can be an effective way to engage the stages of exploration and emergence.

As discussed earlier, the transition out of the survival stage of psychosynthesis seems most often marked by some crisis of transformation that breaks through our status quo. In terms of subpersonalities in the survival phase, this can mean a subpersonality reaction that finally becomes too much for us, as perhaps a reaction to authority that endangers our job; or an anxiety or rage that disrupts our lives; or perhaps a powerful event—positive or negative—that shakes our world.

However it occurs, when this unconscious functioning is disrupted, we move toward empathically connecting to our subpersonalities and allowing them to become authentic expressions of who we truly are. We are then ready to move out of survival into the next phase of developing a relationship with subpersonalities—recognition.

RECOGNITION

After our survival mode is disrupted in some way, we can develop a careful mindfulness toward our ongoing inner experiences. This introspective focus leads to the discovery that our moods and passions and feelings and thoughts are not simply inexplicably random events but expressions of deeper organizing structures—subpersonalities. For example, we may, over the course of a day, find that we are feeling critical, then later on move from that experience into feeling loving, and then after some time has passed may find that we are feeling sad. But these are not simply fleeting, unpatterned experiences.

Tracing the experience of feeling critical, we may uncover a judgmental subpersonality, a part of us with a particular value system, specific emotional tone, unique history in our lives, and even a characteristic body posture and visceral sense.

Exploring the feeling of love, we may recognize a lover subpersonality, one who has over the years learned to love in a particular way, to have particular likes and dislikes, and to feel and act physically in certain ways.

Looking into our sadness, we may discover a younger, sensitive part that feels our pain and the pain of others, that believes the world is a desolate place, that remembers our losses, a part whose affect is melancholy and whose physical manifestation is a certain downcast of shoulders and head.

Here are subpersonalities within us, each with their own unique and abiding pattern of physicality, affect, thought, and behavior. They move into and out of our awareness from the middle unconscious (see Chapter 2), and they operate in our lives whether we are conscious of them or not.

This exploration into subpersonalities amounts to an emergence of the consciousness aspect of "I," as described in Chapter 3. Here arises an ability not only to observe our passing experience but to see the patterns that organize this experience. Dynamically,

> The starting point is the complete immersion in each sub-personality, with degrees of awareness of the incongruity of the situation. The goal is the freed self, the I-consciousness, who can play consciously various roles.
>
> —Roberto Assagioli

the process of recognizing subpersonalities is quite like that stance adopted when doing meditation or contemplation in which we simply observe the passing contents of consciousness without becoming involved in them. The difference here is that instead of observing only the contents of consciousness, we are observing the organizing structures or contexts of our consciousness as well.

By practicing this deeper mindfulness over days, months, and even years, we can learn to recognize and affect these abiding structures of our inner worlds. An expression of "I" thereby begins to emerge that is distinct-but-not-separate from both the contents and structures of consciousness; this emergence heralds a deeper engagement with and full expression of the many aspects of ourselves.

Many Paths to Recognition

Once we are willing to observe our experience in this mindful manner, recognition of subpersonalities may occur in any number of ways. Working with nocturnal dreams, we may realize that what appears as a threatening figure in a dream is actually a subpersonality emerging from the unconscious that can eventually add valuable new qualities to our lives. Or we may begin to feel phony or dishonest in realizing how radically different we are with different people, only gradually discovering that these are simply multiple parts of ourselves. Or perhaps other people will give us surprising feedback about our behavior: that our seemingly innocent comments have a cutting, hurtful edge to them, or that we hide a wonderfully creative or gentle side of ourselves, or that we always seem to become humorous whenever emotionally loaded issues come up.

In fact, when we become willing to become conscious in this way, it is quite easy to begin recognizing subpersonalities. It is important, then, in the recognition phase, to remember the principle of fractional analysis, discussed in Chapter 3. That is, the idea is not to uncover as many subpersonalities as we can, because this would simply tend to confuse and overwhelm us:

> So recognizing most subpersonalities is hardly ever a problem. In fact it often takes less work to find new ones than to deal effectively with the ones we already have recognized. When people are first acquainted with the idea of working with subpersonalities, they often tend to do just that, becoming so fascinated with uncovering a teeming cast of thousands that the more fruitful work of understanding and integrating the central ones is neglected. (Vargiu 1974b, 77)

The aim in the recognition phase is not simply to discover all of our subpersonalities (even if this were possible) but instead to focus on those perhaps two to six that seem to be naturally emerging in our lives. This allows the exploration to remain meaningful and gives plenty of time to develop empathic relationships with each of them.

Subpersonalities often are recognized in counseling and therapy. Here, looking carefully at the deeper patterns underlying our lives, we will find the hidden world of subpersonalities. Let us look at Mark, who began to recognize two important subpersonalities.

Mark in Recognition

Here are the words of Mark, a twenty-seven-year-old graphic designer who entered psychosynthesis therapy struggling with a conflict between career and relationships:

> I hate relationships. Well, not totally. At first it's great, but then it begins feeling like they're too much emotionally. So then I sort of let it fall apart,

not doing much about it, and eventually it's over and I can get back to my work. Yeah, work's a pain sometimes, but at least I'm good at it. Then I start feeling lonely again, wanting someone.

In the above quotation, we can hear a work-oriented subpersonality and a relationship-oriented subpersonality who are in strong conflict with each other. As painful as this conflict is, Mark is at least somewhat aware of these two dissonant attitudes within himself. Formerly he had been caught in an unconscious survival personality pattern in which he cycled through periods dominated by work, then relationships, then work, and so on. During this time his partners were aware of mixed messages: at times his behavior would be saying, "I want to be close to you," and at other times, "Go away and leave me alone." Thus his inner conflict, even though he was not yet aware of it or its effects on his life, was causing hurt and confusion for other people.

For years Mark moved unknowingly between these two parts of himself, oblivious of the conflicting motivations within him. So in some ways this was inwardly a very harmonious time for him; he cycled unconsciously between career and relationships with no overarching awareness embracing both parts—no sense of "I" that could include these two inner structures of consciousness. When in one mode, he knew little about the other, so there was no sense of inner dissonance. The idea that he might have an inner duality would have seemed quite foreign to him at this point; if his contradictory behaviors had been pointed out to him, he might have argued quite honestly that he was simply acting differently at different times. These two subpersonalities were important elements in his survival personality, hiding the uncomfortable dynamics underlying his conscious experience; the subpersonalities were like atoms making up the molecule of the survival personality.

But as time passed, the repetitive pain of failed relationships grew, his loneliness became more intense, and his work began to suffer. Eventually the unconscious harmony of the survival personality was broken, and he entered a period of turmoil in which he began to encounter inexplicable feelings of loneliness, anxiety, and depression—a crisis of transformation, leading him toward hitting bottom. The intensity of his pain and confusion led him to consider the possibility that something might be happening *within* him that was causing this chronic, painful state of affairs. For the first time he began to consider that the problem may not be "relationships" or "the world" but something within himself, something of which he knew nothing at all.

Returning to Mark as he spoke the words quoted above, we can follow him as he begins to recognize the subpersonalities underlying his turmoil. The following occurred in the therapy session shortly after his earlier statement:

Therapist: So how does it feel when you're lonely?

Mark: I don't know, like it would be nice to have somebody and not be alone all the time.

T: Would you like to explore this a bit?

M: Sure, anything to get rid of it.

T: Okay, then, first, do you feel this loneliness in your body?

M: I guess so. Yeah, it's like an ache in my chest, my heart.

T: Let yourself experience that if you are willing to.

M: It actually hurts a little. My chest and throat feel all tight.

T: If you're willing to, let yourself keep feeling that, tune into it even more.

M: (Pause.) I feel a tightness all through here (indicates his chest area). It feels constricted. There's tension in my neck and shoulders too. Feels hot.

T: Let yourself stay aware of this. Close your eyes if you want.

M: (Closes his eyes.) It's just tight, tight, like a ball. It's a little bit scary. Hmm, now I feel sad. That's weird. Sad, real sad. It feels totally alone too. There's no one. (A tear rolls down Mark's cheek.)

T: Are there words?

M: Just that I feel real, real alone.

T: If you let an image come for that one who is alone, what would you see?

M: I just see this lonely guy in the dark, no one around. He's got his head down in his hands.

T: How do you feel towards him?

M: He sorta repulses me. He's like, wallowing in self-pity. He's the wimp in me.

Mark has clearly recognized a part of him with feelings of sadness and loneliness, which at this point he called a wimp. To review the steps of this recognition, it began with his conflict between career and relationships, moved to his loneliness, and then to the physical sensations associated with the loneliness, and finally to the subpersonality who felt lonely. With guidance, here Mark has begun an intentional exploration into the depths beneath the surface layer of his conscious experience—the emergence of largely middle unconscious material into awareness. Mark's inner experience at this point in the session is illustrated in Figure 4.2.

Here we see his personal essence—"I"—embedded within the part that dislikes the loneliness and sadness; that is, his consciousness and will seem to originate from within this part, conditioning how he views and responds to the lonely part (note that his field of consciousness and will extends only to the outer layer of the lonely part).

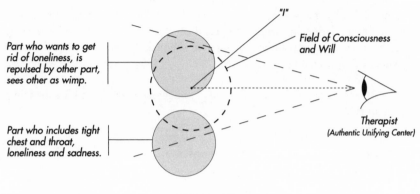

FIGURE 4.2

The therapist acts as an authentic unifying center, seeing Mark not as identical to either part but as one who is distinct but not separate from the parts. As we shall see, this empathic connection will allow Mark to actualize a potential for moving among the parts and working with them.

But Mark now faces the next phase in developing a relationship with a subpersonality—*acceptance*.

ACCEPTANCE

The phase of acceptance is the beginning of an empathic concern for the subpersonality, a beginning respect for the subpersonality "as a person," so to speak. From a foundation of acceptance, an ongoing relationship with the subpersonality can grow, leading eventually to that subpersonality finding its place within the larger community of the personality as a whole.

Note, however, that *acceptance of a subpersonality does not necessarily mean condoning or allowing its behavior.* Often acceptance of a subpersonality is like the acceptance shown by an experienced schoolteacher toward a problematic student: the teacher establishes an empathic bond of trust and respect but sets limits on disruptive behavior, thus allowing the student a safe relationship within which to grow and change. So, for example, subpersonalities who feel impelled to act destructively out of their rage or anxiety may need help in working with their behaviors.

Without this type of empathic acceptance for the various parts of ourselves, we will be ever at war with them, and they with us. As we return to Mark, it becomes clear that he is being challenged in the acceptance phase.

MARK IN ACCEPTANCE

At the point where we stopped in Mark's session above, he is repulsed by the part that was feeling lonely and sad. Acceptance clearly is not yet present, as exemplified by the pejorative word "wimp" itself. When this type of tension is found in a relationship with a subpersonality, acceptance will need to emerge if the inner conflict is to be ameliorated. We pick up the session at the point where Mark is feeling repulsed:

> *M:* He sorta repulses me. He's like, wallowing in self-pity. He's the wimp in me.
>
> *T:* How does he respond to you saying that?
>
> *M:* He just hangs his head and turns away.
>
> *T:* How does that make you feel?
>
> *M:* That's fine with me. Who needs him? He's the one always wanting to be with people and getting us in trouble. I'd rather just focus on my work. That's what's important.
>
> *T:* Try something, Mark. Imagine for a moment that you can become him. Actually enter into him, become him, feel what he feels.
>
> *M:* (Pause.) Okay, I'm the wimp.
>
> *T:* How do you feel?
>
> *M:* Hmm. Sad, lonely, and pissed at that Worker guy for saying those things. The hell with him. Let him work and die alone, for all I care.
>
> *T:* Tell him that.
>
> *M:* I did, and he's surprised. He didn't think I had it in me (chuckles).

Since the therapist is holding Mark as distinct but not separate from both parts, Mark is free to move from his initial identification into the experience of the lonely part in order to get to know this subpersonality better.

This shift of identity is illustrated in Figure 4.3, in which "I" is shown located now within the lonely part. He is now conscious and willing from within the lonely part. From this new perspective, he is, in effect, looking at the former identification, the part he has now named "that Worker guy." Through this shift, Mark has further discovered some of the inner experience of the lonely part, uncovering anger as well as loneliness and sadness.

Let us now return to the session, as the therapist invites Mark to continue his exploration by shifting his perspective between the parts. Note again that such an invitation can be extended because the therapist is still focused on Mark as one who is distinct but not separate from both parts, that is, "I."

> *T:* Okay, now become the Worker guy again. How do you feel towards the lonely guy now?
>
> *M:* Well, yes, surprised he's got so much umph. I guess he's not a wimp after all. I sort of respect him for that.

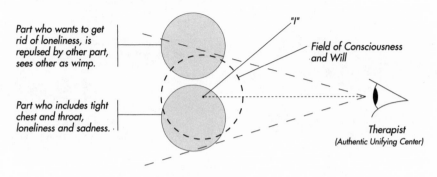

Part who wants to get rid of loneliness, is repulsed by other part, sees other as wimp.

Part who includes tight chest and throat, loneliness and sadness.

"I"

Field of Consciousness and Will

Therapist
(Authentic Unifying Center)

FIGURE 4.3

T: Ask him what his name is.

M: He says he's the Lover.

T: How is it to hear that?

M: Good. It's sure different than "wimp." He sounds interesting.

T: Want to go a little further with this?

M: Sure.

T: Okay, try stepping back from the Worker *and* the Lover, so that you can see both of them. What do you see?

M: (Pause.) I see two guys facing off each other. (Chuckling.) The Worker's real intense, sweaty, with his sleeves rolled up. They're in a stalemate. (Pause.) I guess that's where I've been for a long time now, right? Whew.

T: How do you feel towards them?

M: Good. Sort of fatherly. Compassionate.

As Mark discovered, he had begun the session identified with the Worker subpersonality; his sense of "I" had been merged with the viewpoint of the Worker. Identified with the Worker, he couched his problem as a conflict between himself and the problematic subpersonality later revealed as the Lover. From this initial identification, the Lover was "the problem" rather than the issue being the conflict between two parts of him.

However, *disidentifying* from the Worker and entering into the Lover (Figure 4.3), he could then directly contact the world of the Lover, fully experiencing the sadness, loneliness, and finally the anger toward the Worker. Then, as he disidentified from both the Worker and the Lover (illustrated in Figure 4.4), he found an inner stance that could accept and include both the Worker and the Lover.

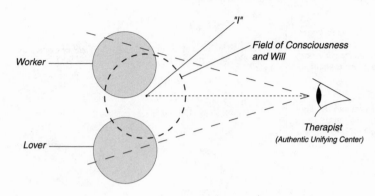

FIGURE 4.4

Through disidentification, Mark finds a position from which he can connect empathically to each part more deeply, facilitate their relationship, and eventually move toward a resolution of their conflict. His sense of identity is no longer caught up in either part, and he is free to extend his consciousness and will to each part as needed. Paradoxically, this allows him to uncover heights and depths in both parts that would have remained hidden by an identification with either of them. Again, this is facilitated by the therapist seeing *Mark* and not simply the two parts or their conflict.

> . . . the observer is not that which he observes.
>
> —Roberto Assagioli

NAMING SUBPERSONALITIES

Note that names for the subpersonalities emerged as the session progressed, following closely Mark's own descriptions of them. Naming can be an important step in developing an ongoing relationship with subpersonalities, as can learning the name of someone new in our lives. An infinite variety of names seems to exist for subpersonalities, for example, The Student, The Judge, Supermom, The Mystic, The Thrill Seeker, Savior, The Pragmatist, The Crone, The Jock, Dreamer, Guardian, or Thinker.

It is important when naming subpersonalities, however, to keep in mind that the purpose is to develop an empathic relationship with these parts of ourselves. For example, inaccurate or demeaning names will need to be changed over time as recognition and acceptance deepen. Nor is it helpful to objectify subpersonalities by the use of standardized labels or categories for them; again, the focus is on respect for the uniqueness of each part.

SUBPERSONALITY TECHNIQUES

Note that Mark's approach to his subpersonalities via body sensations, imagery, feelings, and dialogue is only one way that such work can be carried out. For example, one might act out the two parts and their relationship in the form of a psychodrama; or, as in Gestalt therapy, use pillows or chairs to represent the two subpersonalities, moving physically between them as the relationship develops (psychosynthesis would add a third chair representing the disidentified point); or move nonverbally among the different positions exploring the experience through the body alone; or develop a relationship with the parts using painting, clay, drawing, writing, or small figurines, as in sand tray work.

Subpersonality work can be carried out using a tremendous variety of techniques drawn from virtually the entire spectrum of different schools of psychology. In fact, individual practitioners who understand the overall process of subpersonalities have frequently created their own techniques on the spot to meet the specific needs of a particular client.

Given the variety and availability of techniques, finding a technique usually is not a problem. Problems can arise, however, if we become distracted by the techniques and forget the purpose they are to serve: to begin developing an empathic relationship with these various aspects of ourselves. Let us now move on to the third phase of personality harmonization—*inclusion*.

INCLUSION

Once we have recognized and accepted a subpersonality, we are in a position to receive that part into our personality as a whole, to welcome it as a valuable aspect of who we are, and to allow it to become a part of our lives. This involves an even deeper level of empathic connection, a phase that we have called *inclusion*.

A key to beginning the inclusion phase is to become increasingly intimate with the subpersonality so that we begin to move beneath its superficial presentation to the deeper needs that motivate it. We can see this deepening of empathy as Mark's individual session continues:

T: How do you feel towards them?

M: Good. Sort of fatherly. Compassionate.

T: Ask the Worker what he wants.

M: He says he wants to work, work, work, to get ahead, to make something of himself. He's very strong.

T: How do you feel about that?

M: I like his drive, but he's sorta got tunnel vision.

T: Tell him that, how does he respond?

M: He likes being liked.

T: Ask him what he most essentially needs from you.

M: He says he needs me not to forget him, to let him create and express. Also it seems like he's scared somehow about not making it in life.

T: Okay, now turn to the Lover and ask him what he wants.

M: He says he wants the Worker to go away. Forever.

T: How does that make you feel?

M: Kinda sad. The Worker seems an okay guy.

T: How does the Lover respond?

M: He gets it in a way, but doesn't know what else to do.

T: Ask him what he needs from you.

M: He says he just needs me to be with him, not to judge him.

T: Are you willing to meet these deeper needs they have?

M: Sure, especially if they'll stop fighting.

T: How are they doing now?

M: They're both just standing there. They're more relaxed. Tolerant of each other. They're glad I'm here.

Here there is a movement from the more surface level of behaviors and wants to the more essential level of needs. Contacting this deeper level means that Mark is not faced with the impossible task of dealing with the Worker's rigid demand for "work, work, work" and the Lover's impossible demand that the Worker "go away forever." Instead, Mark can deal with the much more flexible need of the Worker, "to create and express," and the Lover's, "to be with me." His empathic connection here reaches beyond the surface to the depths of the subpersonalities, touching a level at which right relationships can be formed.

This stance—of Mark relating to each subpersonality in an empathic manner—is fundamental to the inclusion phase. He is not so much addressing the relationship between the subpersonalities as he is establishing a direct connection with each one from a more objective and compassionate point of view. The subpersonalities do not have to trust each other at this point; they only have to trust Mark. It is this direct empathic connection that will allow each to heal and grow, to be included in the personality, and eventually, in the next phase of synthesis, to perhaps come to a new, creative relationship with each other.

LIVING WITH THE SUBPERSONALITY

Mark has done some fine work in this session, but if his transformational experiences with the subpersonalities are to actually manifest in his life, his active involvement with them will need to continue into his daily living; subpersonalities do not disappear when the session is over! In fact, it can be said that in a session we only glimpse potential, creating a template or pattern for possible change, and for this potential to actualize, this pattern must be acted upon, made manifest.

Such active manifestation is termed *grounding* (Vargiu 1974b), because insights and experiences from sessions are hereby grounded in ongoing daily living. Lack of attention to grounding is a criticism often leveled at psychotherapy in general, to wit, that psychotherapy only produces insight without any meaningful life change. However, grounding bridges insight with action, new experiences with ongoing experience, sessions with daily life.

In Mark's case, he maintained a mindful stance toward the Worker and Lover over the course of his day. This involved some amount of *time-sharing*

> However, the simplest and most frequent way in which we discover our will is through determined action and struggle.
> —Roberto Assagioli

(Vargiu 1974b) between the two subpersonalities, as he made sure each had some share of time in his life. Devoting quality time to the Worker, he was able to become more creative and expressive at work, and maintaining contact with the Lover, he was increasingly able to find times in which to enjoy his friendships and to begin to date once again.

This time-sharing was not easy, because there were periods in which he became lost once more in the Worker, becoming obsessed with work and ignoring relationships. This put him back into the conflict with which he began, but at least he knew where he was, how he got there, and how to proceed. Invariably this involved him reconnecting with the Lover, saying he was sorry, and then making amends, usually by giving the Lover (and so himself) more quality relationship time.

The ways that people find to include subpersonalities in their lives are as numerous as the subpersonalities themselves. From taking a nature-loving one to the ocean or the mountains; to buying art materials for an artistic part; to taking a class, playing a sport, or learning a craft; to challenging a friend whose remarks are hurtful to a vulnerable subpersonality; to watching particular films or reading particular books; to beginning to be aware of, and to express, one's feelings; to simply being with subpersonalities when they are in need—all such concrete actions, infused by empathic concern, are ways of including the many parts of ourselves in our lives. Such acts represent a commitment to change our lives in concrete ways so that all of who we are can find the space to live and express—the burgeoning of authentic personality.

THE HIGHER AND LOWER UNCONSCIOUS

For Mark, this type of ongoing empathic relationship involved getting to know his subpersonalities at even more profound levels of intimacy, uncovering their roots in the higher and lower unconscious.[3]

Relating to the Worker, he learned about the abuse suffered at the hands of his hypercritical and demanding father. Mark could never do enough to gain his father's respect, and the compulsivity of the Worker was an attempt to manage the pain of this primal wounding (lower unconscious material) by working harder and harder. But, too, Mark could now discover the gifts of personal integrity, self-respect, and power in the Worker, a contact with the higher unconscious that allowed him to meet his deadlines in a creative, more relaxed way. At one point, he reported that his work no longer felt like "a matter of life and death."

Relating to the Lover, Mark found many memories coming to him from his high school years, experiencing feelings such as shame, isolation, and grief, which took him eventually to early childhood memories of emotional and physical abuse—an exploration of the lower unconscious dynamics underlying the Lover. But as this empathic relationship with the Lover continued to grow, the Lover also became much more able to express qualities such as sensitivity, humor, and play, which long ago had been hidden away in the higher unconscious. His relationships became relatively free of the desperate push from the underlying loneliness and much more lighthearted and fulfilling as these transpersonal qualities were given expression.

Using Assagioli's oval-shaped diagram, the higher and lower unconscious areas of these subpersonalities might be represented as in Figure 4.5. This diagram illustrates that both the Worker and Lover contain aspects of themselves

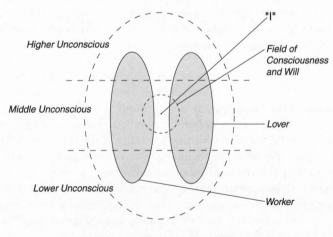

FIGURE 4.5

in the higher unconscious and lower unconscious. As Mark disidentified, he could empathically connect not only with the immediate manifestations of these subpersonalities in the middle unconscious but could reach as well to their heights and depths. His consciousness and will were free to relate to each and to guide each.

So rather than Mark unconsciously bouncing between these two parts of himself, or suffering their intense conflict, he now began to experience them as valuable modes of self-expression that added richness to his life. Formerly, the transpersonal qualities had been split off, repressed, and blocked by the conflict; now, with Mark's sense of "I" playing an active, nurturing role, these two subpersonalities began to unfold.

SYNTHESIS

The phases of recognition, acceptance, and inclusion seek to establish a direct, one-to-one, trusting relationship with a single subpersonality and to include it consciously within the personality; this holds true even when working with more than one subpersonality at a time, as Mark was doing. Although the first three phases may involve ameliorating a conflict between subpersonalities, this is done primarily to give each subpersonality a safe, nonconflictual space in which to heal and grow. This is an important principle, because often subpersonalities need to develop into their own unique identities before exploring their relationship with other subpersonalities.

Although there is not often a clear boundary between inclusion and synthesis, we might say that to the extent a subpersonality has blossomed within the secure holding of our empathic concern, it is ready to explore a more creative relationship with other subpersonalities—the phase of *synthesis*. This phase has to do with how subpersonalities interact with each other, how they may work together to form a more harmonious inner and outer expression of the personality as a whole. Clearly, this can happen only to the extent that the subpersonality is secure in its deeper connection to "I" and its place within the family of the personality.

Synthesis As a Continuation

Working with subpersonalities will not only reduce feelings such as anxiety, anger, and depression created by inner conflicts, not only heal these parts of us and unlock their treasures, but gradually may allow a new synthesis to emerge among the parts. Just as discrete learnings and gifts are brought together to form a subpersonality, so the subpersonalities themselves may be brought together to form a larger expression. That is, it is possible to look toward an even more developed pattern arising from an intimate communion among the parts.

For example, as the Lover and Worker resolve their conflict and begin to trust each other, they may begin to appear *together* in certain situations. At work, Mark might find that the Lover brings a certain playfulness and inter-personal sensitivity to his relationships with coworkers and clients, making work much more enjoyable and productive. In his social life, Mark may dis-cover that the Worker's qualities of integrity and self-confidence are quite helpful, creating a much more pleasurable and satisfying experience.

This communion or "dance" between the two parts may eventually give birth to a new subpersonality, who might be called the "Artist." This new sub-personality will be able to manifest the qualities of both the Lover and the Worker within a single expression. For example, the Artist might be extremely focused on a project while at the same time sensitive and responsive to the people around him; or the Artist, in synthesizing initiative, planning, and love, might allow Mark to express his caring and concern in creative ways, truly touching the people he loves. Here the two subpersonalities work together to create a larger conscious expression, embodying potentials that neither could manifest alone. A synergy between the two creates a whole that is greater than the sum of its parts.

Note that this process of synthesis is again the same one that we have seen from the earliest months of life. Mark's bringing together the Lover and the Worker in a coherent expression is dynamically the same as the infant syn-thesizing various schema into a smooth, thumb-to-mouth behavior, or bring-ing together different experiences into a coherent sense of self and other, or Assagioli's piano player developing from technique to artistic expression. In this process of synthesis, prior structures can become elements within a larger whole, forming a broader expression of who we are.[4]

SUBPERSONALITIES ARE PRESERVED

It is important to note in the phase of synthesis that as we begin to express this communion of subpersonalities, we may not be as directly conscious of the individual subpersonalities as we were in earlier phases. The reason for this is quite simple—the middle unconscious. What happens in such a synthesis is that our awareness shifts to a level of expression that the subpersonalities sup-port from behind the scenes, from within the middle unconscious. But it is not that the subpersonalities have disintegrated and disappeared. The Artist does not demand the extinction of the Lover and the Worker any more than a sports team demands the extinction of the players or an orchestra demands the extinction of the musicians. In fact, the synthesis or team can only mani-fest as the individuals maintain their own individual integrity. *Synthesis implies that individuality at all levels is preserved.*[5]

This notion of synthesis-as-community holds too when this team is not based on the especially close interplay seen between the Lover and the Worker. Often the new synthesis may be simply a generalized pattern of personal coherence in which subpersonalities cooperate in the living of a single life (this can be true for people with true multiple personalities, for example). This would be the case if Mark remained able to shift between the Worker and the Lover as needed and, similarly, among all of his other subpersonalities.

Any appropriate shifting among various parts implies synthesis, an esprit de corps, a higher-order organizing principle operating among the parts. Here there are less debilitating inner conflicts and more fluidity and responsiveness, which again indicate the emergence of a team or community with an overall life direction. In short, synthesis and psychological health do not demand some seamless fusion of all of the parts but rather the parts form a cooperative community in which the gifts of each of the parts are recognized, valued, and included within a meaningful life direction.

Having said all of this about the preservation of subpersonalities, we must add that there are times that can be characterized as the death of a subpersonality. This occurs when there is a subpersonality whose structure must de-integrate so that a new structure may arise. Often this seems to involve a subpersonality who has been highly structured and focused on a particular role or function, a role or function that the subpersonality no longer needs to fulfill. These times can be poignant, involving an appreciation for the service of that part and a grieving of its passing. Of course, the talents and skills of the old form will then become available in the growth of a new structure, so this is in fact a death and a rebirth. Nevertheless, the pain and grief are quite real and need to be engaged as this transformation proceeds. Even subpersonalities can have crises of transformation.

> Here the biological analogy is illuminating: there is no material fusion of organs or apparatus of the body—they remain anatomically and physiologically distinct—but their fusion is a functional unity.
>
> —Roberto Assagioli

Finally, the phase of synthesis implies an overall expression of the personality that is in alignment with the deepest currents of meaning in our lives (i.e., the expression of authentic personality). Just as a subpersonality discovers a unique part to play within the whole personality, so we may look to discover the unique part that we can play in the unfoldment of life around us. By analogy, it is as if we each are subpersonalities within a larger personality—whether a friendship, couple, group, or the world at large—and have a unique place within this larger whole, a call or vocation to express our gifts within this wider arena. To speak of this call, of course, is to speak of Self-realization, a developing relationship with Self in all aspects of our lives. We have outlined Self-realization in our discussion of the stages of psychosynthesis in the previous chapter, and we shall again take up this subject in Chapter 8.

But now let us turn our attention to the one who emerges in subpersonality work, the one who can be present and responsive to any and all subpersonalities—our essential identity, "I."

FIVE

THE NATURE OF
PERSONAL IDENTITY

> During and after this assessment of the sub-personalities one real-
> izes that the observing self is none of them, but something or
> somebody different from each.
>
> —Roberto Assagioli

In Chapter 2, we saw how Laura was able to relate to her Little One subpersonality, to take responsibility for this part of her, and finally to heal and nurture this part. Then, in Chapter 3, we followed Ellen as she moved through
the painful disintegration of who she thought she was toward a completely
new sense of herself. Finally, in Chapter 4, Mark began a session believing
that he was a worker in conflict with a problematic subpersonality, but then
he discovered that he *had* a Worker subpersonality who was in conflict with a
Lover subpersonality.

It is clear that there is a someone in all of these cases who has the ability
to move among these various personality patterns and is therefore somehow
distinct-but-not-separate from them. There is a someone who can relate to
the Little One, who can emerge from Ellen's seeming total disintegration of
identity, and who can disidentify from the Worker and Lover subpersonalities
and work with them.

This "who" is assumed by many different psychological approaches, from
the psychoanalyst asking us to observe and describe our inner-mind stream, to
the cognitive-behaviorist encouraging us to notice and manage our feelings and
thoughts, to the humanistic or transpersonal therapist inviting us to engage and
express our authentic experience. Western psychology has implicitly recognized
this "who" in terms such as Freud's (1978) *ego splitting*, Anna Freud's (1946)

endopsychic perception, Richard Sterba's (1934) *therapeutic dissociation*, Assagioli's (1965a) *disidentification* and, more recently, Arthur Deikman's (1982)
observing self.

Furthermore, many spiritual practices of both East and West assume this
same distinction between the essential person and the contents and states of
consciousness. Such practices involve sitting quietly and simply observing the
flow of experience without becoming caught up in this flow. This ability to
assume a stance of inner observation is, for example, fundamental to Western
contemplative prayer, as well as to Eastern approaches such as vipassana meditation and zazen.

It is fascinating that such seemingly dissimilar systems—secular and spiritual, East and West—all carry the assumption that we are not identical with
any particular content or state of consciousness, and that we are in some way
distinct from these. All of these differ-
ent approaches thus constitute unifying centers that see us as distinct-but-
not-separate from the contents of our
experience; they, to a greater or lesser
extent, mirror the someone who exists
among intrapsychic processes and who
can observe and choose in relationship
to these processes. Within the "gaze"
of such unifying centers, we discover the ability to put our awareness where
we will, whether in service of describing inner events, affecting these, or simply remaining uninvolved in them, as in meditation.

> . . . the inner experience of pure self-
> awareness, independent of any content
> or function of the ego in the sense of
> personality.
>
> —Roberto Assagioli

A DISIDENTIFICATION EXERCISE

Take a moment right now to explore this "who" for yourself by carrying out
the following experiment:

1. Close your eyes and become conscious of your physical sensations, the
    sounds you hear, your breathing, sensations of hot and cold, tension
    and relaxation. Notice that these sensations come and go in your
    awareness. Then ask yourself, "Who is aware? Who am I who remains
    among this change, who is somehow distinct-but-not-separate from
    this change, who can be present to each changing sensation as it
    arises?" The idea here is not to find the answer in an intellectual way
    but merely to pose the question and let go of it, allowing your own
    direct experience to respond.

2. Then become conscious of your feelings. How do you feel right now?
    Calm? Excited? Irritated? Sad? Happy? Notice that feelings can change
    continually in quality and intensity, coming and going in your awareness.

Again, ask yourself, "Who is aware? Who am I who remains among this change, who is somehow distinct-but-not-separate from this change, who can be present to each feeling as it arises?"

3. Next, become conscious of your thoughts. Notice how thoughts and images come and go in awareness in a constant flow. Your mind can think of this, then that, then be reminded of that, then conjure up images of what was and what may be. Now once again ask, "Who is aware of this constant flow? Who am I who remains among this change, who is somehow distinct-but-not-separate from this change, who can be present to each thought and image arising?"

4. Last, choose to become as conscious as you can of your right foot. Concentrate your awareness on your right foot, noticing as carefully as you can its position, the sensations of sock or shoe, whether and how it meets the floor, the bend of your toes, the feel of your instep, and any cool or warm sensations.

    Then move your consciousness again and become aware of your left knee. Notice if there is clothing around it, if you feel pressure at various points, at what angle it is bending, or if it is comfortable or uncomfortable. Take some time to become fully aware of your knee.

    Then move your awareness once again to become conscious of your right hand. Concentrate your attention on how your right hand feels right now, whether relaxed or clenched, hot or cold, touching and being touched, and how your fingers are being held.

    Now ask yourself, "How did I just move my awareness from my right foot to my left knee to my right hand? What is this ability I have to place my awareness where I want it?" Again, let your experience respond. You might explore this further by moving your awareness at will. Focus inwardly, perhaps, on things such as your breathing and bodily sensation, or focus outwardly, on different objects in your environment. Practice moving your consciousness wherever you choose. How do you do that?

    This ability you have to direct your consciousness, to place it where you wish, is what Assagioli calls *will*.

In psychosynthesis, this essential "you" who can be aware and who can make choices is termed *"I"* or *personal self* and possesses the two functions of *consciousness* and *will*. Let us look more closely at the nature of this mysterious "I" who seems able to be conscious of and to dynamically interact with the various contents of the personality.

EMPATHIC "I"

Think of times you have spent with a close friend, someone who knows you well, accepts you, and with whom you feel free to be yourself. Notice that in the presence of this friend you can, for the most part, allow your spontaneous inner experiences to be felt and shared. You can be relatively nondefensive and unguarded, can feel safe being happy or sad, angry or hurt, serious or playful. The two of you can relate spontaneously and authentically, talking about virtually any topic that comes to mind and perhaps laughing good-naturedly at the foibles of your humanness.

In moments of such intimate empathic connection, you are profoundly seen, heard, and met by the other. Your friend does not see you in a limiting or constraining way; you are not expected to fulfill a role, maintain a particular belief system, or express a particular emotional tone. Your friend, acting as an authentic unifying center, sees and accepts *you* with all of your different parts.

This empathic relationship, in turn, allows you to be empathic with yourself—you are free to allow all parts of yourself to come and go, to be aware of all of them as they arise, to move easily among them, and to express them at will. As psychosynthesis therapist Chris Meriam (1996) puts it, "Empathy begets empathy."

DISIDENTIFICATION

This empathic experience with your friend also can be called an experience of *disidentification*. That is, you are not stuck in, *identified* with, any particular pattern of feeling, thought, and behavior but can shift and move among all of them. You are clearly distinct-but-not-separate from the various contents of your inner world, that is, *disidentified* from them all. You are someone who, because distinct from the contents of your inner world, can potentially interact empathically with any and all of these contents.

In other words, here there is an emergence of the essential empathic you—"I"—with the functions of consciousness and will. This meeting with your friend might be diagrammed as in Figure 5.1.

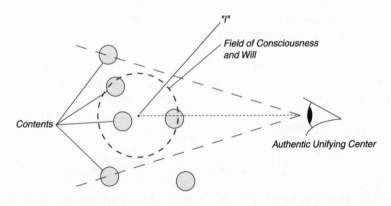

FIGURE 5.1

The seeing eye illustrated at the right side of Figure 5.1 represents your friend and the empathic gaze with which you are seen. Note, *you* are seen— the horizontal dotted line is focused directly upon "I," not on any one particular content of experience (thoughts, feelings, sensations, subpersonalities, etc.). You are not seen as this or that content but as the one who is experiencing these various contents.

The changing contents of our consciousness (the sensations, thoughts, feelings, etc.) are one thing, while the "I," the self, the center of our consciousness is another.

—Roberto Assagioli

Furthermore, all of the contents (shaded circles) that move into awareness also are seen and accepted by the other (an acceptance represented by the two broken lines radiating from the eye). This empathy allows the contents to then flow freely into and out of your field of consciousness and will, with no need to censor or control them. You—"I"—remain disidentified from any particular content and are free to relate to all of them. This diagram thus represents an openness to— *and a full engagement with*—your ongoing, spontaneous experience as it arises in the moment.

(In an empathic relationship, this empathic gaze often is reciprocal, each person functioning as an authentic unifying center for the other. We have, for simplicity's sake, only illustrated one side of the relationship.)

Note that you do not experience "I" as simply another content of your awareness. "I" is not another shaded circle of which you can be aware. In fact, you do not experience "I" at all! While you can be aware of a thought, an image, an intuition, a feeling, or a physical sensation, you cannot be aware of "I" in the same way; you cannot experience "I" as an object of your awareness, any more than you can see the back of your retina. "I" is ever the one who is aware, the experiencer not the experience.

To put it another way, you do not have an "I." You *are* "I." You, "I," are the someone who experiences all of the changing contents of experience, moves among them, and affects them. From this point of view, "I" is not a "self" or "an I" at all but no-self, no-thing.[1]

IDENTIFICATION

The above experience with a good friend is quite different from one in which you relate to someone who does *not* see and accept you but who is open to only a limited range of who you are.

In the case of Ellen in Chapter 3, for example, it is clear that for most of her life she had been seen simply as the role she played in her family, not as someone with a life of her own. Within the nonempathic family environment, she developed a survival personality that was motivated to ignore her own needs and to serve other people.

Over the years, Ellen became *identified* with this survival personality, believing that this was who she truly was. She was not aware of her personal needs, passions, pain, or anger—all of these were kept out of her awareness by the identification with the survival personality. This type of nonempathic relationship is illustrated in Figure 5.2.

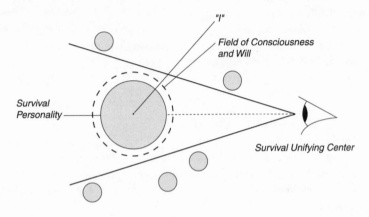

FIGURE 5.2

The eye depicted on the right side of Figure 5.2 now represents the non-empathic mirroring from Ellen's family system—the survival unifying center—which does not see Ellen ("I") but rather sees only the self-effacing survival personality (the horizontal broken line from the eye reaches only the survival personality, not "I").[2] Here "I" is identified, embedded within the survival personality; Ellen can only use her consciousness and will from within the world of the quiet, dependent, helper role.

Note that "I" is not free to move spontaneously throughout a natural range of experience. Contents of experience that are not consistent with the survival personality (the small circles) are blocked from entering Ellen's consciousness (the unbroken lines radiating from the eye are barriers). For her to be aware of contents outside of the self-effacing identification—her own needs and passions, for example, or the guilt and shame directed at these—is simply too dangerous, as this places her, in effect, outside of her role and thus outside of the family. To the extent that she breaks her role to engage these forbidden contents, she will experience psychological isolation and abandonment by the family—an unthinkable prospect for a child.

> . . . self-consciousness is generally hazy, because of its many identifications.
>
> —Roberto Assagioli

This situation is, of course, what we have been calling primal wounding, the wounding caused by not being seen as who we truly are. Ellen is not seen, so she must dissociate certain parts of herself. Later in her life, when the bounds of her survival personality are breached by her experience with her boss, she confronts this wounding in a journey toward wholeness and authenticity.

Survival personality is held in place even after childhood, because the survival unifying center is internalized. This survival orientation is further reinforced, because it guides the selection of career, friends, romantic partners, and spouses. Survival personality builds a lifestyle around it, creating a life that reflects the early environment in subtle and not so subtle ways.

THE TURMOIL OF DISIDENTIFICATION

There is a further important insight about disidentification to be gained from Ellen's experience. While disidentification can be associated with experiences of freedom, peace, and serenity (e.g., Mark in Chapter 4), Ellen's experience reveals that it may just as easily involve turmoil, inner conflict, and anxiety. That is, on the surface she was much more serene while she was still identified with her survival personality. She was relatively content, experiencing little or no inner conflict; her inner world, though severely contracted, was at least stable and secure.

However, when she was passed over for the promotion, the contents from outside of her identification became so energized that they burst into her consciousness in a very upsetting manner. She entered a crisis of transformation. No longer the eager helper with no needs, she found, to her distress, that she was feeling pain, rage, and an impulse to violence. This was a bursting of the bounds of her survival personality and led to her moving forward in her growth by expanding the range of her personal experience to include much of her hidden heights and depths.

> . . . the last and perhaps most obstinate identification is with that which we consider to be our inner person.
>
> —Roberto Assagioli

Thus for Ellen disidentification was not a calm, quiet, centered experience. Quite the contrary, in disidentifying from her calm, quiet, survival personality, she found herself plunged into the intense, tumultuous experiences so long hidden by her chronic identification. She began grappling with the unconscious inner structures that had been conditioning her sense of identity all of those years. Disidentification simply moves us toward a deeper experience of our existence, and this may or may not be serene or even pleasant.

THE IDEALIZATION OF DISIDENTIFICATION

Unlike Ellen, on the other hand, we may indeed have a particular experience of disidentification that feels liberating, gives us a sense of serenity, or allows a feeling of expansion. Such experiences will occur especially when we disidentify from patterns that are oppressive, chaotic, or constricting. *But it is important not to make the mistake of then equating disidentification with these particular experiences.*

That is, we must not then assume that disidentification *is* an experience of liberation, serenity, or expansion. As Ellen discovered, disidentification can just as easily mean engaging difficult experiences as well.

If we confuse disidentification with any particular type of experience, there is a danger that we will begin to confuse "I" with particular types of experience: "When I disidentify, I feel _____ , therefore, 'my true I' is _____ ." The problem here is that "I" is becoming objectified. "I" is understood not as who we are but as a psychological place, an attainment, a certain type of experience. In other words, "I" is misunderstood as a potential *mode* of consciousness rather than as the *one who experiences* all modes of consciousness.

Confused by this objectification, we may make statements such as: "When I am identified with my I, I feel free," or "I feel serene when I am in my I," or "I feel expanded and enlarged when I am in the I-space." But then, who is this "I" who "identifies with my I," or "is in my I," or "is in the I-space"? Suddenly there are two "I"s running around here. Befuddled by this misunderstanding of the nature of disidentification and "I," we may then begin to seek these freeing or serene experiences and to ignore less pleasant ones, thinking that these pleasant experiences constitute who we essentially are— *and thus we begin to form a survival personality based on acquiring and maintaining these experiences.*

Ironically, of course, you can never become "I," identify with "I," or move toward "I," because you always *are* "I" and cannot be other than "I." Whether feeling liberated or oppressed, serene or conflicted, expansive or contracted, identified or disidentified, on the heights of a unitive experience or in the depths of despair, merged with the Divine Ground or experiencing the Void, you are "I." To think "I" is a place to get to or a goal to attain completely misses the essential nature of "I." Again, "I" is not any particular experience but the experiencer. You are already, right this instant and forevermore, "I."

THE TRANSPERSONAL IDENTIFICATION

It is important to understand that there can be many different levels of disidentification, that we can be disidentified at one level yet identified at another. This is seen quite clearly in cases of *transpersonal identification*, identifying with aspects of the higher unconscious while remaining largely dissociated from other dimensions of the psyche-soma. Such an identification can be developed after powerful peak experiences, immersion in religious and spiritual study, and/or in becoming adept at practices such as prayer and meditation.[3]

Within a transpersonal identification, we may, in meditation, become masters of allowing all thoughts, feelings, and sensations to pass through our awareness without becoming caught up in them—we are disidentified from this flow of inner experience. However, we may find that even with this acute ability to disidentify, we are nevertheless controlled by unconscious structures within us. For example, we may yet be caught in destructive addictions, dependencies, and interpersonal styles that cause difficulties for ourselves and for those around us.

In these cases it is quite true that we are observing the flow of inner experience, that we are disidentified from these contents. Yet we are, at the same time, observing through the colored lens of a transpersonal identification that is preventing a direct, unmediated engagement with other levels of us. Jacob Barrington, a Buddhist priest who entered Al-Anon, a twelve-step program for those dealing with the painful effects of relating to alcoholics, says:

> In the two years since I joined Al-Anon I've experienced more healing and personal transformation than in my 17 years of pre-Al-Anon Zen practice.
>
> In all my years of sitting zazen, I got pretty good at forgetting the self, at letting go. Pleasant and painful memories, fear, nostalgia, anger, resentment, joy, worry, delight, jealousy, longing, sadness, would all arise in my mind as I sat, and I let them go with the greatest of ease. They didn't matter, I knew. They were only illusions. Ironically (and not coincidentally), however, this was exactly the message I had received from my parents growing up—that what I felt and thought and wanted didn't really matter. What I was doing in meditation wasn't letting go at all, it was repeating the denial I had learned as a child—and denial of my real self was the root of my sickness. (Barrington 1988)

While Barrington was clearly adept at one level of disidentification, this disidentification was itself conditioned by a deeper identification. In his case, a transpersonal or spiritualized identification kept him from fully engaging the nature and impact of his wounded childhood. We see a similar dynamic in Jack Kornfield's account of his return to the United States after five years of practicing as a Buddhist monk in Asia:

> What I found upon my return is that there are compartments in the mind. Although I worked well in certain compartments, when I got into an intimate relationship again, I was back exactly where I had left off: I was saying and doing the same old things. What was horrifying and interesting was that I could see it very clearly. Things that had been themes in my life—loneliness, fear of abandonment—were very, very visible. The same issues and fears not only remained but came back in spades. (in Simpkinson 1993, 37)

Of course, as practitioners of meditation and contemplative prayer know, these practices may, in many cases, take us to deeper levels of disidentification and to an encounter, for example, with our primal wounding. Psychotherapist James Finley says, "The contemplative attitude involves a weakening of one's defense mechanisms, not a strengthening of them" (Finley

1988). This is similar to Jack Engler's statement that insight meditation functions in some ways like an "uncovering technique," as found in psycho-dynamic therapies (in Wilber, Engler, and Brown 1986, 34) and Mark Epstein's (1995) recognition that meditation can reveal early wounding.

Yet this mindful observation of the inner flow of contents, while clearly a functioning of "I," may remain at only one level within us. We may be truly disidentified from the contents of our awareness yet still quite identified with, and controlled by, deeper structures of the personality that organize our expe-rience. But then we encounter troublesome compulsions or addictions, prob-lematic intimate relationships, or profound life crises that impact aspects of ourselves beyond the range of the present identification. Such crises of trans-formation will call us to disidentify from the former level of disidentification and expand the range of our experience to include these new experiences. We here, with many others, discover that we are far more than we thought we were, that the world is far more than we thought it was.

SPIRIT, SOMA, AND PSYCHE

As we observed in the exercise above, we are distinct-but-not-separate from physical sensations as well as thoughts and feelings. This points to a distinc-tion between "I" and both soma and psyche, both body and soul.

"I" is distinct from the world of soma or body, that is, from the public world of the physical body and outward behavior. This means simply that "I" cannot be reduced to any aspect of the physical organism, nor to any patterns of observable behavior. We might put it this way: "I am distinct, but not sep-arate, from my physical experience."

However, "I" is not only distinct-but-not-separate from soma but from psyche or soul as well. That is, private inner events such as feelings and desires, images and thoughts, dreams and visions, and peak and abyss experiences are distinct from "I" as well. We might say, "I am distinct, but not separate, from my soul experience."

Again, you can verify this distinction between "I" and psyche-soma or soul-body by noticing your own experience. There are times when you are acutely aware of your physical presence within the immediate physical envi-ronment and less aware of your inner experience. For example, when attempting to learn a physical skill or to perform a precise movement, you may be focused on these and relatively oblivious to your inner feelings. But then, at other times, perhaps listening to music or watching a film, you are more aware of your thoughts, feelings, and images than you are of your physicality; you may even forget where you

The "self," that is to say, the point of pure self-awareness, is often confused with the conscious personality . . . but in reality it is quite different from it.

—Roberto Assagioli

are in physical space-time and be transported to a realm of fantasy and feeling. We are distinct-but-not-separate from our soma and our psyche, so we are able to move between these two realms of experience or, if we wish, to experience them simultaneously.

"I" is therefore different from the Freudian *ego* when defined as "a coherent organization of mental processes" (Freud 1960, 7), because "I" is distinct from any "organization" or "mental process." Neither is "I" to be confused with the ideas or images we have of ourselves, whether we call these *self-images, self-representations*, or *I-thoughts*—"I" is distinct from ideas, images, and thoughts. This notion of "I" also is different from Fairbairn's (1986) *central ego* or *I*, which is seen as comprising elements split off from the *original ego*; from Winnicott's (1987) concept of *True Self*, which is defined as "the summation of sensori-motor aliveness"; and from Kohut's (1977) idea of *nuclear self*, which is thought of as a "structure" made up of "constituents." "I" is to be thought of as distinct from any summation of parts, from any sort of structure fashioned from contents or processes of either soma or psyche—otherwise we cannot conceptualize the fact that "I" can move among all such contents and processes.

This view would thus hold the human being not as a soul with a body, nor as a body with a soul, but as a living spirit immanent within *both* the body and soul. Human spirit is one and the same event embodied in two worlds: body and soul, soma and psyche.[4]

TRANSCENDENCE-IMMANENCE

Given our discussion so far, it seems obvious that "I" is highly elusive and difficult to conceptualize. While it seems safe to say that "I" has the functions of consciousness and will, there is yet a mystery surrounding this human spirit. This mystery revolves around the seeming paradox that we have the ability to observe and to engage in the same moment. That is, we can disidentify, realize that we are distinct from content and process, but by this very ability, we also embrace a far greater range of content and process than when identified. Our very ability to transcend particular identifications makes us able to be present to, to be more engaged in, areas of experience beyond that identification.

A term that holds this paradox is *transcendence-immanence* (Firman 1991; Firman and Gila 1997). That is, "I" is transcendent of content and process (the root of transcendent means "to climb over"), but by this transcendence, "I" can be immanent within content and process (the root of immanent means "to remain in or near").

Of course, transcendence and immanence are terms commonly used to refer to God, Spirit, or the Divine. However, it seems that the common usage of these terms often is misleading. For example, a "transcendent God" often is thought of as being far away, while an "immanent God" is thought to be close at hand.

But from our experience of disidentification, we see that this is a false dichotomy, because transcendence and immanence go hand in hand: to the extent that "I" is disidentified from a particular pattern—is transcendent of a particular pattern—"I" is *more* able to engage both that pattern and areas of experience beyond that pattern, that is, "I" is *more* immanent. Transcendence and immanence are not separate poles but appear together, two sides of the same coin, two descriptions of the same reality—the human spirit, or "I" (and as we shall see later, these terms describe deeper Self or Spirit as well).

> The Supreme Value, Cosmic Mind, Supreme Reality, both transcendent and immanent.
>
> —Roberto Assagioli

TRANSCENDENCE-IMMANENCE APPLIED

So, for example, Laura (Chapter 2) discovered that she was transcendent of her Little One subpersonality, and so she became more immanent—opening herself up to an adult perspective that could care for the Little One. Or Ellen's journey (Chapter 3) made her realize that she was transcendent of her survival personality, so she found herself immanent within a whole new range of experience. Mark, in the previous chapter, came into psychosynthesis therapy identified with the Worker subpersonality, eventually realized he was transcendent of both the Worker and Lover subpersonalities, and thus he was able to be immanent within both.

Staying with Mark's situation a moment, note that his original identification with the Worker subpersonality can be called *dissociation*, because he is relatively oblivious of the experience contained in the Lover. Dissociation—a nonempathic relationship with an aspect of ourselves—is a function of *identification*. In contrast, disidentification (transcendence) will create more empathy, more of a connection with the parts (immanence). *Dissociation is a function of identification, not disidentification.*

Within the ongoing empathic holding of psychosynthesis therapy, Mark initially disidentified from the Worker and thus became more directly aware of the Lover. But going further, he eventually found the inner space to reach beyond an identification with either subpersonality, and in so doing he was able to more fully engage each of them. (This disidentification was illustrated in Figure 4.4.)

> When this center has been experienced . . . then it is possible to synthesize the different aspects from which one has dis-identified oneself.
>
> —Roberto Assagioli

From this new inner stance, Mark could embark on an in-depth exploration of both subpersonalities. He discovered that the Lover had feelings of shame, isolation, and grief from early childhood; he also found the Lover's sensitivity, humor, and play, which had been repressed in the higher unconscious. Exploring the Worker, he discovered the wounding that he had received from his father; he also began to contact the personal integrity and self-respect hidden within this part. So, clearly, Mark's transcendence here allowed a full immanent experiencing of, and empathy with, both of these parts of himself. *Transcendence and immanence occur together.*

IDENTIFICATION VERSUS EXPERIENCING

It also is important to notice that when Mark was identified with the Worker, he was not only dissociated from the Lover but from the heights and depths of the Worker as well. This may seem strange, because one might think that to identify with something would mean to fully experience it. But no, identification is a technical term in psychosynthesis, meaning that we are trapped unknowingly within a pattern and believe the pattern to be all that we are; it does not mean that we are fully experiencing the pattern.

Quite the contrary, identification actually *limits* our ability to experience the pattern with which we are identified. Identification kept Mark trapped in a single, narrow sector of the Worker, unaware of the brokenness and gifts hidden within this part. But disidentification meant that he could fully enter into the experience of the subpersonality, to connect empathically with the hidden heights and depths therein. In other words, transcendence implies immanence.

On the other hand, Mark's work also illustrates how immanence implies transcendence. As he moved more deeply into the experience of each, realizing more immanence, his sense of transcendence increased as well. That is, his full exploration and experience of both parts led to a sense of being distinct from the parts—he could better observe them, empathically connect with them, and eventually guide them toward fulfilling their potential. Although it is true that entering into the direct experience of a particular pattern is an important aspect of increasing disidentification, we probably should avoid the word "identification" to refer to this direct experiencing.

The fact that immanence generates transcendence, and vice versa, helps demonstrate that transcendence and immanence are one, that they are simply two descriptions of the same human spirit, of "I."

TRANSCENDENT-IMMANENT MIRRORING

For disidentification to take place, we need authentic unifying centers that can mirror the transcendence-immanence of human spirit. We need some inner or outer context—whether a person(s), a natural setting, an art form, a psychology, a philosophy, or a sacred tradition—that can reflect back to us who we are, that can hold our essential selves. It is within such empathic environments that the transcendence-immanence of "I" emerges.

However, if Mark was continuously seen by himself and others as the Worker and nothing more, he would have had little room to discover that he was identified with the Worker. Such nonempathic mirroring ignores that Mark is distinct from—transcendent of—his experience. Here, as with any survival unifying center, there will be pressure to remain identified with a single, limiting way of being, until perhaps a crisis of transformation breaks the identification and a new unifying center is found.

This objectifying misperception of each other is, of course, endemic in daily life. We see people as stereotypes, as their roles, as objects to be used or discarded; we often focus not on the person who experiences but only on particular aspects of the person. In other words, we ignore that people are distinct but not separate from their psyches and somas.

But mirroring can become just as nonempathic by ignoring that we are embodied and engaged—immanent—within our lived experience. Here a unifying center may misperceive us as only pure essence, as a disembodied spirit, as an entity not essentially related to psyche-soma existence. An example of this was recounted by Prilly Sanville (1994) during a diversity presentation: a Caucasian woman told her African-American friend that she simply liked her as a person and did not even think of her as "black"—thus offending her friend, who said something like, "But I *am* black!" Another example of ignoring immanence can be seen in the following conversation between a recovering alcoholic and a friend:

> *Friend:* Why do you call yourself an alcoholic—that's so limiting and negative. Can't you just disidentify?
>
> *Recovering alcoholic:* But I *am* an alcoholic. If I don't recognize and accept this fundamental fact about myself, I will live a life of bondage.

But do not statements such as "I am black/white," or "I am an alcoholic/addict," or "I am gay/lesbian," or "I am a man/woman" represent identifications that keep us trapped in a narrow range of experience? Quite the contrary, more often than not such statements indicate basic truths that form our authentic personality. These truths are not all that we are, but they are certainly integral to who we are. So no, these statements need not point to identifications that limit our authentic experience; instead, they may be important personal truths whose recognition is fundamental to an authentic life.

For us to treat such statements as being in any way less than integral to the person constitutes an empathic failure, for example, "I don't even see you as black, as an alcoholic, as religious, as gay, and so on." Here we fail to mirror the person in his or her full transcendence-immanence. You cannot see me if you do not see that I am embodied in my grief and joy, my thoughts and beliefs, my body and gender, my disability and language, my family background and age, and my ethnicity and values. These are not irrelevant to who I am but integral aspects of my being in the world, of my transcendence-immanence. In a very real way, these *are* who I am (though not *all* I am).

Transcendent-immanent mirroring is a recognition of each other as distinct-but-not-separate from, neither different from nor the same as, our manifestations. We are seen as transcendent-immanent human spirit, as "I." In turn, this mirroring allows us to realize that this is indeed who we are.[5]

TRANSCENDENCE-IMMANENCE EAST AND WEST

Transcendence-immanence is recognized in many spiritual practices from different traditions. Note the similarity in the following two quotations, one from the East and the other from the West:

Having the semblance of the qualities of all the senses,
    Yet freed from all the senses,
Unattached, and yet all-maintaining;
    Free from the Strands, yet experiencing the Strands (of matter).

(*Bhagavad Gita*, XIII.14)

> For we are not discussing the mere lack of things; this lack will not divest the soul, if it craves for all these objects. We are dealing with the denudation of the soul's appetites and gratifications; this is what leaves it free and empty of all things, even though it possesses them. (St. John of the Cross, "Ascent of Mt. Carmel," Ch. 3, No. 4)

The words of the *Bhagavad Gita*, "free . . . yet experiencing," and St. John's, "free and empty . . . even though it possesses them," imply only a distinction—not a separation—between the human spirit and contents of experience. We are not told to get rid of all contents of experience but to realize that we are not identical to these. It is the identification with them, the attachment to them, that is addressed here. Taoist Lao-tzu follows suit:

Hence always rid yourself of desires in order
    to observe its secrets;
But always allow yourself to have desires in order
    to observe its manifestations.
These two are the same
But diverge in name as they issue forth.

(Lao-tzu 1968, 57)

According to Lao-tzu, realizing that one is distinct from desires is "the same" as having desires, that is, transcendence and immanence are one. These two concepts are contradictory notions that seek to model aspects of one paradoxical phenomenon. Again, we have the ability to be aware of psyche-soma contents and processes but not to be caught up in them—that is, disidentification. We are transcendent-immanent.

TRANSCENDENT-IMMANENT WILL

In the purity of formal disidentification practices such as meditation and contemplative prayer, it can appear that "I" is consciousness alone. We just sit, observing the contents of consciousness flow by, and we experience simple, pure consciousness of the moment. However, we are *choosing* to maintain this focus of our consciousness. And, in fact, we may need to bring our consciousness back to the present moment after becoming lost in a tangential train of thought or a vivid flow of imagery. In other words, "I" is not simply consciousness but has a dynamic function as well. "I" can choose to constrict consciousness, expand consciousness, focus consciousness, and even alter consciousness. "I" has both consciousness and will.

> I am a center of awareness and of power.
>
> —Roberto Assagioli

Thus the realization that "I" is distinct from psyche-soma contents and processes often is accompanied by an increased experience of freedom—if we experience ourselves as being distinct from sensations, feelings, thoughts, images, and so on, we are not only more aware of each but are potentially less controlled by them as well. Assagioli writes:

> We are dominated by everything with which our self is identified. We can dominate and control everything from which we dis-identify ourselves. (1965a, 111)

His use of the word "dominate" here is unfortunate, in that it mistakenly may be read to mean a forceful, repressive type of inner control—not what he means at all. Rather, Assagioli is attempting to indicate the freedom that can emerge when we are not identified with the limited perspective of a single part of ourselves.

For example, Mark's disidentification from the Worker and Lover allowed him the freedom to draw on either in response to life's changing circumstances. We are more able to experience and express the richness of our multiplicity rather than limit ourselves to one aspect of our personalities alone.[6]

Again, this disidentification is not a dissociation nor a "standing back and deciding what to do" (although one may be free to do even this as well!). Rather, this is moving naturally and easily as "I," as that "who" not limited to a single part of our personality, who can thus potentially engage them all. Here it is clear that we are not identical to any one part, or even all parts together, and so we are able to engage the whole—we are transcendent-immanent. This inner freedom, the freedom to express more and more of our inner resources in the world, is will. Will often is experienced as a graceful inner freedom and empowerment derived from an openness to all that we are.

Therefore, Assagioli's idea of will should in no way be confused with the harsh repression of aspects of ourselves represented by the puritanical or Victorian notion of "willpower." This latter is not emanating from I-amness; it is a force wielded by one strong aspect of the personality against others:

> The Victorian conception of the will . . . [is] a conception of something stern and forbidding, which condemns and represses most of the other aspects of human nature. But such a misconception might be called a caricature of the will. The true function of the will is not to act against the personality drives to force the accomplishment of one's purposes. The will . . . balances and constructively utilizes all the other activities and energies of the human being without repressing any of them. (Assagioli 1973a, 10)

Having said all of this about the freedom of will, we must point out too that this increased potential for freedom at times can mean an increased experience of weakness and helplessness—we are free to accept such abyss experiences as well. There are times in life that call us to accept our very real human limitations, to come to grips with the fact that we are far less in control of ourselves than we would like to think that we are.

For example, many of the deeper layers of our psyche contain wounds from traumatic experiences of helplessness and victimization. Thus when these levels within us begin to reemerge and to disrupt our lives, it often is necessary to enter into a full experiencing of the powerlessness characteristic of the original painful events. In this way we can accept these experiences and begin to heal them. Plumbing these depths shows true disidentification, because here we actually may choose to give up for a time any sense of independence and freedom in order to embrace and redeem wounded aspects of ourselves.

If during these times we attempt to maintain a centered, choosing, self-actualizing persona, we are, in effect, dissociating from the depth of our own humanness. And this is dissociation, not disidentification; it is an identification with survival personality. If, on the other hand, we accept such helplessness, we can then disidentify from survival personality and move toward a deeper experience of ourselves—we "lose self to gain self."[7]

> The conscious and purposeful use of self-identification—or dis-identification —is basic in psychosynthesis.
>
> —Roberto Assagioli

In conclusion, we can say that "I," or human spirit is distinct-but-not-separate from—transcendent-immanent within—all contents and processes of the psyche-soma, and that it possesses the functions of consciousness and will. "I" is who we are in essence and thus can neither be sought nor attained.

At this point, we may well ask, "If 'I' is who I am, and so I can't reach toward this because I already am this, how do I discover or develop myself?" The next chapter will address this question at some length. The key is recognizing from whence "I" comes, how "I" is held, and so, how "I" flourishes.

SIX

A PSYCHOSYNTHESIS
DEVELOPMENTAL THEORY

But "outgrowing" does not mean "losing." You can and should
keep the child in yourself—not killing the child. You see, the child
remains, the adolescent remains, and so on.

—Roberto Assagioli

As we uncover and include the many different aspects of our personalities,
there is a deepening of empathy across an increasingly broad range of experience and an increased freedom to respond within this range—in other words,
there is a burgeoning of the consciousness and will of "I."

We become more aware and responsive to our physical experience,
whether in the form of our physical needs or the felt sense of our bodies in the
moment; to the changing inner atmosphere of our feelings, whether anger or
excitement, grief or joy; to the many aspects of our mental experience, from
the shape of our here-and-now thinking to the levels of inspiration found in
creative expression; and to the inner community of subpersonalities. All of this
experience can become a part of the larger meanings in our lives, enriching
ourselves and our relationships with others and the world.

BIGGER THAN WE

At some point, however, we may come up against something in ourselves that
resists all of our attempts to resolve it. I may, for example, find that I am
unable to prevent my internal critic from berating and shaming me, that this
incessant, hypercritical voice simply will not let up, leaving me in a chronic,
depressed mood. Or, I find that my rage keeps getting me into trouble, that

certain seemingly small interactions with others unaccountably make me lose my temper, leaving me regretful and perplexed afterward. Or, I may discover that my spiritual persona continually prevents me from intimacy with others, that while my spiritual practice moves along well, my relationships with others are superficial, unsatisfying, or conflictual.

When we find patterns and reactions in us that are bigger than we are and that seem to run us, there is a need to reach empathically to an even deeper layer of the psyche. Why is that inner critic in me so incessant, so insistent? I may discover that this voice is desperately trying to keep me from making a mistake. To what end? Because to make a mistake will make me feel isolated, abandoned, and worthless—like it felt when my father punished me for my mistakes.

What about my temper? Upon looking carefully, I may discover that just before each flare-up of rage, there is a moment in which I am feeling disrespected, ignored, and shamed—precisely how I often felt in relationship to my mother.

And why do I prefer the spiritual heights to the crucible of intimacy? I am afraid to let people know me, to open up authentically, because they will find that I am very small and empty inside, and I will be attacked—a feeling that I have carried since grade school, when I was mercilessly taunted for being awkward and overweight.

As we have mentioned at various times in the preceding chapters, all of these traumatic experiences are instances of primal wounding. Patterns that seem entrenched in us, that react in ways beyond our ability to guide them, will be found to have their roots in primal wounding. This chapter explores the hidden depths that underpin our daily experience. We shall see how optimum human development takes place, how this development is derailed by wounding, and how these wounds may be uncovered and healed.

In presenting a psychosynthesis developmental model, we need to be clear that, to our knowledge, Assagioli never elaborated a detailed developmental theory. The developmental model that we shall present here, although arising directly from Assagioli's original thinking, has evolved from our own work over the past ten years, with invaluable assistance from Chris Meriam (see Firman and Gila 1997; Firman and Russell 1994; Meriam 1996; Meriam 1994). We hope that this material will help fill the need for a psychosynthesis developmental theory and spark further efforts in this important area; there also are many implications here for psychosynthesis personality theory and clinical theory, as we shall see.

OPENING THE INNER DOOR

In order to approach the depths within, we must confront a guardian standing at the gates of the inner world. This guardian is not a dragon or an ogre but a simple and pervasive idea. This idea is that our lives take place along a

FIGURE 6.1

time line that began at some point in the past and extends away from the point of origin into the future. This is illustrated by the arrow in Figure 6.1.

This ubiquitous belief places infancy and childhood "far, far away" from adulthood—at the extreme other end of this long line, moving us inexorably further and further away from early life. Human growth seems here a matter of leaving those early years behind, of "growing up" and not being so "childish," "immature," or "infantile."

This model, of course, has its place—it represents the fact that we no longer look like infants, that we have learned to walk and talk, and that we have adult responsibilities in our lives. However, it is only one way of looking at our development, and it leaves out crucial aspects of human experience.

Under the sway of this model, childhood seems a vague, shadowy land of half-remembered moments and elusive feelings—it is "far away." We may only glimpse this misty, forgotten time when looking at an old picture album or indulging in nostalgia with family and friends. The idea that childhood is not only still with us but dominating our lives seems farfetched from this point of view.

However, since the entire history of Western psychodynamic psychology shows us that childhood is in fact not "far, far away" but utterly present in the moment, there must be another model of human development as well; there must be a model that includes the past in the present. Such a model is implicit in any depth psychotherapy, and was voiced by Assagioli to John Firman in this way:

> But "outgrowing" does not mean "losing." You can and should keep the child in yourself—not killing the child. You see, the child remains, the adolescent remains, and so on. Outgrowing does not mean eliminating. Of course that is the ideal process, but we are too stupid and try to kill or repress the past ages. There is the notion that one has to kill the child in order to become mature, or to repress the previous stages. (Assagioli 1973c, edited from audio tape)

Assagioli maintained that each developmental age was not left behind but formed an aspect of the whole personality in a process that he called the *psychosynthesis of the ages* (1973b). Based upon a sketch made by Firman during the above conversation with Assagioli, this process is diagrammed in Figure 6.2.

In this developmental model, infancy and childhood are not distant but are at our center, similar to the annual rings of a tree. For example, there might

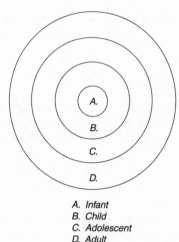

A. Infant
B. Child
C. Adolescent
D. Adult

FIGURE 6.2

be a six-year-old child within you who feels small and vulnerable among "grown-ups," or who feels that life is too vast and complex, or who feels sometimes like playing with crayons and clay. Or there might be an adolescent in you who feels painfully shy and awkward around potential romantic partners, or who feels rebellious and angry toward authorities, or who seeks freedom and adventure. And so on.

The point is that thinking in terms of the concentric-ring model allows us to become more conscious of our inner world. These major sectors of ourselves are not people we have been but people we *are*. They do not live in a long-lost time but in the immediate present. Here the word "childhood" does not mean "that time long ago when we were kids," but rather, "a deeper substrate of our here-and-now experience."

Of course, the time line arrow model often is favored by many of us as adults, because it can be a way of pushing into the background the feelings and thoughts of the infant, child, and adolescent. Adhering to this more linear model, we will assume that such "immature" thoughts and feelings have been left behind, and it may even be an affront to our self-image to realize that they exist within us, often seemingly unchanged by the passage of time.

Again, the insight held by the ring model is that all stages are present, all can be engaged, and all have something to offer our current lives. We might then visualize the growing personality as expanding harmoniously outward through the various life stages, accumulating the human potential unfolding at each stage. In the words of psychologist Gina O'Connell Higgins, "Like an extensive set of Ukrainian nesting dolls, we are a collection of selves, simultaneously encompassing all of our previous versions" (1994, 70).

In the presentation of this model, note that the different developmental stages represented by the rings in the diagram are only named in general terms (e.g., infant, child, etc.). We make no attempt here to define the various life stages beyond this, and we focus instead on dynamics that pertain to growth in all stages. Actually, almost any developmental stage theory could be represented by these expanding rings.[1]

As we shall see shortly, the key here is that with good enough nurture at each stage of growth, there is an

... he regresses to his psychic origin in childhood. Once there, he does not uncover sexual dreams of his childhood as might be expected. ... Rather, he returns to the positive, creative basis of his life.

—Roberto Assagioli

ongoing inclusion and expression of all of the multiple perspectives and abilities of the different ages—the blossoming of authentic personality. Let us now explore how this takes place.

AUTHENTIC PERSONALITY

The unfoldment of the personality through developmental stages is of course a matter both of inherited endowment and social interaction—of both "nature and nurture." Our focus, however, is on the nurture side of this relationship. Here what is crucial in development is that one is recognized, acknowledged, and understood. That is, one needs to be seen as the unique, individual human being one is, rather than as something to meet the purposes and plans of others. I must be seen as "me" by my parents, and not as, for example, "the one who will grow up and make us proud," or "the one who will save our marriage." Only if I am seen as uniquely "me"—and not an object of someone else's desires, fantasies, and plans—can I have a sense of myself as a unique person living my own life.

British pediatrician and psychoanalyst D. W. Winnicott, among others, called this type of empathic relating *mirroring*. Mirroring occurs as the mother (or caregiver) can look at the infant and recognize the unique, individual human being who exists before her. As the infant experiences his or her self reflected in the other's gaze, the infant is able to realize that she or he *is* indeed a unique, individual human being. In Winnicott's words, "When I look I am seen, so I exist" (1988, 134). This type of empathic attunement to the child, generalized to the whole early nurturing environment—called a *holding environment*—provides for the development of what Winnicott calls a "continuity of being" and a blossoming of the *True Self* of the child.

The American analyst and founder of self psychology, Heinz Kohut (1977, 1971, 1984), recognized this type of relating as an empathic responsiveness to the child on the part of the caregivers. Empathy allows the understanding of another from the other's point of view, a seeing into the other's world of experience ("vicarious introspection"). If caregivers relate to their child in this attuned way, the child is able to develop a sense of self that has "cohesion in space" and "continuity in time." Where Winnicott speaks of a true self, Kohut posits a deep *nuclear self* that will unfold its unique destiny or *nuclear program* in response to empathic attunement from the nurturing other.

EMPATHIC MIRRORING

So it is through a mirroring or an empathic connection to others that we receive an awareness of ourselves as whole, volitional, and continuous through time—what in psychosynthesis can be called "authentic personality." This mirroring process is illustrated in Figure 6.3.

The rings here are the same as in the earlier diagram, representing the many developmental ages that form the personality. The seeing eye represents all of those people and situations by which we are seen for who we truly are: perhaps parents and family early in life, then particular schoolteachers and peers, and then the friends, colleagues, mentors, and life partners of adulthood.

If at each stage of life we receive this mirroring, we are able to recognize, accept, and include the unfolding aspects of our experience at that stage. This is precisely the same dynamic that we explored in the last chapter, using the example of spending some time with a good and trusted friend (see the section "Empathic I"). Your friend empathically connected with you, so you were able to recognize and include all of your spontaneous experience within the relationship. You could be all that you were.

The same relational process happens over the course of development. That is, if our developing independence, sexuality, or cognitive abilities are

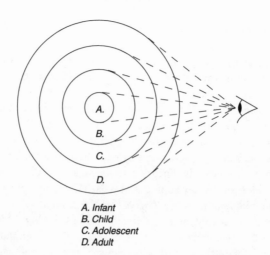

A. Infant
B. Child
C. Adolescent
D. Adult

FIGURE 6.3

mirrored, we will be able to recognize these as valid aspects of ourselves: "I am my own person," "I am a sexual person," "I am a thinker"—in other words, these unfolding developmental abilities become expressions of our authentic existence, our essence, our I-amness.

Through this mirroring we can actualize all of the richness of our unfolding human potential in an ongoing way; the developmental stages form the "rings" of our personality, each subsequent age of life enduring as an important part of the larger whole.

This development can be termed *authentic* in that the blossoming personality is a true expression of who we really are. It is as if the mirroring other is a gentle wind fanning the spark of "I," allowing "I" to glow and come to life, fully expressing that unique individuality through the unfolding developmental stages. "I" might be imagined in Figure 6.3 as being among the various rings, able to engage each and all of them as we live our lives.

Of course, this is not a passive process in which we are empty holes being filled up by the empathic regard of others. Within these empathic relationships, we learn to give and receive, to contact and withdraw, and even to influence the responses of the mirroring other (as when an infant's responses cause caregivers to modify their behavior). This mutuality of relationship between caregiver and child has been called *mutual influence* (Beebe and Lachmann 1988), a dynamic, changing process influenced by all parties involved.

SELF AS THE SOURCE OF EMPATHIC MIRRORING

Just as when spending time with an empathic friend, empathic relationships over our lifetime allow the emergence of "I" with the ability to include all of our ongoing experience. So mirroring or empathic attunement allows the flowering of I-amness throughout the life span, a "continuity of being," creating authentic personality. It is as if our very being flows to us through the empathic relationships in our lives.

However, as we discussed in Chapter 2, and as we will explore further in the following chapters, Assagioli (1965a) held that the ultimate source of personal selfhood is a deeper Self. He speaks of "I" as a reflection or projection of Self, and thus "I" in effect flows from Self.

This implies a tremendous intimacy between "I" and Self. "I" is continuously dependent on Self for existence, as a reflected image is dependent upon the subject reflected. This intimacy in turn implies a profound empathic connection of Self to "I." Assagioli writes that one may think of Self as a "spiritual Self who already knows his problem, his crisis, his perplexity" (1965a, 204).

It stands to reason, therefore, that these mirroring others in our lives, so crucial to the blossoming of personal being, are somehow conduits, channels, or manifestations of this I-Self connection. In Assagioli's terms, these empathically attuned others would be called *external unifying centers*. The

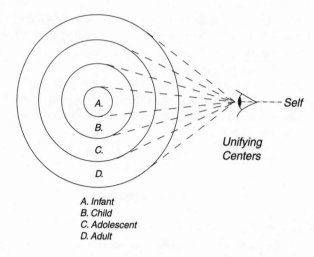

A. Infant
B. Child
C. Adolescent
D. Adult

FIGURE 6.4

relationships between Self, external unifying centers, and the unfolding authentic personality are diagrammed in Figure 6.4

"I" can be imagined in Figure 6.4 as transcendent-immanent among the rings of the unfolding personality. As "I" is accurately seen by the unifying centers, and so the I-Self connection is intact, "I" is able to engage all of the various life stages as they unfold. All of these stages of development become part of our authentic expression (i.e., become authentic personality).

Of course, this diagram represents optimum human growth; this would be like having good and trusting empathic relationships with all of the significant figures throughout our entire lives. As we shall see, this optimum process is indeed interrupted by primal wounding.

EXTERNAL AND INTERNAL UNIFYING CENTERS

In ideal human development, then, we would at each stage of life experience the primary connection between "I" and Self as facilitated by different empathically attuned or mirroring others. Each stage of growth would have attendant external unifying centers—external others who act as the facilitating medium for the I-Self relationship. In Assagioli's words, such an external unifying center is

an indirect but true link, a point of connection between the personal man [or woman] and his [or her] higher Self, which is reflected and symbolized in that object. (1965a, 25)

The external unifying center is a "true link" or conduit for the I-Self connection. Thus the optimal external unifying center of early childhood would be the matrix of empathic connections with the caregivers and the extended family system. This early holding environment would mediate the I-Self relationship, allowing the experience of healthy personal selfhood, a sense that "I exist as a unique, worthy, and choosing person, just as I am."

Later, this sense of self might be facilitated by schoolteachers, peers, and other validating and mirroring contexts such as social, cultural, and religious milieus. At each point in growth, one would be realizing oneself through the different empathic connections at that time in life, as illustrated in Figure 6.5.

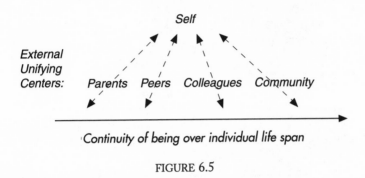

FIGURE 6.5

The external unifying centers listed in Figure 6.5 are only a few examples of many possible nurturing life contexts. No particular number or type of external unifying centers is being put forth here and, in fact, it may be that in exploring such centers, we may continually discover new and unique ones. Besides significant other people, external unifying centers can be such things as pets, cherished objects, professional disciplines, political and business associations, nature, and religious or philosophical beliefs.

The point of the current discussion is that a series of relational systems exists—external unifying centers—crucial to the development of the human being. Each center in a different way facilitates the I-Self relationship, supporting the expression of authentic personality.[2]

Furthermore, as each stage of life is supported and held by the appropriate, empathic, external unifying center, the active interaction with that external unifying center conditions the formation of an *inner* representation or *inner* model of that center—an *internal unifying center.* That is, the experience with the external center would condition the development of an inner center capable of serving many of the same functions fulfilled by the external one.

In psychoanalytic parlance, the internal unifying center might be called an *internalized object* or *object representation,* and it develops according to the principles outlined in the section on the middle unconscious in Chapter 2 (cf. Piaget, Stern, and Bowlby). In Winnicott's terms, the emergence of such an inner center could be described as the outer holding environment conditioning the formation of a similar *internal environment* (1987, 34). This same process also can be seen in Kohut's *transmuting internalization* (1971, 45).

The internal center may be experienced as actual inner symbolic figures, as when we inwardly "hear" the advice of a parent or mentor, or we carry on an inner dialogue with an image of wisdom. But these internal centers also include the beliefs, values, and worldviews developed in relationship to the external centers over our lifetime.

Internal unifying centers thus constitute a context or matrix, an internal holding environment, within which one derives a sense of individual selfhood, personal meaning, and life direction. Like the external unifying centers, the inner centers also are "indirect but true links" or points of connection between "I" and Self, as seen in Figure 6.6.

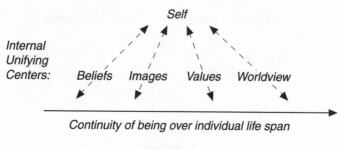

FIGURE 6.6

Note that Self is not to be equated with any particular internal (or external) unifying center. Self is distinct from them all, yet present in them all. We can relate to Self through many different internal unifying centers: an image of a loving grandparent, a spiritual teacher, or a mandala; a masculine or feminine God-image; a sense of responsibility, values, and conscience; or a philosophical stance toward the world. Self is not only distinct from the multiple internal unifying centers but provides a continuity of being throughout all of our inner experiences, from the peak of ecstasy to the abyss of despair. The I-Self relationship is transcendent of all particular inner contents, yet immanent within them all—it is transcendent-immanent.

The continuity of external and internal unifying centers amounts to a continuous relationship to Self and thus facilitates the experience of continuity in personal being. To say it another way, authentic personality is the authentic expression of I-amness, in union with Self, manifested through the person's unique genetic endowment and facilitating environment. Figure 6.7 is another way of picturing this continuity throughout the life span.

To use an early psychosynthesis metaphor kept very much alive in the teachings of psychosynthesist Philip Brooks (2000), this abiding empathic connection to authentic unifying centers allows the unfoldment of the "oak

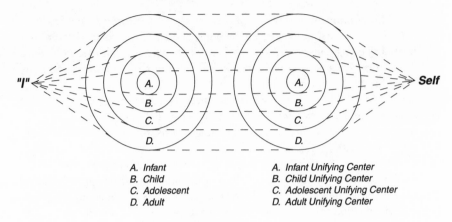

A. Infant   A. Infant Unifying Center
B. Child   B. Child Unifying Center
C. Adolescent   C. Adolescent Unifying Center
D. Adult   D. Adult Unifying Center

FIGURE 6.7

within the acorn," that is, of the unique character and life direction of the person. The unfolding of authentic personality seems akin to what has been called *individuation* by Jung (1969a, 1971); the realization of the *nuclear program* of the *nuclear self* by Kohut (1984); the actualization of the *True Self* by Winnicott (1987); and the realization of one's *personal idiom* manifesting the *destiny drive* or "an internal sense of personal evolution through space and time" by Bollas (1989, 34).

But if the primary I-Self connection, facilitated by unifying centers, creates our experience of personal existence, what happens when the unifying centers fail? What happens if our unifying centers are broken or violating? What happens when the unifying centers are damaged "links" to Self, preventing an intimate relationship with Self? Then the unifying center cannot mirror I-amness, and instead of facilitating the experience of personal existence, it creates the experience of personal nonexistence—not the experience of being but nonbeing.

PRIMAL WOUNDING

As stated above, Winnicott's phrase, "When I look I am seen, so I exist," describes well the process in which mirroring facilitates the formation of authentic personality: the empathic regard of the other allows a sense of personal being as "I" emerges to include and express the unfolding layers of the personality.

Conversely, we can use the phrase, "When I look I am *not* seen, so I do *not* exist," to describe how psychological wounding disrupts human development: here nonempathic regard creates the experience of not existing, of nonbeing. Winnicott used the powerful term *annihilation* to refer to the experience of not being mirrored—one is torn from being and plunged toward nonbeing.

This nonmirroring is what self psychology calls *empathic failure* or *selfobject failure*—events, moments, interactions, and so on in which we were not treated as living conscious human beings but as objects, as things. In Kohut's words, here we are faced with "the indifference of the nonhuman, the nonempathically responding world" (1984, 18).

In Martin Buber's (1958) terms, these failed relationships create not empathic *I-Thou* experiences but cold, impersonal *I-It* experiences. In these moments, the experience of personal being is broken, and our sense of existing is wounded.

In psychosynthesis terms, such I-It experiences indicate a failure of the unifying center to facilitate a healthy I-Self connection. Since personal being or "I" in effect flows from Self via the unifying centers, a broken unifying center will disrupt this flow and create the experience of not existing. Thus moments of nonmirroring or empathic failure hold the potential for uprooting us from selfhood and personal being, as we face the unimaginable prospect of personal nonexistence, annihilation, nonbeing.[3]

WHY "PRIMAL"?

We call the effects of these empathic failures primal wounding, not because this wounding is early or primitive, but because it breaks this primal—that is, fundamental or essential—connection to the ground of our being. Some experiences that have been associated with the primal wound of nonbeing include anxiety, disintegration, worthlessness, isolation, shame/guilt, emptiness, and despair (in the following chapter, these experiences will be explored more fully as being characteristic of the lower unconscious).

Have you ever been ignored by someone you looked up to? Have you ever poured out your heart to someone only to find that he or she was not listening? Have your personal boundaries ever been disregarded or violated? Anger can exist in these moments, true, but beneath this is a feeling of not being seen, recognized, and respected as a human being—the list above outlines where we may find ourselves at those times.

Moments such as these can be devastating to adults, so how much more so for the small, vulnerable child who experiences them? Instances of major failures in mirroring for a child will inflict psychological wounding to the child's deepest sense of self; they are disruptions in the continuity of being, moments of nonbeing.

HOW WOUNDING OCCURS

The events that create primal wounding may be either direct and overt or indirect and covert. The overt type includes obvious violence, sexual abuse, or physical abandonment, but the covert category is perhaps even more pervasive. The more covert types include such things as emotional battering, psychological incest, and identity enmeshment; bigotry (sexism, racism, etc.);

compulsions and addictions that remain unrecognized and untreated in the caregivers; denial in the family system vis-à-vis any important aspect of human life (e.g., sexuality, spirituality, death); or a constant, unresolved tension between caregivers.

Even the apparently healthy family can covertly inflict debilitating wounds in the children through the unconscious wounding of the caregivers and others. Such wounds constitute blind spots in the mirroring function that create areas of nonbeing in the child—"When I look I am not seen, so I do not exist." Here caregiver psychological blindness to certain sectors of human experience leaves vacancies in the child—holes of nonbeing, so to speak, in the unfolding personality. In this way, wounds can be inflicted by the very process of bonding to the wounded personality of the caregiver.

A common, covert wounding, hidden by its often positive appearance, occurs when children or their achievements are idealized and inflated. Here, out of the caregiver's own fantasies and desires, a child may be seen as a special prince or princess, or as a heroic savior and champion, or even as a best friend or surrogate partner. This idealization is not simple appreciation, praise, and affection but instead the covert demand that the child become this inflated image; the child becomes an actor in the caregiver's fantasy, the object of the caregiver's needs. Here, again, the actual individual child—unique and common, ordinary and special, vulnerable and powerful—is not seen, and primal wounding occurs. This wounding can be difficult to recognize for all concerned, because it appears that the caregiver is simply being loving and supportive.[4]

WHO IS TO BLAME?

It is crucial here to point out that this level of psychological trauma can occur with no conscious intention on the parts of the ones who wound us. As we have said, the mechanism for the wounding can be the unconscious, empathic blind spots of the caregivers, which are in turn the effects of their own wounding.

Given that historians have pointed to the severe lack of empathy for children in ages past (Ariès 1962; deMause 1974; Tuchman 1978), we can imagine a river of wounding flowing down to us through the generations, a river that takes on collective proportions:

> So this historical flow of wounding is a social, political, and cultural phenomenon also. We do not believe there truly can be good enough caregiving without a good enough society. For example, if infant girls are seen as less valuable than infant boys by the culture, this attitude will be transmitted by the caregivers at some level, whether conscious or unconscious. We are talking here about wounding from the whole interpersonal matrix of the growing child—any and all of the unifying centers which make up the broadest of holding environments. We are not talking only about those of us who have been obviously abused and neglected, but about the human condition itself. (Firman and Gila 1997, 97)

Primal wounding thus surrounds us from conception, a fundamental matrix in which we grow throughout our entire lives. Our lives are filled with moments when significant unifying centers—intentionally or not—have treated us not as human beings but as objects, as "Its" rather than "Thous." These wounds might be imagined as empty holes in the developing personality, inflicted at different ages within us. Drawing upon the ring model of the person, primal wounding is illustrated in Figure 6.8.

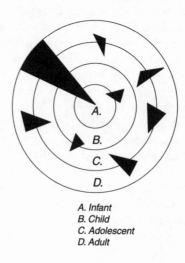

A. Infant
B. Child
C. Adolescent
D. Adult

FIGURE 6.8

Here the personality, rather than expanding in an unbroken way through the stages of development, is seen riddled with primal wounding suffered at different ages (represented by the dark triangles). These wounds of nonbeing are unbearable moments of isolation, fragmentation, and pain that are subsequently pushed out of awareness. The longer triangle in the diagram represents wounding through all ages, which occurs, for example, when we grow up in a family atmosphere of incest, addiction, or violence; or in a society that denigrates or idealizes our gender; or in a culture that is hostile to our race, ethnicity, religious beliefs, or sexual orientation.

Rather than experience those instances of nonbeing, we cut off those aspects of ourselves that were impacted by them, developing what Winnicott (1987) called a *false self*. Instead of being who we are—which is unseen or violated by the environment—we will become what we must become in order to survive the wounding. As mentioned in earlier chapters, this dynamic is the process of turning what we call *authentic personality* into *survival personality* (Firman and Gila 1997).

SURVIVAL PERSONALITY

The hallmark of survival personality is survival in the face of nonbeing or primal wounding. Rather than the environment being empathic and welcoming of who we are, we are forced to conform to a narrowed sense of ourselves to accommodate the environment. In Winnicott's words, "The False Self has one positive and very important function: to hide the True Self, which it does by compliance with environmental demands" (Winnicott 1987, 146–47). Survival personality represents the best that we can do to find some sort of existence in spite of nonempathic or nonmirroring responses from the environment.

The trouble is that to the extent we develop survival personality, we cannot manifest authentic personality. We quite literally forget who we truly are. Charles Whitfield describes what we would call the loss of authentic personality to survival personality:

> When our alive True Self goes into hiding, in order to please its parent figures and to survive, a false, co-dependent self emerges to take its place. We thus lose our awareness of our True Self to such an extent that we actually lose awareness of its existence. We lose contact with who we really are. Gradually, we begin to think we *are* that false self—so that it becomes a habit, and finally an addiction. (Whitfield 1991, 5)

It must be emphasized that since primal wounding seems inevitable, survival personality (Winnicott's "False Self" and Whitfield's "false, co-dependent self") is the starting place for all of us to a greater or lesser extent. Survival personality is not merely a one-dimensional façade, an empty shell devoid of depth and richness; in fact, it often can function well above the average level, commanding truly impressive talents and abilities. Winnicott claims that the False Self can closely imitate the expression of True Self (1987, 147). But even with this high functionality, there is a hidden sense of lack, a feeling that something central is missing in our lives.

Recall the case in Chapter 3 of Ellen, whose survival personality manifested as a talented, committed, worker who was successful in the workplace. Hidden beneath her high-functioning personality was a level of grief, anger, and pain from her childhood, which eventually emerged into awareness. The following statements help illustrate the range of survival personality:

> Every time I succeed at something I tell myself it must have been a fluke, that I put one over on people, that who I really am couldn't do these things.

> Although I've been in therapy and have some good recovery, it seems like something is missing, like after all I've never truly found out who I am.

> I have a fulfilling spiritual practice and am held in high esteem in my religious community, but whenever I approach intimacy in a relationship I am stopped by feeling scared and overwhelmed.

These phrases represent well-functioning survival personalities that integrate the true gifts and skills of the person, but we also can sense the wounding beneath the identifications—the feelings of success as a fluke, or not knowing who I am, or feeling scared and overwhelmed. Of course, when we are totally identified with such a personality, we are not aware of the experiences indicative of wounding, remaining instead contained within the limits of the functioning identification.

Clearly, survival personality is not merely a superficial role or social persona with which we meet the world. We can even undergo a surprising amount of psychological and spiritual growth and yet remain well within the grips of survival personality. We can engage depths of past wounding, abreacting memories of childhood abuse (lower unconscious); feel released from many different psychological patterns and subpersonalities (middle unconscious); or move into the heights of the sublime, enjoying the complete transcendence of ego in a union with the Divine (higher unconscious)—*and do all of this with the survival personality remaining intact.*

Survival personality is not simply one subpersonality within the personality but represents a general conditioning of vast areas of our entire conscious expression. We cannot easily gain distance from and reflect upon—disidentify from—survival personality as we can from many other personality contents. Different subpersonalities and complexes are elements contained *within* the larger context of survival personality. We can therefore disidentify, become "centered," and mindfully observe the flow of inner processes, all the time remaining well within the confines of survival personality (see, for example, our discussion of transpersonal identification in Chapter 5).

Many of us can live a long while lost in an identification with survival personality, especially if this mode is well functioning, adaptive, and capable of success in the world. However, in many cases, survival personality sooner or later eventually wears thin, revealing the hidden chasm of nonbeing on which it is built. Just because primal wounding is buried does not mean that it is inactive. The pressure from such hidden wounds can and does eventually wreak havoc in our lives and in the world.

ADDICTION/ATTACHMENT

In order to maintain survival personality and to avoid the threat of nonbeing, we are increasingly driven to behaviors and attitudes that become out of control and destructive to ourselves and others. In short, we become attached, addicted, obsessed, or compulsive (for our purposes here, these are treated as synonymous). These attachments/addictions seem endless in variety, and they include such things as compulsive sexuality, alcohol and drug addiction, destructive overeating, obsessive gambling, overinvolvement with the Internet, relationship addiction, and compulsivity in prayer or meditation—in short, virtually any pattern of human thought and behavior can become obsessive.

To the extent that our patterns of living become obsessive, we are using them to manage, to survive, prior primal wounding. Here we become trapped in compulsions and addictions in a vain effort to escape the hidden wounds from the past:

> How would I feel if I did not seek comfort and stimulation in compulsive sexual activity?
> I would feel lost, alone, abandoned. (threat of nonbeing)
>
> How would I feel if I quit my all-consuming, driven job?
> I would feel empty, isolated, worthless. (threat of nonbeing)
>
> Why don't I leave this abusive relationship?
> Because I would feel lost, abandoned, helpless. (threat of nonbeing)
>
> What would happen if I didn't maintain perfect fidelity to my religious practices?
> I would feel like a bad person, ashamed, worthless. (threat of nonbeing)

So the tremendous power of these attachments derives largely from the fact that they offer ways of avoiding the hidden threat of nonbeing caused by nonempathic responsiveness from others. These are not simply habits and tastes casually gathered over the course of living; they are desperate strategies by which we attempt to avoid nonbeing, to survive primal wounding. This partially explains the perplexing tenacity of addictions, even in the face of pain, public humiliation, illness, and physical death itself—none of this pain is as terrible as nonbeing, annihilation.

Using three different random examples, Figure 6.9 shows the relationship between nonbeing experiences and attachments or addictions.

The arrows in Figure 6.9 illustrate a movement away from nonbeing into the relative safety of the different addictive processes. The negative feelings embody the threat of nonbeing, forming the foundation or "basement" of the addiction.[5]

In the psychosynthesis literature, therapist Victoria Tackett has pointed to this wounding beneath addictions, saying, "To anesthetize these interpersonal

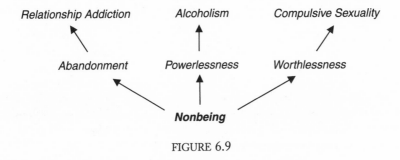

FIGURE 6.9

wounds, we are rapidly becoming a nation of addicts" (1988, 15). Within the Recovery Movement, this same connection between wounding and addiction has been made by Charles Whitfield (1991). According to Whitfield, early wounding causes feelings such as abandonment, shame, and emptiness, which finally give rise to compulsions such as chemical dependence, eating disorders, and relationship addictions (Whitfield goes on to maintain, as we do, that wounding underlies many other psychological disturbances as well).

In our terms here, all addictions, attachments, compulsions, and obsessions are manifestations of the survival personality and its imperative to avoid contact with the earlier primal wounding. Although survival personality, supported by addictive patterns, may allow the management of primal wounding for a time, its protection will eventually falter. Then we are thrown into a crisis of transformation that may feel like the "end of the world"—we are brought to our knees by a major addiction, by a brush with personal mortality, by self-destructive relationships, or perhaps by the loss of a job or loved one. Survival personality begins to deintegrate, and we begin to feel the wounds that were present all along. Here, hitting bottom, we have a chance to reach to the depths to rekindle the development of authentic personality.[6]

CONTACTING EARLY WOUNDING

Since the true expression of ourselves—authentic personality—has been impacted by primal wounding, we need to accept that our authentic life story now includes the wounds from many ages of life. It is of course true that in reaching to the wounded layers we will regain many lost gifts—new sources of spontaneity, wonder, and creativity, for example—but we also must engage the anxiety, isolation, and abandonment we suffered at various times in our lives. That is all a part of our story, our path in life, our wholeness. We must find a willingness to enter into the world that we have seemingly left behind, the world in which those wounded layers dwell, even now.

In other words, contacting wounded layers or reaching toward authentic personality is a matter of mirroring, of empathic attunement. *It was a disruption in empathic connection that caused the splitting off of these layers, and thus it is only empathic connection that can heal them.* This is one of the most important points of this entire book and the central organizing principle of all effective work in psychosynthesis. Both wounding and healing are a matter of empathic connection; both wounding and healing are a matter of relationship.

SIMPLE BUT NOT EASY

This approach to healing may seem obvious, simple, and humane, but it is precisely what all our survival tactics have been designed to avoid. The whole raison d'être of survival personality is to function without feeling primal wounding, therefore, an empathic connection to the wounded layers in us goes directly against this prime directive. So while it seems simple and humane, we in fact face our worst terrors.

For example, say my life is being disrupted by anxiety or depression. My survival personality will want to fix these problems so that my life can continue in the way it sees fit. The first thing I will do is blame the environment: "It's my parents, my boss, my spouse, or my friends who are causing these feelings." But perhaps after changing bosses, spouses, and friends several times, it may just dawn on me that the issue has to do with me too.

> . . . the recognition of the depth and seriousness of human life, of the place of anxiety in it and of the suffering which has to be faced.
>
> —Roberto Assagioli

After this first line of defense fails, I might fall back upon, "I must find the right medication, the powerful technique, the breakthrough therapy, the correct spiritual practice, which will get rid of these feelings and let me live my life in peace." Here begins a phenomenon in which survival personality plunges into various approaches to therapy and personal growth, seeking to alleviate these feelings. This may in fact work for awhile, offering new insights and self-knowledge, but nevertheless the wounded layers themselves will remain largely hidden. Why?

The reason is that if I am approaching these young, wounded layers of myself with the idea that I am going to fix them or even heal them, I am setting up the same type of relationship that caused the wounding in the first place—a relationship in which the child is not treated as a Thou but as an object, as an It. The wounded layer here becomes simply an obstacle blocking my way to the life *I* (survival personality) want. There is still no vulnerability on my part, no patient listening to this inner voice, no willingness to change my life in order to touch and be touched by my authentic being. Without a nonjudgmental, empathic, mirroring atmosphere, the wounded layers—and their gifts—will simply not emerge.

So the phrase "healing the inner child" is a bit of a misnomer, while perhaps "healing my *relationship* with the inner child" is closer to the mark. We must be willing to let go of survival personality, face our worse fears, and gradually allow our younger parts to live with us. It is not a matter of fixing a problem or curing a disease; it is a matter of making a place in our lives for the young, vulnerable aspects of ourselves. Again, *empathic failure wounds us, and it is only empathic connection that can ultimately heal us.*

Let us now look at the four mutually overlapping phases of working with these levels of wounding: *recognition, acceptance, inclusion,* and *synthesis.* These are the same phases of personality harmonization that we explored in the chapter on subpersonalities, although here they apply in a special way to these deeper layers within us.

RECOGNITION

Very seldom, it seems, do we turn to the wounded layers within ourselves, except out of some dire situation in our lives. Survival personality is tremendously resilient and can operate throughout a range that extends from what might be called psychopathology to high-functioning self-actualization to genuine spiritual or transpersonal states of consciousness. Most often our foundations must be shaken, we must be crushed down by life, and we must be plunged into the realization of personal vulnerability.

Early in the history of Alcoholics Anonymous (AA), so the story goes, the alcoholics recovering in the fellowship would not accept a person as a true alcoholic unless that individual had lost everything: house, car, spouse, family, career. Not having lost all of these things, one would not have hit bottom and so could not have found the willingness to completely surrender to something greater than ego—the first step in recovery (or on any spiritual path). Later in the history of AA, it recognized "high bottoms" who had not lost everything but who had met with such suffering that there was authentic willingness to face the truth of their lives.

Much the same can be said about reaching to the wounded aspects of ourselves. It seems unlikely that those who have not entered what we have called a "crisis of transformation" will be motivated to look at the dark forces that drive their lives. This is, after all, the gift and curse of survival personality: to carry on, to survive the wounds, and to remain in control by ignoring or smoothing over personal vulnerability, wounding, and pain.

However, as survival personality begins to falter in the face of life's buffeting, we may become willing to look. This willingness is the beginning of the *recognition phase* of healing. The next question becomes: "Who are we looking for?"

"KING BABY" AND "THE VICTIM"

In beginning to recognize our young, wounded aspects, a common mistake is to believe that the infant, child, or adolescent in us is simply a self-centered, demanding aspect of our personalities. Psychoanalysis would in fact understand such self-centered structures as archaic, infantile remnants of the early developmental stage of primary narcissism. Freud reportedly used the term, "His Majesty, the Baby," to describe the supposed inherent narcissism of the infant (Cunningham 1986, 4).

In our view, however, any grandiose narcissism is *not* an inherent characteristic at all *but the result of primal wounding*. In fact, these self-centered parts of ourselves are none other than aspects of survival personality that developed in response to early empathic failures. Playing off Freud's term, chemical dependency counselor Tom Cunningham describes what we call survival personality as *King [or Queen] Baby*:

These feelings of worthlessness, self-blame, and I-don't-belong become a central part of our personalities. King [or Queen] Baby—a selfish, demanding being—emerges as a reaction to these feelings of shame and inadequacy. As we childishly strive to be accepted and to please other people, we begin to seek things from the outside to feel better inside. Designer clothes, fast cars, attractive girlfriends or boyfriends, drugs, and the excitement of life in the fast lane help salve our pain. We develop attractive, magnetic, charming exteriors to get our way. Pleasure-seeking, power-seeking, and attention-seeking devices are used to fill the void, but the void remains. (1986, 4)

Note carefully that in this passage Cunningham is *not* describing a primary structure, *not* an inborn attitude, but a way to survive shame, inadequacy, and an inner void—characteristic effects of primal wounding. We were not born this way. We formed ourselves in this way to manage profound violations of our spirit. So, no, these attitudes and behaviors are not "childish"—they are not intrinsic characteristics of childhood, *but are the expressions of wounding.*

The same can be said of a survival pattern sometimes referred to as *The Victim.* This unfortunate pejorative term, as well as "poor me" and "self pity," often denotes a wounded personality. Here there is an identification with the suffering of the past in a way that supports a dependent, passive stance toward life (which, as we shall see, is quite different from a dynamic, responsible engagement with our wounding). Beneath this dependence there often is a feeling that the world owes us something because of early abuse or neglect. There can even be a sense of prideful entitlement here, an arrogant demand that claims, "You owe me."

But, again, like King Baby, The Victim is not a primary reaction to life by an unmolested human being. Both of these are survival formations developed in response to early wounding. These so-called "narcissistic" aspects of ourselves are not the authentic formative layers of our personalities; they are desperate, driven, and ultimately self-destructive attempts to manage assaults to the human spirit.

An irony of these kinds of problematic attitudes is that the world *does* owe us something; it owes us a recognition of, and response to, the severe damage inflicted upon us when we were helpless to defend ourselves. This is called justice. However, the tragedy of survival personality is that often the very behavior developed to manage the wounding prevents the wounding from being addressed. These extreme attitudes do not in fact expose the wounding and allow healing but instead constitute addictions that actually prevent the wounds from emerging and being healed.

SEEING THROUGH SURVIVAL PERSONALITY

It is important in recognition, then, to be able to see beneath survival personality to the underlying wounds. But often our disdain for these types of personality patterns prevents us from doing this. Indeed, disrespectful and abusive names such as King Baby and The Victim effectively block our empathic connection to the depths of these personality patterns (not to mention words such as "infantile," "childish," "narcissistic," "primitive," "immature," and "archaic"). If we demean these patterns in ourselves or others, we can effectively cut ourselves off from recognizing, engaging, and healing the wounding beneath them.

All too often *any* speaking of our wounding, *any* expression of our pain, is discounted by the assumption that it is simply indulgent whining and self-pity. But we must be able to distinguish true pain from an identification with suffering, distinguish true victimhood from a victim identification. We all *are* in fact victims. We all have *actual* wounds that need to be recognized. And it just may be that we have to grieve long and hard as we touch these wounds, experiencing a confusing mix between authentic and survival experiences.

In the dialogue that follows, Tom, a client in a psychosynthesis therapy session, sees through the survival personality to the wounds beneath. He had been struggling with compulsive bragging, a part of him who always felt compelled to let others know how great he was:

Tom: I've discovered my inner child. I call him my inner brat. He's the one who is always bragging. It's embarrassing.

Therapist: How does the child feel, hearing that?

Tom: He's angry and sulking.

Therapist: How does that make you feel?

Tom: A little guilty, I guess. I don't know. I just can't stand him always needing to be the big cheese all the time.

Therapist: Ask him how he feels when he doesn't get to brag.

Tom: He says he feels like he doesn't matter, that no one sees him.

Therapist: Is that a familiar feeling?

Tom: Yes. That's how I felt as a kid in my family. I always had to be bigger than life to get any attention.

Therapist: How do you feel towards the kid now?

Tom: I feel sad.

Therapist: How does he respond to that?

Tom: He's crying. We both are. (Long pause.) He doesn't seem so prideful now. Just sad and being with me.

Therapist: Is there anything you would like to say to him?

Tom: I'm telling him I can be with his pain if he'll just stop bragging all the time. He *is* good. He doesn't need to prove it.

Therapist: What's he say?

Tom: He's smiling. He's willing to try.

Tom formed an empathic connection to the actual level of wounding that was driving the compulsive bragging survival behavior. Over time, he was able to significantly diminish this behavior by connecting to the wounded world of the child but also—and this is important—by actively setting limits on the problematic behavior. He took time to notice when the behavior recurred and to apologize for it when it was disruptive. Survival personality must sometimes be dealt with in a firm way, much as a good parent sets limits on a child's behavior, yet remains empathic to the inner feelings that triggered the behavior.

Note, too, that Tom's work illustrates a point made earlier: his bragging behavior was not some sort of archaic, primitive holdover from a supposed early narcissistic stage of human development; it was a structure designed in desperation to prevent and survive primal wounding.

The recognition phase, then, involves looking for the authentic younger parts within, seeing through any protective, self-centered, driven, demanding behaviors to the deeper shame, inadequacy, and emptiness underlying this stance—to the primal wounding. There, beneath the protection of the shell of survival personality, the depths of the inner children hide.

WILLINGNESS IS ALL

When there is a willingness to see, and a clarity about what we are looking for, many different avenues to the wounded layers magically appear. We may gain insight from books and tapes on the subject; attend inner-child workshops, self-help groups, or enter therapy; become more aware of our vulnerability and hurt in relationships; find memories of childhood spontaneously emerging; be moved by a film or play touching upon our lifelong issues; or have revelations about early experiences in conversations with parents, siblings, or relatives.

However, these younger parts of ourselves appear perhaps most directly in intimate relationships. Remember that we have been wounded by faulty, intimate connections with others. So where might we expect these wounds to surface? Precisely in intimate connections with others.

An intimate relationship tends to bring to the surface all of the many inner levels within us, all of the many inner rings of the personality (see Figure 6.2). Such a relationship is not limited to the adult levels but invites all of the many psychological ages into expression, from the touching and cuddling of the infant, to the spontaneity and play of the child, to the adventure and emotionality of the teen. However, as these various levels emerge into expression, so too will any wounding carried at these various ages (see Figure 6.8).

It is extremely common, for example, that two apparently well-adjusted people will get married and in a short time find themselves immersed in violent and painful feelings toward each other. Suddenly, "small things" that never mattered before become hurtful and intolerable; tones of voice, mannerisms, and habits of our partner now begin to make us feel disgusted and angry, and we find ourselves acting in strange and unusual ways, fighting over superficial things.

But these are not small things. They are only small because we do not recognize the deeper waters in which we are now swimming. We are used to the adult surface of ourselves, not to the younger world hidden in the depths. But within the empathic resonance of intimate relationships, the hidden vulnerabilities and wounds of the younger parts surface (along with the gifts and abilities). Within such intimate closeness, the comment that at one time was a "harmless joke" is now a knife in the heart of a vulnerable child; the thoughtless criticism is no longer insignificant but is felt as an assault on one's deepest self.

While all of this may be alarming and disconcerting, it is to be expected—we cannot be truly intimate with another without these hidden, inner vulnerabilities emerging. (The root of the word "intimacy" itself means "within.") Intimate relationships call forth each person's wholeness—all of the rings of the personality are invited into the relationship. Indeed, this is a fundamental dynamic in psychosynthesis individual sessions; individual sessions establish an intimate, empathic resonance within which relational wounds may surface and be addressed.[7]

This often painful emergence cannot be avoided in true intimacy. It is only by forging a bond between survival personalities—via mutual addictions, compulsive patterns, and shared illusions—that a relationship can avoid the emergence of deeper material triggered by an intimate, empathic resonance.

From this point of view, a central task for an intimate couple is to accept the vulnerable layers of each partner and to create a safe, secure environment for these aspects of the person. Here we accept that "playful joking" may cause great pain to a wounded child; or that sullen withholding may throw the other into a profound sense of abandonment; or that normal sex may be felt as harsh and abusive due to childhood wounding. Such activities may need to be modified or even at times forsaken for authenticity to grow in the relationship. The couple's challenge is to welcome these younger parts, to create a safe atmosphere for them to engage their experience, to hear them and respect them, and thus to allow them to find a home within the new relationship.

But we are getting ahead of ourselves. Let us return to the phases of this healing process. After hitting bottom and recognizing the wounded layers in the recognition phase, we are ready to move into acceptance.

ACCEPTANCE

The phase of *acceptance* speaks more directly to the need for the younger parts to be heard and understood, to be mirrored. This often entails working with the subpersonalities who tend to criticize, discount, and belittle these younger ones. We have seen the terms *King Baby* and *The Victim* used in this way, but even when we mutter angrily to ourselves, "You idiot," when making a mistake, a vulnerable child will feel this and instantly withdraw. Or if we deny or make fun of our softer feelings of hurt, sadness, or joy, the adolescent will not feel accepted and will remain hidden. Or if we find ourselves fed up with our vulnerability, and demand of ourselves that we "stop whining and grow up," the infant within us will not reveal himself or herself. This type of self-empathic failure is diagrammed in Figure 6.10.

This diagram illustrates that the adult level—dominated by the survival orientation—is sending messages (arrows) designed to suppress the younger layers of the personality. Whether through negative criticism, beliefs, or attitudes, the child is kept down and, more importantly, so too is the primal wounding (dark triangle). As long as the inner atmosphere is polluted by these negative dynamics, the child and the nonbeing wounds will remain inaccessible.

The repressive arrows in the diagram do not only represent failures in self-empathy but failures in the environment as well. If there are people in our lives who ignore or belittle our vulnerabilities, these relationships also operate to maintain the break with our inner layers: "Big boys/girls don't cry," "Quit being a victim and grow up," "You're too needy," or "Get over it."

Under the onslaught of these inner and outer messages, survival personality will remain in power, and we will continue to be susceptible to addictions, compulsions, and destructive interpersonal relationships. Remember, ignoring these wounds does not mean that they are inactive, but quite the contrary—that we are unconsciously controlled by them.

In short, until we can be open to these younger parts of ourselves without pressure to change, without shaming, and without hurtful criticism, there is no way that we will ever rekindle the unfoldment of authentic personality.

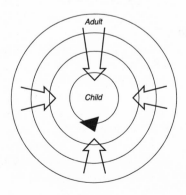

FIGURE 6.10

ENTERING THE CHILD'S WORLD

Perhaps the biggest challenge at the acceptance phase is to be with the actual direct experience of the younger levels within us. Ironically, this experience often eludes us not because it is far away from us, *but because it is so very close to us:*

> A man and woman were reading side by side in bed one evening, when the man reached over and began caressing the woman softly on the arm. Slightly irritated, she said, "Stop that," pushed his hand away, and continued reading. Inwardly the man felt hurt and angry, but said nothing. They continued reading as before, and an outside observer would have noted nothing remarkable in this small interaction.
>
> Nor did the woman notice anything until later, when she found him withdrawn and uncommunicative. She asked him if anything was wrong, and he sullenly said, "No," and rolled over to go to sleep. The woman felt guilty but had no clue as to what she might have done. They both lay there in silence, she feeling guilty, confused, and abandoned, he feeling hurt, angry, and vindictive.
>
> She finally broke the silence and vehemently demanded to know what was happening, and he angrily countered, "Nothing! Can't you just leave me alone and go to sleep?!" This then escalated into a long fight about everything in the world except the small, subtle, and now forgotten interchange that began the entire incident.

This is a good example of early wounding beginning to emerge within an intimate relationship. Here the comment by the woman—"Stop that"—inadvertently touched upon a hidden vulnerability of the man's childhood level. Unbeknownst to the man, there was an important aspect of his relationship to his mother in which he was rejected by her, and a child layer in him was still carrying this wound. Thus the woman's action did not feel like a mild rebuff but a devastating disparagement of himself as a person. He felt that his reaching out in love and openness had been met with cold, violent rejection. He felt unseen, shamed, and discounted—the primal wounding he unknowingly had received from his mother.

Furthermore, his sullen reaction in turn pressed upon the vulnerability of a wounded younger part within the woman. Her feelings of guilt and abandonment flowed from the wounding she had suffered in her relationship with her father, who had been inappropriate with her sexually as she was growing up. Indeed, her initial rejection of the man's caresses also was an unconscious reaction to her father's mistreatment of her, and the irritation in her voice was the visible tip of her rage toward her father. So she too was reacting from her early wounding, and the stage was set for an explosive conflict whose intensity seemed out of proportion to the observable triggering event. Each was, in effect, stepping on the hidden vulnerabilities of the other's younger part, and both were struggling in the dark to protect themselves from being retraumatized.

PROJECTION?

Some would call this interaction an example of *projection* occurring on both sides. According to this view, these two have merely projected their earlier relationships onto the current relationship. But it is more complicated than that. First of all, the woman's "Stop that!" and the man's sullenness *were* in fact empathic failures vis-à-vis the other. So, no, this is not simply a case of projecting or transferring a past relationship onto the current one; there actually *are* empathic failures occurring in the present. These empathic failures, however, are felt strongly by each person because of the vulnerability from this earlier wounding. *This is not a projection of the past onto the present but the retraumatizing of long-unhealed wounds in the present.*

Clearly, it is difficult to be with the feelings of the childhood level here because these feelings can be painful and overwhelming. These are not the feelings of two adults having a mild disagreement at bedtime, but those of two young people living in a world of violation, abandonment, and despair. To engage this existential level of experience directly, much less to accept it, is to leave the safe, well-lit surface of the adult world to step into a dim, strange, and sometimes terrifying world.

On top of this, however, acceptance of this inner world means a threat to our adult identity and perhaps to relationships with other adults. For these two people, to accept the magnitude of their feelings means that they may appear "overly sensitive," "childish," or "in a victim role"—not at all conforming to their image of themselves as mature adults, nor to the image each may wish to maintain in the eyes of the other. Owning the depths of their inner worlds means to risk appearing weak, vulnerable, and dependent, belying the notion that they are adults who are in control and grown up. And then the question may arise: "Will my partner accept these feelings in me, or will this be the end of the relationship?"

THE SURVIVAL CONTRACT

Acceptance, then, of early wounding is no small matter, but another challenge can still exist in the acceptance phase, a challenge brought by the question: "How did I come to have wounds such as abandonment, rejection, and loss in the first place?" This may threaten long-held images of our childhood, ourselves, and our families.

For example, if the man in the above example enters therapy and begins exploring the experience of rejection, he might be shocked to realize just how rejecting his mother was of him as a small child (especially if she was outwardly loving and supportive). As he explores this rejection further, he may feel as though he is betraying his mother, that he is going against a sacred taboo. This sense of betrayal or disloyalty, a common feeling in this process, arises because he is breaking the contract that founded his survival personality: a contract to see himself and his mother in a certain way in order to be accepted by her. To break this implicit contract, to speak about the hidden, destructive side of the relationship, means the younger parts will face being ostracized by this crucial early caregiver—they face nonbeing, annihilation.

Survival personality is based on psychological contracts that require us to be a certain way in order to be accepted by the early caregivers. Think of Ellen's contract to be the self-effacing helper within her family (Chapter 3), or Mark's contract to be the Worker to gain his father's respect (Chapter 4). These contracts offer security, a sense of belonging and identity, a knowing who we are—and so an avoidance of nonbeing. But the price we pay for this secure identity is the repression of authentic personality, a disowning of important aspects of our experience. And if we begin now to listen to the actual experience of these younger layers, we may begin to uncover a whole experiential world that reveals our early lives as being far more difficult or destructive than we or anyone else had ever realized. This revelation will challenge our secure identities, again bringing up the ancient threat of nonbeing.

"But my family was fine. Sure, we weren't perfect, but all in all, I had an okay childhood." This may be absolutely true for aspects of our childhood. This does not rule out, however, deep sectors of abandonment, violation, and pain; there seems to be no caregiver or other unifying center that can be connected to the experience of children in a completely empathic way.

> It has been found that the refusal to accept suffering can often create neurotic conditions, while generous acceptance of unavoidable suffering leads to insight, growth, and achievement.
>
> —Roberto Assagioli

However, let us be absolutely clear that accepting the full phenomenological world of early wounding *does not mean blaming our caregivers for everything wrong in our lives.* True, empathy with ourselves may mean clearly seeing our parents' destructive side or accepting deep rage toward them, but blaming has nothing to do with this. What matters here is honestly understanding and accepting the childhood layers within us, wounds and all.

Note, too, that an awareness of these early layers is not necessarily a matter of remembering the exact events that caused the wounding. Keep in mind the concentric ring model of the person—we do not have to go anywhere but into our here-and-now experience to recognize and accept the deeper layers within us. The task confronting the couple in our example is not to regain memory of the past, it is to uncover the deeper feelings and thoughts underlying their conscious interactions. The focus here is not upon remembering the past (although remembering often is a by-product) but upon connecting empathically to the younger parts that live within us now.

THE HEALING ENVIRONMENT

In any type of healing environment, such as counseling or therapy, for clients to break the survival contract and accept the experience of early wounding usually depends on practitioners who have done these things in their own lives. Only if we have wrestled with our own survival personality and faced our own wounding are we equipped to mirror the wounding of another.

If we are unaware of our own wounded layers, remaining controlled by our own survival personality and survival contract with our caregivers, we will find it difficult to connect empathically to these layers within the client. In fact, if we are confronted with emerging wounding in a client, we may in all good faith attempt to help by moving the client *away from* the experience of the vulnerable child. The client may, for example, be encouraged to sympathize quickly with the plight of the early caregivers, to undergo techniques designed to gloss over the pain before truly understanding its depth and meaning, or to engage a premature process of forgiveness. Therapist and author Alice Miller says:

> The religious notion that a "gesture of forgiveness" will make you a better person has also found its way into psychoanalytic treatment. As if this gesture could do away with something slumbering deep within a person since childhood that can be articulated only in neurosis. (1984b, 213)

Such misguided attempts at healing actually amount to the repressive dynamic illustrated in Figure 6.10. They prevent the younger parts within us from finding a new empathic connection, may lead to further wounding, and will further entrench survival personality. So for practitioner and client alike, acceptance of these deeper layers often demands personal transformation.

In the acceptance phase, then, the task is to open ourselves up to the phenomenological world of the wounded layers without allowing survival personality to cover this up. But let us acknowledge that accepting the broken world within us can be tremendously anxiety provoking and should proceed at its own pace. As we have seen, the entire process is hemmed in by the threat of nonbeing, and only respect and safety can support this uncovering and acceptance. *This process is not something one can force.* Throughout this work, we are simply attempting to become more and more empathically attuned to the world of the younger ones within, and we cannot establish an empathic relationship through pressure, clever techniques, or coercion.

So, having hit bottom, recognized the world of childhood wounding, and attained some amount of acceptance of this world, it becomes possible to include the younger aspects of ourselves more fully in daily living.

INCLUSION

The phase of *inclusion* also can be called the phase of "living with." A useful metaphor here is that you have found an abandoned infant, child, or adolescent, have adopted him or her, and have brought this young person home to live with you. Perhaps this is more than a metaphor. Take a moment and think about this: if you brought a sensitive child home, a child who would be with you every second of your day, what in your life would need to change?

Inclusion is an ongoing, moment-to-moment process, whereby we adopt the younger parts of ourselves and begin to live our lives in an intimate relationship with them. Inclusion does not mean that these inner children are "integrated," in the sense that they become submerged within the larger personality, nor does it mean changing them to suit the needs of survival personality; rather, it means making whatever lifestyle or attitudinal changes necessary to accommodate them in our daily living. Only by creating such a space in our lives will these younger parts find a new unifying center, a new empathic holding environment, by which to heal and grow.

EVALUATING RELATIONSHIPS

In bringing these inner children consciously into our lives (they have always been present and active unconsciously), it often will be necessary to evaluate how current personal and professional relationships affect them. Do we have friends who criticize and belittle us "all in good fun"? Do our partners give us the message, in word or deed, that our vulnerability and sensitivity are not okay? Do our supervisors or coworkers set a nonempathic, even an abusive, tone in the workplace? Such questions can point to ways in which our lives need to change so that the younger parts within us have a place to live and grow.

An example of this type of change is Ellen, whose journey we followed in Chapter 3. Having had some amount of recovery and healing, she began to realize how destructive her workplace was for her. Initially, identified with survival personality, she simply could not see the sexual discrimination, unreasonable workload, and high pressures that surrounded her—to do so meant feeling the pain of it all and so placing her at odds with the workplace survival contract. In retrospect, Ellen reported brief moments in which she was aware of these injustices, but she had quickly reasserted the "Everything is okay" of the survival stance—her survival-contract role in her family of origin and now in the workplace.

As she worked her way through her crisis of transformation, her awareness grew and she saw the situation more clearly. She began remaining connected to her inner child, giving the child what she needed in her off hours so they could make it through another stressful workday. However, the situation finally was revealed as being intolerably unjust, and she began to challenge her employer's behavior and policies. Although she did make some changes in the situation, she ultimately chose to find a new job in a much healthier environment.

It is of course not always possible to alter the situation as Ellen was able to do. We often have to learn to survive in oppressive environments. But can we do this without forsaking these younger, more sensitive aspects of ourselves? Can we find for those younger parts within us—the inmost layers of our personality—places of safety and nurture in our lives?

Many life relationships of course will easily change so that the younger parts may be included. Simple, direct statements and requests about our needs may be honored by those who respect us, and our inner children can find space to live within such relationships.

Note again that the emphasis here is not on "shaping up," "fixing," or even "healing" the child so that he or she will fit neatly into our current relationships. The emphasis is on *changing* our relationships so that the childhood layers are welcomed, made safe, and thereby allowed to emerge, heal, and grow.

TAKING TIME

Having a new child means making parenting a priority. Spending time with the child is crucial if you expect to get to know this new addition to your life. Relationships only blossom with attention and care, so you both need time to sit down and communicate with each other.

Through a variety of different methods we can learn to communicate with these younger parts and gradually develop an understanding of their wants and needs. Is there a need for time alone? More peace and safety during the day? Time to play? More adventure? More intimacy? The needs of these deeper layers of us usually are quite easily satisfied within the course of normal living. In fact, meeting the needs is not nearly as hard as remembering to create the time and space to meet them.

For example, a man in psychosynthesis therapy made an agreement with a wounded inner child to spend an hour hiking in the hills during the next week. At the next session the client reported that the child had not been around all week, and that compulsive, self-destructive behaviors were beginning to reassert themselves. As he explored this, it turned out that he had forgotten to spend that hour hiking. He had become caught up in a busy work week, the agreement had been forgotten, and so the child had withdrawn. Here is a small retraumatization of the child, an empathic failure that moves in the direction of survival personality. As it turned out, the man discovered that he was treating the child just as his father had treated him when he was young. The survival, workaholic personality of the father, and now of the son, had not been able to see and meet the child.

So the inclusion phase is an ongoing process. It is not one moment of insight, one breakthrough experience, or one important abreacted memory (although these may be valuable aspects of the process). Inclusion means *relationship*. It is consciously living with the children in us and making daily choices so that they—with no pressure to change—can live securely in our lives. Again, since empathic failure split off these inmost levels of us, it is only through empathic relationships that we will be able to reconnect with them.

HEALING RELATIONSHIPS

Throughout this ongoing inclusion we will of course make mistakes, committing empathic failures under the sway of survival personality. An important point here is that these failures need to be mended. For example, the man who forgot to hike with the child needed to apologize to the child and do something else for the child in order to make up for the broken agreement.

Empathic failures such as inner self-criticism, indulging in rages, forgetting the child by immersion in T.V., radio, newspapers, or other media (media addiction), or exposing the child to abusive situations all need to be owned and healed. In fact, any addiction or attachment blocks our access to these inner layers of ourselves. As with any relationship, making amends forms a resilient foundation of respect and safety that allows us to navigate the mistakes that will surely occur over time (if the amends are followed by real change, of course).

Taking responsibility for survival personality also can include making amends for interpersonal pain when our criticism, revenge, or dark humor hurts other people. And as many have learned in twelve-step programs, this making of amends for the transgressions of survival personality can be taken into the past as well, with great healing effects. Members of these programs make a list of everyone they have harmed, become willing to make amends to them all, and make those amends, except when to do so would cause further harm (Anonymous 1976, 1985).

Such work is not about the past as much as it is about transforming the present. It helps establish an empathic holding environment around us and allows us to become safe for the deeper layers of other people as well. In this way, empathy and intimacy may begin to infuse many of our relationships, creating unifying centers by which the child may again learn to live and breathe. Here the rewounding of the child is stopped, creating space for the unfoldment of authentic personality.

It thus seems clear that working with these inner layers of ourselves is not only an intrapersonal process but a profoundly interpersonal one. We were wounded in interpersonal relationships, and we need to be healed in them as well. We and our younger parts need the support of empathic others as we seek to heal our relationship with them. Whether friends, family, self-help groups, or therapy, there needs to be a healthy holding environment for healing to take place. Such new unifying centers facilitate the inclusion of the children in our lives and eventually lead toward the formation of internal unifying centers that support the continuous and stable unfolding of authentic personality.

SYNTHESIS

In working with subpersonalities, the phase of *synthesis* is one in which subpersonalities may begin to relate to each other in new and creative ways, forming expressions that respond to the most meaningful values in our lives. This phase marks a development of authentic personality, a movement into more conscious Self-realization (the contact and response stages of psychosynthesis).

Much the same can be said for the phase of synthesis when working with the early levels within us. However, in this case, the phase is most clearly understood as the formation of two fundamental relationships: (1) an ongoing, committed relationship with our early, inner layers; and (2) an ongoing committed relationship with Self.

JAMIE AND PURPOSE

Jamie was a forty-six-year-old lawyer who had been in recovery from drugs and alcohol for ten years. She had been struggling for some time with a sense that she had wasted her life, and that she desperately needed a vocation that would finally give meaning and purpose to her existence. She felt that she had lived over half her years, and that time was running out for her.

She attended courses about discovering vocation, took different aptitude and interest tests, and avidly devoured self-help literature about finding a life's calling. But she simply could not find a life path that drew her, and she was falling deeper and deeper into despair. A religious woman, she also felt angry at God for not showing her the way after she had walked her long, painful journey out of addiction.

Fighting a growing depression, Jamie began antidepressant medication and psychosynthesis therapy. In therapy, she all but demanded to find her purpose in life, and she was irritated whenever her therapist seemed to fail in producing this. On the face of it, Jamie was asking a perfectly reasonable question, especially of a practitioner trained to facilitate questions concerning meaning and purpose. But even though the question was approached in a variety of ways—dream work, imagery, creative expression, sand tray, and dialogue with inner figures of wisdom—she constantly received messages about developing patience and listening, which simply irritated her further.

Her frustration grew as time passed, and she began to feel even more acutely the underlying sense that her life was wasted, with attendant feelings of despair and worthlessness. This increased intensity forced her to listen more closely to these feelings, and she found the part of her, a child, who felt this sense of waste and hopelessness. In connecting to this level of herself, she began unearthing the experiential world of this child, a world haunted by an alcoholic father, a severely depressed mother, and an abusive older brother. At this fundamental level she did not feel seen or held in her family system beyond her role as caretaker to her younger siblings. This child felt that she could not live her own life, that her life was being wasted.

As Jamie established a strong empathic relationship with her child, the depression increasingly turned to grief, a grief that spilled out as she saw the plight of this child, the loss, the waste. Through her empathy and fidelity to these feelings, Jamie became an authentic unifying center for this child, allowing her story to be told, heard, and felt, and thus bringing this lost, young part of herself back into her inner community.

An Addiction to Purpose

At the same time, Jamie came to see that her driving need for a vocation was in fact a reaction to the feelings of this important layer within her. Her efforts had not in fact been a simple, straightforward search for a calling in life but were largely desperate attempts to avoid the emerging feelings of the child. In effect, the quest for a calling had become an addiction, functioning as any other addiction in preventing primal wounding from entering awareness.

In retrospect, she also recognized a pride and an inflation that infused her quest—she was looking for a purpose grand enough to wipe out the felt sense of waste and worthlessness, a motivation that had led her to subtly ignore or abhor vocations that seemed unworthy of her.

So Jamie continued living with this childhood layer of herself, and in so doing, she began to respond to the child's wish to do drawing and painting and also to spend more time in nature. In the early stages this seemed like a sidetrack from her quest for a vocation, but as she gradually understood the desperate drivenness of this quest, she became increasingly willing to spend time with and for the child.

Then a quite unexpected thing began to happen. Jamie began to feel a peace and a passion in these times with the child. She became more and more interested in her art. She took classes at a local community college, began experimenting with a variety of media, and eventually even entered local art shows. It was as if the child was a lost seed that, once recovered and nurtured, could now blossom in its current life. And as this direction unfolded, her driven search for a grand life purpose begin to evaporate.

As her pressing need for an exalted vocation waned, so too did her anger with God. Her spiritual practices became times of a felt connection to God, and in fact, she realized that she felt most connected when doing her art. She struggled with this, however. She wondered if "just doing art" was "serving" enough in the world. Honestly facing this question—now without the pressure of finding her "Supreme Life's Purpose"—she realized that what she was doing *was* service. She felt that simply staying with her art was making her a better person and in turn was transforming her relationships with friends and family, society, and the planet as a whole.

To date, Jamie's art remains what others might call a hobby, but it is in fact a powerful authentic unifying center in which she is holding and being held by her deeper nature; it is a central crucible of her Self-realization, an ongoing connection to Self that infuses and guides her relationship to the seeds of her authentic expression in the world.

In Jamie's journey we can see the two fundamental relationships in the synthesis phase. There is a committed, empathic relationship with the wounds and gifts of the deepest layers of our personalities, as well as a committed, ongoing relationship with Self via authentic unifying centers that hold us while we hold ourselves.

These two relationships can be seen emerging during psychosynthesis therapy: the empathic relationship with the therapist operating as an authentic unifying center, holding clients while they uncover their heights and depths; or, working in imagery, clients might find themselves holding a younger aspect of themselves while they sense a larger presence holding both of them; or, even the younger layers of the person—which can have a direct relationship with Self as well—unfolding to give wisdom and guidance to the adult. In all of these ways and more, we can see these two relationships forming the backbone or axis of authentic personality.

PERSONAL, SOCIAL, AND GLOBAL TRANSFORMATION

As authentic personality blossoms through the healing of inner and outer relationships, there is an increased empathic connection with ourselves, with other people, and with the world at large. This can, in turn, lead to social action as we engage a world that often is profoundly nonempathic to human vulnerability. Here we can see the deep, unbreakable connection between the transformation of ourselves and the transformation of world—two levels that are frequently, for some reason, seen as being mutually exclusive.

For example, in the above cases in which Ellen was led to quit her job, or Jamie discovered her calling, we can note a natural progression from personal healing to social healing. They were both led to act in ways that did not support the status quo and that pushed for social transformation. They can be considered active agents of social change, struggling with oppression in their own ways.

Social action arising from personal transformation also can be more dramatic, as when people find that they can recognize and report sexual harassment around them; pursue legal action toward perpetrators of abuse; work politically to pass legislation that protects the vulnerable among us, the young, the poor, the disabled, and the elderly; or fight against the massive abuses of the natural environment that threaten the holding environment that every one of us shares—the planet Earth itself.[8]

Indeed, the very substance of working with the depths within us seems to be addressing abuse and oppression perpetrated by larger systems, beginning with the family. This empathic process of opening up to authentic personality moves naturally from healing the individual and family to healing the wider society and the planet as a whole.

Such concern for the world can of course take the form of economic, religious, artistic, and political agendas beyond the single issue of children. The point here is that a great deal of human suffering is not blamed on the Divine, evolution, nature, or "the way things are" but largely on human empathic failures and/or the structures that embody a lack of empathic responsiveness. And this is a focus about which we can do something. Here we can look deeply into the roots of the broken human condition and begin to discern strategies for healing it. Here service can become a serious effort based on clear insight into the entrenched nature of wounding, suffering, and human evil.

Thus inherent in connecting to deeper levels of our experience, and thereby reestablishing authentic personality, is a larger concern for others and the world. If, however, we refuse to recognize our wounds and our path of healing, we will find it difficult to render true service to a wounded world.

THE PATH OF AUTHENTICITY

As our inner and outer relationships heal, authentic personality begins to unfold. As the blocks to these relationships are unearthed and addressed, as there is more empathic communion among all concerned, and as there is an ongoing commitment to keeping these relationships alive in our lives, we begin to shift away from survival personality and toward authentic personality—into the expression of our true nature, our essential I-amness with other people and the world.

> . . . synthesis . . . tends to transcend the opposition between individual and society, the selfish-unselfish polarity.
>
> —Roberto Assagioli

From the point of view of the individual, empathy is thus the force that "integrates" or "synthesizes" the personality. Through self-empathy we can hold all of the different parts of us, allowing a sense of inner multiplicity and unity at the same time. We have sometimes said that "empathy is the glue of the personality." At a social level, empathic connection functions much the same way; empathy is the source of a solidarity with others and the planet that can hold both unity and differences.

It might even be said that living these inner and outer relationships amounts to our life path or journey—our Self-realization. This journey begins as we grapple with the "egoism" of survival personality and see through the illusions by which we have been living. The journey proceeds into a letting go of addictions and attachments, generated by the survival motivation, toward an acceptance of the profound depths of human vulnerability hidden beneath these.

From this confrontation with attachments, we move into a new relationship with ourselves, others, and the world that is grounded in a sense of the interconnection of all things. In psychosynthesis terms, this is a healing of the primal break between "I" and Self, a communion of personal being with Universal Being.

Thus grappling with our compulsive behaviors and enthrallments and then searching the inner depths for the wounded ones within us can lead to wondrous and creative lives. It is not uncommon to hear someone say, "I am a grateful alcoholic," or, "I am glad to be an adult child of a dysfunctional family," or, "I thank the struggles I have had in my life." As Assagioli (1973c) used to say, "Bless your obstacles."

Such sentiments do not indicate an identity as a victim, a "poor-me" or blaming stance in life; nor do they entail a condoning of the brokenness of the world; rather, here there is an acknowledgment that suffering can be redeemed. Such statements say: "This is the actual road I have traveled to become who I am today, and I am grateful for the goodness I have found on the journey."

This journey from survival to authenticity is not one that we finally complete, finding ourselves eventually in a state of blissful perfection. Authenticity is not an enlightened state to be grasped but a direction to be walked. We will always experience some mixture of survival and authentic personality in our lives; we shall always be human beings in an imperfect world.

The point is that we can be human beings in recovery. We can be people who admit our brokenness, face in the direction of authenticity, and walk with others who are traveling this same path. It may even be that the distance we travel is unimportant, and that the real gifts are the fellow travelers we meet along the way.

IN CONCLUSION

So when we are treated empathically by the unifying centers in our lives, we develop authentic personality. We find ourselves aware (consciousness) and intentional (will) within a broad experiential range, and we have a sense of something greater than ourselves that invites us into meaningful pathways of attitude and action. In psychosynthesis terms, authentic personality is a function of our connection—moderated by unifying centers—with Self.

We have seen too, however, that when this connection with Self is broken by nonempathic unifying centers, we undergo primal wounding. This wounding violates our sense of continuity, self-empathy, and relationship, causing us to split off parts of ourselves—to become nonempathic with ourselves—in order to survive in the face of the wounding. This splitting can later be recognized in the intense conflicts among subpersonalities; in surprisingly strong reactions to impingements by the environment; in a vulnerability to attachments, compulsions, and addictions; and in survival personality cutting us off from deeper layers of ourselves.

However, there is another splitting that we have been encountering throughout this book: the splitting between our heights and our depths, between our wounds and our gifts, between our losses and our blessings. Whether with Ellen engaging the pleasures and pains of a more authentic range of experience (Chapter 3), with Mark discovering the early suffering and creative qualities of his subpersonalities (Chapter 4), or with Jamie uncovering the wounds and gifts of her inner child (this chapter), it seems that healing involves the bridging of a split between our brokenness and giftedness.

These examples all point to a more general splitting within us, which seems to pervade all other aspects of the personality—the splitting of *higher unconscious* and *lower unconscious*. As we shall explore in the next chapter, this split between our heights and our depths is a major effect of primal wounding.

SEVEN

THE HIGHER AND
LOWER UNCONSCIOUS

We try to build an elevator which will allow a person access to
every level of his personality.

—Roberto Assagioli

We have seen how an authentic unifying center facilitates an openness to all
we are, a self-empathy. As in the case of spending time with a trusted friend,
we feel free to experience whatever arises in the moment. We are not identified with any particular aspect of our experience, and so can fully engage a
broad range of experience—the transcendent-immanent "I" blossoms.

We also have seen that this is precisely how optimum human growth
occurs throughout the life span. As we are mirrored, empathically responded
to, we can include all of our developmental gifts and skills as they emerge during our growth. Interacting with the empathic presences in our lives, we
develop the ability to express our I-amness in the world, the mode of being
that we call "authentic personality."

This connection with empathic unifying centers could not be more profound. It is ultimately a connection to Self—what also can be called Spirit, the
Divine, God, or the Ground of Being—a connection that gives us our existence
as well as our sense of place and purpose in the universe. Accordingly, when an
important unifying center fails as an empathic other, when we are treated as an
"It" rather than a "Thou," primal wounding occurs; our lifeline to the source of
being is threatened, and we face a headlong fall out of the universe, a plunge
into nothingness, a seeming rejection by the Source of Being itself.

As we have seen, this wounding leads to inner conflict, addictions and
attachments, and the formation of survival personality, but beneath all of these

149

lies something even more fundamental. Underlying these painful reactions, and infusing them all, is a primal split between our heights and our depths. This chapter will explore this deeper split in our being.

PRIMAL WOUNDING AND SPLITTING

In order to approach the experience of primal wounding, imagine again that you are spending time with a good friend. Trusting the warmth and acceptance flowing in the relationship, you spontaneously speak your love for your friend. But to your shock and embarrassment, your friend responds coldly and withdraws. A silent chill replaces the warmth between you, and you know that your expression of love has for some reason broken the empathic flow between you.

This empathic break makes you feel suddenly disconnected, alone, even abandoned—primal wounding. You may even feel as though you did something wrong and may feel angry that you are being made to feel this way. Your friend's cold withdrawal in the face of your love has sent a message about the limitations of the relationship. Consciously or not, you understand that to maintain this relationship you will need to somehow adjust yourself to fit within certain confines: first, you will need to inhibit your feelings of warmth, acceptance, and love; and second, you will need to ignore the shame and anger you felt in the rejection because, if expressed, this will bring up again the issue that your friend wants to avoid. In sum, for you to have any hope of recapturing that original connection with your friend, these two aspects of your experience must be left out.

Of course, adults often can stand back and discuss such moments of empathic failure. In this discussion you both might find, for example, that your expression of love threatened your friend, touching on a long-standing fear of intimacy, which caused the cold withdrawal. Together you may realize that your friend's need to avoid the fear in effect took precedence over the connection between the two of you. Then you could talk about your own experience—rejection, isolation, shame, and anger—clearing the way for apologies to be made and empathy to flow again, allowing the whole shared experience to be held by both of you.

SPLITTING THE HEIGHTS AND DEPTHS

But if you do not have such a candid discussion, much the same may happen as it does in childhood—the positive, natural self-expression, as well as the feelings resulting from the rejection of that expression, will be pushed out of consciousness, beyond the limits of the relationship. You may simply be aware of an awkward moment with your friend, allow it to pass, and continue as if nothing had happened. But now you will operate under unspoken rules about how you are to feel and act within the relationship, and your connection with your friend will be more superficial.

By ignoring a painful moment of empathic failure in this way the relationship survives—an absolute imperative for the child—but it does so at the expense of distancing you from your heights and depths. Here your friend functions as a survival unifying center, a point of authority informing you of how you are to behave in order to maintain the relationship. And you in turn express survival personality, conforming yourself to the dictates issuing from the survival unifying center.

If the relationship continues, your friend will actually begin to *see* you as someone who conforms to the relationship, as someone who does not experience and express warmth and love nor hurt and shame. In short, your friend will see you as your survival personality.

Similarly, over time, you might begin to see yourself in this way too, losing your ability to experience this range within yourself; in other words, you become identified with your survival personality. Although Assagioli himself never wrote directly about the formation of the higher and lower unconscious, we can use his oval-shaped diagram (Figure 2.1) to illustrate this survival relationship (see Figure 7.1).

In relating to some people in our lives, the condition illustrated in Figure 7.1 might be a passing phenomenon; this dissociation from our heights and depths passes, and we return to our normal experiential range afterward. We can do this largely because we have other unifying centers in our lives—internal and external—that see our heights and depths, mirror our wholeness, and thus allow us to maintain our full, experiential range.

For example, as discussed earlier, if you and your friend were not able to talk about the interaction together, you might go to others who could hear and understand both the love and pain you felt in the interaction. Relating to these others, your experience with your friend could be held, understood, and

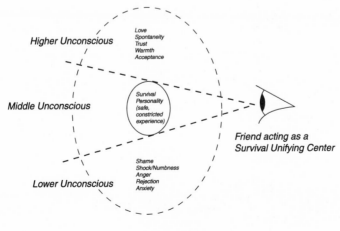

FIGURE 7.1

integrated, and your experiential range would remain intact. In such cases, there is no chronic splitting, because there is only a temporary dissociation of your experience and not a structuralized break within you.

STRUCTURALIZING THE SPLIT

But in childhood a relationship with a survival unifying center may not be temporary at all, and we may not have anyone else to mirror our experience. In fact, our existence often depends on our conforming to nonempathic environments in an ongoing way. We must then find a way to *permanently* split off certain heights and depths of ourselves, to actually become someone who seemingly does not have, and has never had, these heights and depths at all. We cannot even afford an internal awareness of this broader range of experience, because this internal awareness might be recognized from the outside and thus threaten our place in the relationship. We must become someone who knows nothing of these experiences at all.

The way we become such a person is by internalizing the relationship with the nonempathic environment. We then can actually appear to ourselves and others precisely how the environment wishes to see us, no more and no less. By internalizing the relationship, we no longer need to depend on the outer environment to tell us what experiences are not acceptable; we now have the relationship present within us, and so we can conform to its dictates smoothly, automatically, "naturally."[1]

To put it another way, in the face of an *external* survival unifying center, we form an *internal* survival unifying center, as shown in Figure 7.2.

This diagram shows that we have split our natural experiential range in a permanent way by repressing the two ends of the range. Just as the external survival unifying center is blind to our wounding and gifts, so we are now blind to

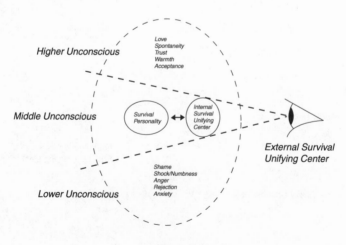

FIGURE 7.2

them as well. Bonded to the internal center, we are in a trance, unaware of the heights and depths within us. However, such splitting and repression allow us to survive primal wounding and secure some sense of stable existence within a nonempathic environment. In a particularly rich passage, psychologist John Welwood describes just this loss of our heights along with our depths:

> As children, the pain of not being truly seen or loved is so *utter* that we contract and thus disconnect from the original openness of our being. This loss of being leaves behind an abyss, a gaping hole [the primal wound], which we cover up with trance—with beliefs, imaginings, and stories about who we are. Our ego structure develops as a survival strategy, as a way of getting by in a world that does not see or support who we really are. It is a protective shell, which diverts our attention from the abyss and loss of being, so that our mind can "step around, across, upon it" without falling in. *Yet the shell of our self-constructed identity also blocks access to the deeper seed potentials—for passion, vitality, joy, power, wisdom, presence—contained in our basic nature.* (2000, 247, latter emphasis added)

In order to become what the environment wants us to be, we now have eliminated our heights and depths from consciousness and have formed what is known as the *higher unconscious* and the *lower unconscious*—two areas of experience that have been repressed by the internal formation of the survival personality and the survival unifying center.[2]

THE LOWER UNCONSCIOUS AND HIGHER UNCONSCIOUS

As we relate to nonempathic environments over the course of development, the higher and lower sectors of our unconscious will continue to grow. Increasingly, one sector of our unconscious will be related to our capacity to experience qualities that arise from empathic holding, such as love, joy, spontaneity, and beauty, and another sector will be related to our capacity to experience qualities associated with empathic failure, such as shame, fear, pain, despair, and rage. By repressing both our higher and lower range of experience in this way we are able to find some stability and safety within the various problematic environments.

Thus Figure 7.2 represents our normal—though not natural—psychological situation. Although we may not be aware of it, our normal, stable, experience of ourselves and others is, to a greater or lesser extent, cut off from our heights and depths by primal wounding. Let us now more closely examine the lower and higher unconscious in turn (see also Chapter 2).

THE LOWER UNCONSCIOUS

If the threat of nonbeing or annihilation (Winnicott) derives from an empathic failure on the part of an external unifying center, it seems safe to assume that every personality is riddled with greater or lesser amounts of primal wounding. Human life is rife with moments and periods of nonempathic response from significant others, whether covert or overt, intentional or unintentional. These confrontations with nonbeing, when split off and repressed, form what we are calling the "lower unconscious."

One way to think of the lower unconscious is that it is a particular bandwidth of our experiential range that has broken away from consciousness. It comprises that range of experience related to the threat of personal annihilation, destruction of self, nonbeing and, more generally, the painful side of the human condition.[3]

When we then repress this range in forming survival personality, it is as if we begin wearing eyeglasses that filter out these types of threatening experiences both within ourselves and in other people. Experiences or qualities associated with nonbeing might include the following:

- Anxiety and disintegration
- A lack of meaning in self or world
- Feeling lost, trapped, or buried
- Isolation, abandonment, banishment
- Feeling overwhelmed, helpless, or hopeless
- Emptiness or hollowness
- Endless despair
- Rage, revenge
- Wanting to die
- Shame and guilt
- Overwhelming terror at the possible loss of another
- A sense of inauthenticity or falseness
- Low self-esteem or worthlessness

All of the above qualities are symptomatic of a break in an empathic connection, causing the threat of nonbeing; they are all related to a potential fall toward annihilation, nonexistence.

The Higher Unconscious

As the lower unconscious represents the loss of an aspect of our experiential range related to the threat of nonbeing, so the higher unconscious represents the loss of an aspect of our experiential range related to being. When we repress our heights in forming survival personality, it is, again, as if we begin wearing eyeglasses. But these limiting glasses now prevent us from seeing *positive* experiences arising from empathic connections with unifying centers in our lives. Just as we did with our friend in the example above, here we remove from our consciousness positive aspects of ourselves and the world.

While the lower unconscious is infused by the type of difficult experiences just listed, the higher unconscious includes quite opposite experiences that in psychosynthesis are called *transpersonal qualities*. Maslow called such qualities *being values* and *being cognitions*, and they can been seen in Richard Bucke's (1967) *cosmic consciousness*; in those moments William James (1961) studied as "varieties of religious experience"; in what Marghanita Laski (1968) explored as *ecstasy*; and in the *peak experiences* researched by Maslow (1962, 1971). Transpersonal qualities are probably infinite in variety, but a partial list was published by the Psychosynthesis Institute in Redwood City, California (circa 1970):

- Beauty, compassion, comprehension
- Courage, creativity, energy, power
- Enthusiasm, eternity, infinity, universality
- Freedom, liberation, detachment
- Cooperation, friendship
- Generosity, goodness, goodwill
- Gratitude, appreciation, admiration, wonder
- Harmony, humor, inclusiveness
- Joy, bliss, light, love
- Order, patience, positiveness
- Reality, truth, service
- Renewal, trust, faith
- Serenity, peace, silence, quiet, calm
- Simplicity, synthesis, wholeness
- Understanding, vitality, will, wisdom

Transpersonal qualities derive ultimately from our connection to Self, the source of our being, potentially facilitated by authentic unifying centers. They are essential properties of this primal relationship which, once repressed, characterize the higher unconscious (of course, many aspects of these qualities are not split off or repressed and have been integrated into ongoing functioning).

THE PROFUNDITY OF SPLITTING

The childhood splitting of positive and negative, good and bad, within the personality has been recognized throughout the history of Western psychology. It was seen by Sigmund Freud (1981), by Melanie Klein (1975) and W. Ronald D. Fairbairn (1986), by James Masterson (1981) and Otto Kernberg (1992) and, in the field of transpersonal psychology, by Michael Washburn (1994). However, most thinkers seem to understand this as a simple splitting of, for example, inner representations of parental figures into good and bad representations, or good and bad "objects," not to mention that these thinkers often hold differing theories about the cause of splitting. But it is vastly more profound than this would imply.[4]

In this splitting and repression we truncate our most fundamental experience of ourselves, of others, of the cosmos, and of Divinity. Remember that the empathic connection with a unifying center—a connection that can be broken or distorted by empathic failure—is ultimately a connection to the source of our being, or Self (see Chapter 6). Thus a break in this connection is experienced as a break in our connection to the Ground of Being, to Source, to God, to Spirit, to the Universe.

As children, then, our connection to a failing unifying center is akin to encountering a God who is giving us our existence and at the same time annihilating us. Faced with such an impossible contradiction, and given no other unifying center to help us hold it, we split the unifying center into a positive God and a negative God, and we repress both. This splitting and repression leave us with a constricted world, one devoid of the heights and depths, but one in which we can find some stability and safety—the world of the survival personality and the survival unifying center.

So the situation represented in Figure 7.2 is that we, right now, at this moment, are radically unaware of the mystery, the beauty, the love, and the Divinity that surrounds us. Although at times we do realize such wonders, our day-to-day experience often leaves us unmoved by the infinite colors of a sunset, the intricate counterpoint of a symphony, the good hearts of those around us, the touch of the Eternal, or our unity with the Divine.

Likewise, we are relatively blind to the wounding around us, whether from our own behavior or that of others. We cannot feel the full impact of the contemptuous comment, the disdain in attitudes around us, the bigotry within and without, and the raw suffering of humanity and of the planet itself. Our empathy, our compassion, for ourselves and others is thereby limited, and our capacity to heal and to serve is likewise limited.

POSITIVE AND NEGATIVE IDEALIZATION

Remember that the higher unconscious and lower unconscious are split off and polarized aspects of a single whole, that is, of our full experiential range by which we can engage both the heights and depths of life. When we are held in being via external and internal authentic unifying centers, this range is intact, and we are able to experience whatever arises in our lives.

However, while each repressed sector represents an aspect of our full experiential range, each also is distorted by its isolation from the conscious personality. Over time, each sector remains insulated not only from the other sector but also from the transformative and integrative effects of daily living; these sectors remain untouched and unchanged by the learning gained from ongoing experience in a world that is in fact both light and dark, bitter and sweet, and full and empty.

It is as if certain positive and negative elements of our experience now exist in pure form; they exist as essences, potent and heady, in a sense extracted from the world like juice extracted from a fruit. Or, to use another metaphor, we have lost the eyeglasses through which we can see both the positive and negative in life, leaving us instead with (1) one pair of glasses through which we can see all of the positive, (2) one pair through which we can see all of the negative, and finally, (3) another pair, that of the survival personality, which excludes broad ranges of both negative and positive.[5]

In any case, the positive and negative now seem to exist in an idealized form. That is, they seem more pure than concrete reality; they are energies or forms that appear to exist beyond our daily living, somehow more fundamental or more true than our normal existence.

POSITIVE IDEALIZATION

It is therefore understandable that when higher unconscious energies suddenly become conscious, the experience often is described as ideal and perfect, seeming to point to a realm that is more pure and grand than daily life—what we call *positive idealization*. Two examples of higher unconscious experience, taken from the many accounts gathered in Laski's (1968) important study, *Ecstasy*, follow:

> . . . the heart leaps like a fountain—a wordless feeling of sudden tremendous expansion, sudden glory . . . it is an end of individuality for a moment, because there's sudden glory in both me and the universe, both inextricably mingled. (383)

> I don't know how to put it into words—forgetting oneself, no, oneself ceasing to matter and no longer being connected with everyday things, with the commercial sort of life one lives—a feeling that for the first time you're seeing things in proper proportion. (387)

We can see here wonder, joy, and expansion as the person feels a perfect, pure holding by a larger reality. There is a sense of an ideal union with this greater reality—a union that moves well beyond the normal sense of separate identity and the details of daily life.

However, especially if the peak experience is a powerful one, it can seem as though the experience reveals a wondrous ideal realm beyond our mundane lives to which we must aspire—a dualism that can be misleading, as we have seen. It is more accurate to say that we have momentarily removed the "lens" of the survival personality and are perceiving reality through the pure "lens" of the higher unconscious. That is, these transpersonal energies do not in fact exist in another, ideal world; they are aspects of *this* world that have been disconnected from it, and they seem so utterly pure because we encounter them initially as separate from their original context in the world.

In a peak experience we regain our ability to experience particular transpersonal qualities, and we suddenly see the beauty, love, and wonder that was always there, in us and in the world. In other words, these qualities are no longer idealized—experienced as dualistically separate from the real—but realized. They may now be integrated into our daily lives which, in truth, is where they existed all along.

NEGATIVE IDEALIZATION

The pure and universal nature of positive idealization can be seen mirrored in what we call the *negative idealization*, characteristic of the lower unconscious. An example of what Laski calls a *desolation experience*, what we would call contact with the lower unconscious, follows:

> Instead of the light of ineffable revelation I seem to be in perpetual fog and darkness. I cannot get my mind to work; instead of associations "clicking into place" everything is an inextricable jumble; instead of seeming to grasp a whole, it seems to remain tied to the actual consciousness of the moment. The whole world of my thought is hopelessly divided into incomprehensible water-tight compartments. I could not feel more ignorant, undecided or inefficient. It is appallingly difficult to concentrate, and writing is pain and grief to me.
>
> As for wickedness, although my mind has not reached the stage of regarding itself as the most wicked person in the world and responsible for all the sin and evil afflicting mankind, I know too well that it can do so. The appalling self-centeredness is the reverse of the delusions of grandeur and power. It leads to the uttermost depths. (1968, 160–61)

When lower unconscious energy emerges strongly in such desolation or abyss experiences, we may feel that brokenness and pain are the substance of the world, that suffering or evil reigns in the cosmos, that we are doomed and worthless, or that all of life is meaningless. So these painful experiences can be every bit as pure as the positive experiences; they too seem larger or more true than life—ergo, "negative idealization." Laski clearly points out that idealization is present in both ecstasy and desolation:

> The only characteristic of ecstasy equally found in these desolation states is feelings of totality; what is felt is total and absolute, affects the whole life, is the most of its kind, lasts for ever: e.g., "thus it will be with it *for ever* . . . abandonment with respect to *all* creatures . . . an object of contempt to *all,*" "I *could not feel more* ignorant, etc. . . . the *uttermost* depths," "doomed to remain there *for ever.*" (1968, 163, emphases in original)

Because of this sense of "totality," of the absolute or universal, desolation experiences can overshadow any points of brightness in life, just as peak experiences can outshine the darkness. In effect, lower unconscious experience results from contact with the distilled essences of our wounding—essences that seem fundamental and universal, because they have been extracted from the concrete events of our lives; in other words, they have been idealized.

Thus both the higher and lower sectors of the unconscious represent distilled essences or pure experiences and, as such, they can be disorienting and difficult to integrate. Just as higher unconscious experience is contact with the heady, concentrated sweetness extracted from the world, so the lower unconscious is contact with the heady, concentrated bitterness extracted from the world.

Clearly, neither of these realms of experience, although they can appear as an idealized totality, are in fact the whole story. For one thing, they each leave the other out—they are split-off fragments of a whole. Life is neither totally good nor totally evil, purely pain nor purely joy. It is a mysterious mix of birth and death, loss and gain, desolation and consolation.

As we begin to integrate the higher and lower bandwidths of our perception, we begin to perceive this

> . . . joy at some level can coexist with suffering at other levels.
>
> —Roberto Assagioli

profound mix that has always surrounded us. In such an integration, we will find positive-negative polarizations becoming less pronounced; we will be better able to feel our joy with our pain, our gratitude with our sorrow, our emptiness with our fullness—the heights and depths of human existence will be more easily available to us. (This integration is the expansion of the middle unconscious, as described in Chapters 2 and 8.)

This integration of higher and lower is far easier said than done. One might even say that life itself is a journey in which we increasingly realize the awesome heights and depths of existence. Furthermore, the challenges to this integration take a wide variety of forms; the higher and lower unconscious can interact in multitudinous ways within the human personality, presenting different sorts of challenges to each of us. When these challenges are sufficient to disrupt our lives, they may manifest as psychological disturbances. Let us now explore some of the more common types of these disturbances, discerning the operation of the higher unconscious and lower unconscious within them.

PSYCHOLOGICAL DISTURBANCES

When discussing how the higher and lower unconscious impact us, it is important to keep in mind the nature of the I-Self connection. A central aspect of this primal relationship is that it gives us our being, our spirit, our ability to exist distinct-but-not-separate within the flow of ongoing experience. As we explored in Chapter 5, essential human being or I-amness is distinct from all content and process (transcendent), and yet it is engaged with content and process (immanent). We are the experiencer, transcendent-immanent within experience.

As discussed in Chapter 6, modern psychoanalysis has at least partially recognized this sense of being and the source from which it comes: psychoanalytic thinkers write of the child's sense of "cohesion in space and continuity in time" (Kohut) and "continuity of being" (Winnicott) emerging within the empathic relationships with early caregivers.

Although our sense of being does indeed emerge vis-à-vis empathic or authentic unifying centers, in our view this sense ultimately derives from a source distinct-but-not-separate from all such nurturing relationships—the Ground of Being, Self. Self is transcendent-immanent within all unifying centers, just as "I" is transcendent-immanent within the contents of experience. So the I-Self connection is ultimately a spiritual connection, one that transcends—and yet is immanent within—other relationships in our lives.

The connection to Self then should not be confused with experiences of ecstasy, bliss, or unitive states of consciousness, nor with any sort of insulated imperviousness to the human experiences of pain, grief, and loss. Self simply holds us in being, so that we may be open to the full range of our experience—good or bad, pleasant or painful, personal or transpersonal, empty or full. Held securely in existence, our experience does not fragment or destroy us; we can be there within it. This is why, held in this way, we can include and integrate all of the experiences, gifts, and modes of being that arise throughout development, in an unfolding of authentic personality.

It follows that as this I-Self connection is disturbed by nonempathic unifying centers—primal wounding—our sense of being is undercut so that we can no longer hold certain heights and depths of our experience. These latter are in effect too big for us to hold, thus we split them off and repress them. We hereby lose this ability to be empathic with the full range of our experience.

Although this higher-lower splitting is largely repressed, its impact is profound and pervasive. The effects can be seen in any and all patterns of attitude and behavior that disrupt our lives, from problematic subpersonalities and painful inner conflicts, to addictions and compulsions, to a wide variety of other psychological disturbances.

THE ROLE OF PRIMAL WOUNDING

Before examining specific psychological disturbances, we should point out that we are not claiming that primal wounding is the sole causal factor in all such disturbances. Psychological disturbances are varied and complex and often will involve genetic, biochemical, and constitutional factors as well as psychosocial ones. We are saying, however, that many common disturbances, whatever their origin, exhibit a problematic interplay between what we are calling the higher and lower unconscious—sectors that, we believe, arise from primal wounding.[6]

Here too we should reiterate our statement in Chapter 6 ("Who is to blame?") that the infliction of primal wounding can be a completely unconscious process and may come from a variety of different sources. Thus even if wounding were found to be the dominant cause of a particular disorder, this would not necessarily mean that caregivers consciously inflicted the wounding; the transmission of this wounding can occur as silently and blamelessly as genetic inheritance or intrauterine infection.

It is beyond the scope of this book to delve deeply into the many types of psychological disturbances, so we will take a shorthand approach by presenting brief statements that illuminate a few common ones. In using this illustrative method, however, let us be clear from the outset that these statements are to be understood as no more than abstract sketches, merely suggestive of highly complex, powerful patterns. *The phrases we shall use are not statements necessarily uttered or thought by those suffering these disturbances and should in no way be thought to minimize the magnitude of these destructive patterns nor the often lengthy and painful recovery from them.* So when we refer to higher unconscious and lower unconscious in these phrases, we are referring only to the qualities of these two areas of the unconscious; they may or may not be unconscious in the particular psychological disturbance that we are describing.

With these caveats firmly in mind, let us look at some statements that illustrate the higher-lower dynamics in a variety of common psychological disturbances.

ADDICTIONS AND COMPULSIONS

A few statements that symbolize the split between higher and lower unconscious as manifest in addictions and compulsions follow:

> I use alcohol not only to overcome my feelings of anxiety and emptiness (lower unconscious) but in order to feel connected to other people (higher unconscious).

Is the alcoholism simply a result of failed willpower, oral fixation, or solely biological determinants? We think rather a deeper dynamic is that alcoholism embodies an attempt to integrate the higher unconscious while avoiding the wounding in the lower unconscious. In the words of William James, "The sway of alcohol over mankind is unquestionably due to its power to simulate the mystical faculties of human nature" (1961, 304). And these higher unconscious positive "kernels" or "nuclei" (Firman and Gila 1997) are apparent in other addictions as well:

> I feel worthless (lower unconscious) unless I'm working, whether at my job or at home; I've got to work all the time because that's how I know I am worthwhile (higher unconscious).

Is the person who works compulsively, causing pain to himself or herself and others, the victim of a powerful instinct for self-preservation? More to the point is that the person is caught in a compulsive pattern that seeks to establish self-worth in the face of the worthlessness brought about by primal wounding.

> I compulsively attach to my partner in order to escape my inner sense of abandonment and despair (lower unconscious), but also because this is the only thing that gives meaning to my life (higher unconscious).

And is the relationship addict simply caught up in an overactive erotic drive or an archaic need to merge with another? No, here again is a desperate attempt to secure essential qualities of human being in spite of primal wounding.

Note that each addictive pattern is a painful synthesis of the types of higher unconscious qualities and lower unconscious qualities outlined above. Here there is a vicious cycle in which we, in effect, seek the higher unconscious, fall into the lower unconscious, seek the higher unconscious again, continually ad infinitum—a cycle that often becomes destructive to ourselves and others. A Buddhist might call this a cycle of *aversion* and *craving*. This is a common experience in addictions, a moving from the euphoria of the addiction into remorse and worthlessness, only to begin the cycle again.

The tragedy is, of course, that the positive qualities ultimately remain out of reach and unintegrated. They can only be experienced within the addiction and are unavailable for any graceful, natural expression in daily life. Here our connection to others is available only when we are high, our self-worth only when working, or our sense of meaning only when we cling to another person. These are toxic syntheses but nevertheless are desperate attempts to manage the deeper splitting in our being.

What these patterns all have in common is that they are bigger than we are; they dominate our consciousness and will. But note again that this domination is not a function of upwelling primitive drives and basic instincts; it is the result of a profound higher-lower splitting caused by wounding to our spirit.

Multiple Personality or Dissociative Identity Disorder

We have seen that there is a natural multiplicity within the human personality, a multiplicity with the potential for forming a coherent expression of ourselves and our life's journey. We have seen too that difficult or problematic subpersonalities arise in response to primal wounding. Such subpersonalities constitute problematic syntheses. They are driven by the "stick" of their underlying pain and drawn by the "carrot" of expressing their positive gifts—aversion and craving. However, the greater the wounding, the more dissociated and polarized the parts may become as the entire personality system responds to the wounds:

> It actually worked well for a long time. Some of us were in charge of different types of functioning, giving some sense of self-confidence and identity (higher unconscious), while other parts were holding different aspects of our abuse (lower unconscious). But finally it wasn't working. There were too many of us and not enough communication. Then, as we came closer together to improve functioning (higher unconscious), the wounded ones (lower unconscious) began to emerge to be included also.

So a pattern of extremely dissociated multiplicity, as problematic as this can become, can in fact be seen as a creative response to primal wounding. Some parts form a functioning system, handling daily affairs, and keeping things together, while others perform the task of holding the wounding. All works well, as long as there is enough communication to function and distance is maintained between the ones who function and the ones who are wounded. The entire system is in fact a synthesis—a painful synthesis when it becomes self-destructive—which embodies an attainment of higher unconscious qualities yet manages the pain of the lower unconscious.

NARCISSISM AND DEPRESSION

We can see this same interplay of higher and lower in other, apparently quite dissimilar, types of disturbances:

> I generally feel I am a special person, even sometimes a pure shining light (higher unconscious, positive idealization), but whenever I get some criticism or meet a defeat, I feel awful about myself (lower unconscious, negative idealization) and angry (lower unconscious) at the person or situation who has done this.

This statement might be called by some a fixation at an early, primitive, narcissistic stage of development. But even if that case were to be made, it is somewhat irrelevant when compared to the paramount fact that here is someone suffering the effects of violence done to her or his spirit. There has been primal wounding here that has demanded an idealized survival personality based on higher unconscious energy—"I am a special person," and so on—an identification that can function to keep the lower unconscious pain at bay.[7]

Another common disturbance that seems quite different from the previous one, yet embodies a similar higher-lower polarity, is described thus:

> I have been so traumatized by significant others that I have been left feeling I am a worthless, bad person. I feel I am a failure and have no right to be alive, I hate myself, I'm simply wasting space on the planet (lower unconscious, negative idealization).
>
> In some ways, though, I feel like by accepting this painful identity I am maintaining a meaningful loyal connection (higher unconscious, positive idealization) to my significant others; in other ways this identity is a way of holding my trauma in the hope that the truth of it may finally be seen and validated (higher unconscious).

These statements are of a type that can be associated with depression. Here we can see the domination of lower unconscious dynamics in the feelings of extreme self-loathing (here quite conscious, of course). However, such feelings are not in fact *self*-loathing, but rather the loathing is coming from an internalized oppressor or perpetrator in the lower unconscious.[8]

Such an inner perpetrator is the internalization of the actual perpetrator(s) in the person's life, the distilled essence of early, nonempathic unifying centers. As painful as this is, the position of slave or victim to this inner oppressor nevertheless embodies higher unconscious qualities such as connection, hope, loyalty, and truth—an important point to remember if one is seeking to ameliorate such a condition.

BORDERLINE AND BIPOLAR

Still other disturbances involve wide swings between the heights and depths of these two realms of the unconscious. A common one follows:

> I can move so quickly between highs (higher unconscious) and lows (lower unconscious). One moment I see the beauty of the other person (higher unconscious, positive idealization), but then when the other person doesn't seem to get who I truly am, it feels terribly hurtful, and I suddenly see them as bad and get angry (lower unconscious, negative idealization).

Here we have a statement that represents what some call a borderline type of experience. But is this most essentially a failure to wrestle an ego from a primitive state located on the border between neurosis and psychosis (thus the term *borderline*)? Is the sensitivity and anger indicative of uncontrolled, innate aggression or envy?

We would say instead that this type of experience is a state of high vulnerability caused by profound wounding. Here we have someone whose wounds are so unprotected that the slightest empathic failure will feel terribly painful and will trigger the emergence of lower unconscious experience. This is like walking around with an untreated abscess that will trigger pain and rage at the slightest touch.

Another experience of dramatic swings between highs and lows might be described like this:

> I'll go along for quite awhile having wondrous experiences, seeing everything so clearly, having great insights, and enthusiastically throwing myself into inspired creative activity (higher unconscious). But then I will crash and become very low energy, down on myself, despairing of life, not wanting to live (lower unconscious).

This type of experience is characteristic of what has been called manic-depressive or bipolar disorder, or the less severe cyclothymic disorder, in which one cycles from the heights to the depths over longer periods of time. But is this a failure to grow beyond the supposed grandiosity and insecurities of the toddler? Clearly, such an explanation completely misses and obscures the most fundamental point: that this is someone who has been traumatized, causing the split between higher unconscious and lower unconscious and leading to an oscillation between these two separate domains of experience.[9]

THE MALEVOLENT, ANTI-SOCIAL, AND VIOLENT

There also is a terribly destructive psychological disturbance in which the person seems to feel no empathic connection with other people and may perpetrate horrific acts of ruthless violence. We often are shocked and confused by these depths of human evil, and we may speak of "senseless acts of violence"—but they are quite sensible within the world of the brutalized personality. This type of disturbance includes the child who guns down classmates at school, the remorseless serial killer, the fanatical terrorist, and the sadistic dictator who oversees torture and genocide; but to a lesser extent, we find similar dynamics in any person motivated by hatred, rage, or revenge.

> I have been so violated by life, so unseen and brutalized (lower unconscious), and so schooled in violence (middle unconscious), that my resultant rage (lower unconscious) is spontaneously expressed in violent ways. The world seems so utterly dangerous that I must assert power (higher unconscious) violently in order to maintain a sense of self that is exalted enough (higher unconscious) to triumph over violent oppression.
>
> Further, my internal and external significant others (unifying centers) support an ethos of violence, and I act in moral union with their values and worldview.

Is this violent behavior, then, the result of an upwelling of innate human aggression? An archaic holdover from a violent, primitive past? No. As many have pointed out, there is a direct relationship between early violent wounding and human malevolence (Athens 1992, 1997; Goldberg 1996; Miller 1984a; Rhodes 1999; Winnicott 1984).

In response to this wounding, there develops a survival personality that uses violence as a primary response to the world. And yes, society

> Many violent patients are infuriated by . . . injustices . . . because they are symbolic of injustices rendered to them in the past.
>
> —Roberto Assagioli

must protect itself from the destructive behavior that this wounding engenders. But can we at the same time hear the abyss of violation beneath these extremes of human evil?[10]

PSYCHOSIS

Finally, can our analysis of psychological disturbances be extended to that perhaps most mysterious disorder called psychosis—disorders of thought and feeling so extreme that they seem simply the chaotic disintegration of the entire personality?

> I have had much neglect and abuse (lower unconscious) in my life which no one, now or then, ever seems to be able to acknowledge. Therefore I

have needed to hold my truth (higher unconscious) symbolically, forming what are seen as crazy and delusional ideas but which for me encapsulate what has happened to me in my life.

Psychotic experience might be considered a failure to grow beyond the supposed autistic or symbiotic stage of infantile development, a failure to differentiate from an archaic, fused state dominated by fantasy and hallucinatory wish fulfillment. We do not think that this is the case, of course, especially in light of the fact that modern developmental research has discounted the existence of such a primary fused state (Stern 1985).

It is quite true that on the face of it the worldview manifest in such experience might indicate that the person is out of touch with consensual reality, confusing the inner and outer worlds. However, as it has been clearly pointed out (Stolorow, Brandchaft, and Atwood 1987), such seemingly crazy worldviews can carry the deeper truth of the person's suffering. Here there is a symbolic expression of the wounding, past and present, that the person has suffered in life, and a desperate hope that this wounding will finally be recognized and responded to.[11]

The power and stability of the psychotic pattern again seem to derive from twin factors: it is an embodiment of a quest for the higher unconscious, a quest for validation, for being seen, for truth, and at the same time, it is an attempt to manage the pain from wounding. In the words of Winnicott, "It is wrong to think of psychotic illness as a breakdown, it is a defence organization relative to a primitive agony" (1989, 90). Psychosis does not appear to be a regression to some sort of primal, undifferentiated state but just another attempt to bridge the higher-lower splitting.

On the other hand, the psychotic process can be seen as a massive crisis of transformation similar dynamically to those discussed in earlier chapters (Ellen in Chapter 3, for example), although far more intense and chaotic. Here a psychotic break may be a complete failure of survival personality to maintain itself, leading to a radical openness to all levels of the unconscious, and finally perhaps to a gradual formation of a more authentic personality.[12]

ON THOSE WHO STRUGGLE

The types of disturbances that we have outlined above involve different responses to primal wounding, different ways of managing the higher-lower splitting that this wounding causes. We hope that you, the reader, can empathize with these experiences. Perhaps you yourself have had these types of experiences at one time or another.

We all have suffered primal wounding and splitting to a greater or lesser extent, and we all face some struggle with these vast, split-off dimensions of our being. Those with diagnosed psychological disorders are not lost in some sort of mad world completely foreign to a normal world; they are simply experiencing—acutely and painfully—particular points on an experiential spectrum that we all share.

It may even be that those who focus on their healing in this way have been called to deal with the collective primal wounding that most of us desperately attempt to avoid. Perhaps they struggle for us, seeking to heal a hidden abscess in our collective spirit that insidiously poisons all of our lives. Perhaps, as Chris Meriam (1999) speculates, through their healing work, they "somehow keep the consensual/collective psyche flexible and moving forward."

> In each of us there are, potentially, all the elements and qualities of the human being.
>
> —Roberto Assagioli

From this perspective, those who so intensely confront our collective wounding are not tragically flawed unfortunates unable to achieve normality but instead are dedicated laborers in the field of human evolution. If grappling with the truth of our lives is the measure of spiritual development, these people may not be in the early stages of this development but in the advanced stages.

PSYCHOLOGY AND SPIRITUALITY

Note, then, that most, if not all, psychological disturbances can at some level be seen as involving a response to primal wounding that has been inflicted by empathic failures of various kinds. This wounding cuts us off from the ground of our being, thereby forcing us to split off the heights and depths of our experiential range, and this splitting in turn seems to infuse the wide range of disturbances outlined above. Thus underlying psychological disturbances seem to be a wounding to our spirit—a *spiritual* wounding.

We posit, then, that such disturbances are not simply the result of basic instincts clashing with society; nor of an inner conflict between powerful drives; nor of a struggle to differentiate from a supposed archaic, infantile merged experience; nor of perturbations in the collective unconscious; nor even of a difficulty integrating split internal objects. While some of such phenomena may be viewed as accompanying primal wounding, we would hold as probable that these disturbances of body and soul are secondary to an essential spiritual wounding underlying them all.[13]

TREATMENT IMPLICATIONS

The notion that primal wounding is involved in psychological disturbances also is a worthy hypothesis for its humanitarian value. That is, if we are holding a hypothesis that does *not* allow for a fundamental wounding of human spirit, then we will not be looking for the wounding, nor will we understand the depth of empathic concern that it demands, nor will we fully appreciate the skills, gifts, and creativity that have been actualized in spite of the wounding.

In other words, we will miss the essential person, "I," the human spirit transcendent-immanent within the wounding and gifts—the one who is experiencing this split in being. We will then actually retraumatize those seeking healing by ignoring the profundity of their experience and, thus, once again, we will give them the experience of not being seen. Trauma researcher Bessel A. Van der Kolk, speaking of "a variety of psychiatric disorders," says:

> However, if clinicians fail to pay attention to the contribution of past trauma to the current problems in patients with these diagnoses, they may fail to see that they seem to organize much of their lives around repetitive patterns of reliving and warding off traumatic memories, reminders, and affects . . . if clinicians deny the essential truth of their patients' experiences, they can only aggravate feelings of rage and helplessness by invalidating the realities of their patients' lives. (Van der Kolk, McFarlane, and Weisaeth 1996, 183–84)

So while research into all of the possible causes of psychological disorders should proceed on all fronts, such research also should entertain the hypothesis that there is a primal wounding present that has been suffered within significant relationships, and that there exists an essential human spirit within these disturbances seeking liberation. As it has been pointed out, much research, even that looking at psychosocial factors, fails to ask the questions that would reveal the role of trauma in psychological disturbances (see Herman 1992; Van der Kolk, McFarlane, and Weisaeth 1996).

The treatment implications for this model are simple but far-reaching ones. In short, *if empathic failure causes this spiritual wounding, then ultimately only empathic connection can heal.* Empathy is fundamental to the healing process. This, of course, is the type of empathic connection that we have been describing throughout this book—the type of listening, respect, dynamic response, and acknowledgment of deeper Self, which allows the emergence of the essential I-amness of the other. So note that this empathy is not mere passive listening, not necessarily being "warm, friendly, and nice." This is a fierce spiritual empathy that demands continual disidentification and personal work by the practitioner so that this essential empathy will not be obscured by responses from his or her own survival personality.

Clearly, too, this spiritual empathy is not a technique or method among many but the context of all technique and method. Most techniques, ranging the entire spectrum from receptive listening to active interventions, can be done empathically—or not.[14]

PSYCHOLOGY IS SPIRITUAL

This view of the human spirit and the wounding of this spirit can perhaps refocus attempts to encourage psychology to expand its scope to include spirituality. For example, although a worthy and needed effort, it can be misleading to include spirituality only in the *Diagnostic and Statistical Manual of Mental Disorders* (First 1994) under the recently appended category of "Religious or Spiritual Problem, V62.89." Rather, *all* disorders involve spiritual problems, because the human being and the wounding of the human being are essentially spiritual in nature. It is similarly misleading to consider bring-ing spirit into psychotherapy as sim-ply adding spiritual and religious practices to therapy; instead, *psychotherapy itself must be understood as spiritual at its very core.*

So, in a very real way, spirit does not need to be brought into psychol-ogy—spirit is already present, however hidden, at its very center. Spirituality

> Such empathy is made possible by the fact of the essential unity of human nature existing beneath, and in spite of, all individual and group diversities.
>
> —Roberto Assagioli

must not be seen as an appendage to psychology, something that we should work to include, but as the essence of all personality, clinical, and develop-mental theory. Psychology has not neglected spirit but has been grappling in the dark with spirit. From the earliest insights of the pioneering psychologi-cal thinkers, to all of the modern differentiations of psychology and psy-chotherapy, we have throughout been attempting to deal with the human spirit. It is interesting to ponder the changes in modern psychology that would occur if this realization became widespread.

EIGHT

SELF-REALIZATION

Just as there is a personal will . . . so there is a Transpersonal Will. . . . It is its action which is felt by the personal self, or "I," as a "pull" or "call."

—Roberto Assagioli

The fundamental importance of "I" and Self has been a major theme throughout this book. It is the I-Self relationship which, facilitated by empathic unifying centers, forms the axis of optimum human development. When this relationship is intact, there is a burgeoning of "I" and an unfolding of authentic personality throughout the life span, a following of one's unique path in life.

Conversely, when this relationship is disturbed by nonempathic response from the environment, primal wounding occurs. This wounding in turn leads to the splitting of the higher and lower unconscious, polarization and conflict within the natural multiplicity of the personality, a lack of meaning in life, and various other types of psychological disturbances.

In this chapter we will more closely examine the nature of "I" and Self, with a particular focus on the dynamic relationship between them, or what is called *Self-realization*. We will see that Self-realization does not denote a state of consciousness, a stage of development, a transformational moment, or any other particular mode of experiencing but rather an ongoing relationship with Self though all experiencing. In order to discern this relationship more clearly, we will later describe the two dimensions of Self-realization, *personal psychosynthesis* and *transpersonal psychosynthesis*.

"I" AND SELF

As we have seen, human spirit, or "I," is able to engage a breathtaking range of different experiences: moving through inner chaos and psychological crises, disidentifying from subpersonalities and other personality structures, engaging the ongoing events of psyche and soma, embracing the heights of unitive experience, experiencing no-self and emptiness, and walking through the valleys of primal wounding.

Throughout, "I" remains distinct-but-not-separate of—transcendent-immanent within—all energies, patterns, contents, processes, images, feelings, thoughts, drives, heights and depths. "I" is ever the experiencer transcendent-immanent within the experience. The essence of who we are should not be confused with our bodies, our feelings, our minds, our roles, or any state of human being.

Given this nature of "I," what might we say then about the source of "I"? Clearly, "I" cannot derive from instinctual drives, physical sensations, dynamics of emotion, patterns of thought, or social conditioning, because "I" is ultimately distinct from all of these. What then might be the source of such a mysterious spirit? It would make sense to posit that the source of this remarkable transcendent-immanent I-amness is an even more remarkable, deeper, transcendent-immanent I-amness. It is this deeper source of "I" that we call *Self.*

> The reflection ["I"] appears to be self-existent but has, in reality, no autonomous substantiality. It is, in other words, not a new and different light but a projection of its luminous source [Self]. (Assagioli 1965a, 20)

Transcendent-immanent personal self, human spirit, or "I," is the direct projection or reflection of transcendent-immanent Self, Spirit, or "Divine I am." Unique human selfhood is not a cosmic mistake, not an isolated ego lost in illusion, but something far more essential that is chosen and sustained by Self.[1]

Further, just as "I" can be transcendent-immanent within many sensations, feelings, thoughts, subpersonalities, and so on, we can posit that Self is transcendent-immanent within all of the contents and processes of the entire personality and perhaps beyond (see discussion that follows). Self would then be present and active at all of the levels of the unconscious—lower, middle, higher—and thus could be met at any level and invite us to any level.

This transcendent-immanent omnipresence of Self makes sense of the fact that many, in following their path of Self-realization, find themselves traversing all levels of experience and not simply ascending into the higher unconscious. Self can meet us anywhere, invite us anywhere. This is an important reason to not picture Self at the apex of the oval diagram and instead assume that Self is transcendent-immanent within the entire diagram (see "Self and the Oval Diagram" in Chapter 2).

SELF AS SOURCE

Note that since Self is transcendent-immanent within all levels, it is not a mere totality, a summation of these levels. Self is not a collectivity, a totality, or an undifferentiated unity from which we must separate in order to attain a sense of individuality. Quite the contrary, Self *gives* us our individuality, is *choosing* our I-amness. To lose the connection to Self would be to *lose* individuality, not to gain it. Think of the analogy we used in Chapter 2, of Self as a candle flame whose image—"I"—is being reflected in a mirror: we might say that losing the connection to Self amounts to interposing an obstacle between the candle (Self) and the mirror reflection of the candle ("I"), thus causing the absolute disappearance of the image (i.e., nonbeing, primal wounding).

Conversely, the more we are in alignment or communion with Self, the brighter and clearer the reflected image will be—"I" will blossom. This is quite apparent in the phenomenon of empathic mirroring: the more we are seen by authentic unifying centers, which are conduits for Self, the more "I" is in evidence.

This view of the genesis of personal individuality differs from a common view found in psychoanalysis, Jungian psychology, and even transpersonal psychology. Some proponents of these approaches posit that our individuality separates from a primordial unity of some sort, whether this is called id (Freud), self (Jung), Spiritual Ground (Nelson 1994), or Dynamic Ground (Washburn 1988)—although much current infant research has strongly called into question the existence of a primary unity from which the infant must differentiate (see Stern 1985).

In any case, Self here is not considered an undifferentiated unity from which we must separate to gain individuality. Self is in no way and at no time inimical to individuality but the direct and immediate source of this at every moment. A disconnection from Self undercuts our being; a connection with Self gives us our being. Psychological disturbances are not caused by an inability to differentiate from Self but from an experienced disconnection from Self caused by primal wounding. (Of course, a relationship to Self potentiates "I" and therefore can put survival personality into crisis, so yes, that type of identity can be threatened—remember Ellen in Chapter 3.)

The I-Self Union

In Assagioli's conception of "I" as a projection of Self, we also can see that "I" and Self exist in a profound, unbreakable union. Think again of an image reflected in a mirror—the image is in complete union with the object imaged, the "projection" in union with its "luminous source." Furthermore, since both "I" and Self are transcendent-immanent, it seems clear that their union too is transcendent-immanent. The I-Self union exists at a depth beyond all things. *In fact, from this point of view primal wounding—the apparent breaking of the I-Self connection—is an illusion.*

That is, the I-Self union cannot in actuality be broken—or improved—because this is transcendent-immanent of anything that might conceivably disrupt or improve it. In the words of the great mystic, Meister Eckhart, "there is something in the soul so closely akin to God that it is already one with him and need never be united to him" (Blakney 1941, 205). What does occur, of course, is that we *experience* a disruption through empathic failures in our lives, and as we have seen, we undergo many tremendous changes in order to manage this perceived threat to our spirit.

This transcendence-immanence of the I-Self connection helps explain how primal wounding is finally healed. Such healing of course involves reestablishing an empathic connection with the wounded layers in ourselves as they emerge during Self-realization, our empathy dispelling the night of nonbeing. But those who feel deeply the hurt, fear, and loneliness of these younger parts often discover a surprising thing: their essential nature was never in fact hurt, they were never truly alone, and they were never in danger of annihilation:

> I was angry that God had deserted me in this abusive family. It wasn't fair. I shouted at God a lot, raging at the betrayal. But gradually I began to see something amazing. If God had deserted me, how is it I could now live to tell the tale? I am here, undamaged at some level, at some deep level from which I can see what happened to me and have compassion for myself. God got me through. So God did not actually desert me, though it felt that way at the time.

In remaining empathic with such traumatized layers of ourselves, there often is the realization that Self was in fact ever-present, holding us in being, saving our soul. It is simply that the abuse or neglect cut us off from conscious contact with Self at the time. Healing often is a matter of returning to these moments, to those parts of us, and seeing through the illusory absence of Self to the unbroken connection to Self.

SELF AS EMPATHIC

This transcendent-immanent union of "I" and Self also illuminates why this relationship is quintessentially empathic. As direct reflections of Self, continuously in union with Self, we are known by Self in the most intimate way possible. In fact, although we ourselves may be unclear about who we are, as we are caught up in various roles and identifications or immersed in the details of our daily lives, Self continuously knows us at the level of spirit, of "I." The following statements show this spiritual empathy operating through authentic unifying centers:

> My grandmother really knew me. She always seemed to know what I really needed before I did.

> My high school coach accepted my doubt and fear, but saw through this to the athlete in me. I blossomed.

> She's awesome. I can't put one over on her; she knows me too well. She sees through my dramas and gets me to laugh at myself.

> There was this tree I used to sit in for hours when I was ten years old. No one seemed to know my loneliness but the spirit of that tree.

And even more clearly:

> I feel like God has always known me, from the womb and before, and through all the moments of my life, even when it seemed God wasn't there.

These statements show the operation of a transcendent-immanent empathy that can reach our essential nature. While we may not be seen and understood in much of our lives, even by ourselves, empathic Self remains clear about who we truly are. To paraphrase St. Augustine, "God is more intimate to us than we are to ourselves."

Transcendent-immanent empathy is a fundamental aspect of the I-Self relationship. As we have seen, to the extent that this empathy is manifested by unifying centers throughout our development, we are able to experience whatever arises in our lives and to hold these experiences meaningfully—we gain self-empathy. Within the radiance of this empathy our sense of transcendent-immanent I-amness blossoms, and we show up for our lives in an expression of authentic personality.

> ... his spiritual Self who already knows his problem, his crisis, his perplexity.
>
> —Roberto Assagioli

SELF AS UNIVERSAL

From the deepest point of view, Self can be conceptualized as universal much along the lines of Jung's statement that "self is not only in me but in all beings, like the Atman, like Tao" (Jung 1964, 463), or as in Wilber's description of what he calls Spirit:

> Spirit transcends all, so it includes all. It is utterly beyond this world, but utterly embraces every single holon in this world. It permeates all of manifestation but is not merely manifestation. It is ever-present at every level or dimension, but is not merely a particular level of dimension. Transcends all, includes all, as the groundless Ground or Emptiness of all manifestation. (1996, 38)

Wilber's "transcends and includes" is what we are calling transcendence-immanence, and in the universality of Self, this transcendence-immanence would embrace "all of manifestation." This universality would be one possible explanation for the fact that Self can be present to us through such a staggering variety of unifying centers: oceans and mountains, animals and plants, blankets and teddy bears, people, real and fictional, symbols and beliefs, and so on.

Of course, as Assagioli (1973a, 125–26) points out, such a profound omnipresence of Self would be beyond the human mind's power of comprehension, so the universality of Self cannot finally be proven or denied intellectually. However, he would point to the fact that one can have an "intuitive, direct experience of communion with the ultimate Reality" (125), and that this type of experience constitutes an observable fact (see Bucke 1967; Laski 1968; Maslow 1971). This is akin to Jung's statement that, "God is an obvious psychic and non-physical fact, i.e., a fact that can be established psychically but not physically" (Jung 1969b, 464).

Whether Self is understood as pervading all levels of the personality, the collective unconscious, and/or the entire cosmos, here we can see that Self-realization does not entail "identifying with Self" or "becoming Self," as it is sometimes held. If this were in fact possible, it would mean becoming directly aware of all contents and processes existing at all of the levels of the unconscious—and perhaps beyond—simultaneously, presumably an overwhelming experience inconsistent with healthy human functioning. Rather, Self-realization can be seen as involving the development of an increasingly conscious communion with Self in our daily living, in other words, the development of authentic personality.

> The Supreme Value, Cosmic Mind, Supreme Reality, both transcendent and immanent.
>
> —Roberto Assagioli

HOW TO DESCRIBE SELF-REALIZATION?

This I-Self connection or axis is then transcendent-immanent within the entire range of human experience, including the depths of our pain in the lower unconscious, the more accessible structures of the middle unconscious, the higher unconscious heights of unitive and peak experiences, and beyond. But if Self-realization is not to be confused with any particular point along this tremendously broad spectrum of human experience, then how are we to describe it?

In our discussion of the stages of psychosynthesis (Chapter 2), we outlined the process in which Self-realization can be supported by exploration and work with the middle unconscious, the higher unconscious, and the lower unconscious. Although Self-realization cannot be reduced to engagement with these levels of ourselves, it seems apparent that these levels form the psychospiritual terrain through which our unique journey of Self-realization will pass. To put it another way, since Self is transcendent of, yet immanent within, these sectors of the unconscious, Self-realization may entail engaging material from any and all sectors at different times.

In order to bring Self-realization into sharper focus, then, let us now examine working with these various levels of the unconscious, understanding this work as occurring along two developmental lines—*personal psychosynthesis* and *transpersonal psychosynthesis*.

PERSONAL PSYCHOSYNTHESIS

Human healing and growth that involves work with either the middle unconscious or the lower unconscious is known as *personal psychosynthesis*. In Assagioli's words:

> This [personal psychosynthesis] includes the development and harmo-
> nizing of all human functions and potentialities at all levels of the lower
> and middle area in the diagram of the constitution of man [and woman].
> (1973a, 121)

In this quotation, Assagioli is referring to the oval diagram, and he is
indicating the middle and the lower unconscious as the areas involved in personal psychosynthesis. Of course, there is seldom an aspect of the human journey that does not include material from all of the levels of the unconscious.
Personal psychosynthesis, while more obviously engaging the lower and middle unconscious contents, will involve higher unconscious material as well—
for example, one quite often encounters higher unconscious content when
working through early trauma. Indeed, we can think of personal psychosynthesis as simply referring to where one is currently focused in the overall healing of the split between the lower and higher unconscious.

Personal psychosynthesis does not necessarily involve the application of
formal methods of education, counseling, or therapy—surely it most often
occurs simply in the living of our lives. In the process of rising to meet the
challenges of our personal and professional lives, we overcome feelings of
unhealthy guilt and shame, transform fears and anxieties, and develop more
harmony within our personalities. In an effort to live authentically, we often
will find old wounds healing and personal wholeness blossoming. But in many
cases, too, much time and struggle can be saved by consciously working at personal psychosynthesis with a trained professional.

THE PROCESS

In Mark's initial work with his Lover and Worker subpersonalities (Chapter
4), we saw an example of personal psychosynthesis occurring at the level of the
middle unconscious. In his case, more or less conscious aspects of his personality—the Worker and Lover—were recognized and brought more sharply
into consciousness. This type of work can of course involve a variety of different techniques and methods from the entire range of therapeutic and growth
modalities available today.

The deeper aspect of personal psychosynthesis can be seen as Mark
uncovered the early abuse, shame, and grief underlying these two subpersonalities—a healing and an integration of material from the lower unconscious
into the conscious personality. Here we are not dealing only with subpersonalities but also with deeper structures comprising experiences, attitudes, motivations, and life scripts conditioning the personality as a whole.

The manifestations of this deeper level may include phenomena such as self-destructive patterns; compulsions, addictions, and dysfunctional attachments; depression, anxiety, and rage; and disturbing experiences of early abuse and neglect. Personal psychosynthesis at these more primary levels is a long-term process, and it may involve the following:

1. The growing awareness of problematic life attitudes and behaviors as they affect daily life, and an awareness of the chronic survival strategies that have been hiding the damaging effects of these attitudes and behaviors.

2. A developing acceptance that these chronic attitudes and behaviors will not transform easily, nor disappear through dramatic breakthrough experiences, but will involve a commitment of time and energy.

3. The gradual recognition and acceptance of the thoughts and feelings of the earlier traumatized levels of the personality.

4. An ongoing living with the emerging material in such a way that our authentic personal potential is actualized in the world.

Such growth often will mean incremental change in habitual ways of relating to ourselves and others, and in the very way of living itself. Personal psychosynthesis that involves much lower unconscious work therefore is best done within the context of stable, secure life structures—authentic unifying centers—such as counseling and psychotherapy, psychosynthesis therapy, ongoing support groups, and an empathic circle of family and friends.

THE HIGHER UNCONSCIOUS

Whether addressing the middle or lower unconscious, personal psychosynthesis tends to lead toward, among other things: less debilitating conflict within the personality; a growing awareness of the physical, emotional, and mental aspects of experience; a sense of freedom and spontaneity; less toxic self-criticism; increasingly realistic self-acceptance; and a sense of personal choice and responsibility.

Note that personal psychosynthesis includes the integration of higher unconscious content as well. Higher unconscious qualities such as creativity, freedom, self-confidence, and spontaneity are included in conscious functioning. We might, for example, be working with an anxious, closed-off subpersonality who, after some amount of empathic connection, begins to manifest playfulness and creativity. Here we initially have moved into the lower unconscious, then into the higher unconscious, and finally we begin to form a healthy new structure in the middle unconscious. So we need not think of personal and transpersonal psychosynthesis as being completely separate; each ultimately implies the other, because each addresses complementary dimensions of our growth.

Furthermore, as many have discovered, personal growth moves quite naturally into a more overt intensification of transpersonal growth. People working on their psychological healing may encounter unexpected moments of profound serenity, ecstatic joy, and spiritual insight; or, plumbing the depths of psychological trauma, they may find a deeper presence that has been holding them always, even at tremendous depths of isolation and pain.

On the other hand, as we proceed further along the personal dimension, we may find a growing emptiness and boredom gnawing at our lives—a crisis of transformation, called the *existential crisis* (see Firman and Vargiu 1977; Firman and Gila 1997; Firman and Vargiu 1980). Such a crisis triggers a search for something more, something that has meaning beyond our individual lives and will lead us eventually into the transpersonal dimension of growth. Thus whether surprised by joy or surprised by lack of joy, we often find that the path of personal psychosynthesis intersects the path of transpersonal psychosynthesis.

TRANSPERSONAL PSYCHOSYNTHESIS

Whereas personal psychosynthesis involves the integration of material from the middle and lower unconscious, transpersonal psychosynthesis (or *spiritual psychosynthesis*) is aimed at integrating material from the higher unconscious. In Assagioli's words:

> The specific therapeutic task . . . is that of arriving at a harmonious adjustment by means of the proper assimilation of the inflowing superconscious energies and of their integration with the pre-existing aspects of the personality; that is, of accomplishing not only a personal but also a spiritual psychosynthesis. (1965a, 53)

As with personal psychosynthesis, transpersonal psychosynthesis often may occur gracefully, with no need for any conscious attention or work on our part at all. Whether in striking peak experiences or in a gradual shift in consciousness, the higher unconscious reveals itself, and we begin an active engagement with this realm. Through meditation, prayer, ritual, music, art, service, and community, we seek to contact and express this dimension of existence.

And as we become more familiar with higher unconscious energies, we may automatically transform our attitudes and behaviors to express these energies in our daily living. We gradually become more compassionate, wise, and inclusive, and we are less controlled by separative attitudes such as greed, rage, and envy. Perhaps a new appreciation for the natural world, an experienced solidarity with other human beings, or a love of the Divine here infuses our lives with little or no disturbance of our personal equilibrium.

However, higher unconscious experiences can be difficult to integrate at times. For example, if we have an intense experience of solidarity and compassion for all humankind, this may lead afterward to a heightened awareness of our feelings of hatred or revenge—feelings that obstruct the expression of compassion. Or perhaps a strong experience of our unity with nature may reveal the personal attitudes and beliefs that caused us to violate this union in the past—attitudes and beliefs that are obstacles to a right relationship with nature. It is as if the older habits, attitudes, and feelings that would obstruct the concrete expression of the new experience are thrown into stark relief in light of the experience itself.

> All the rocks and rubbish, which had been covered and concealed at high tide, emerge again.
>
> —Roberto Assagioli

This dynamic in which obstacles to our growth are energized by a potential step in our growth is called *induction* (Firman 1991; Firman and Gila 1997). The notion of induction is meant to convey the idea that the energy of a forward step activates both the higher unconscious and lower unconscious material that will be needed to manifest the new potential. Induction is, in effect, a call to wholeness, and it often reveals that the higher and lower unconscious are two sides of one split, so that an engagement with one sector often will invite—or demand—engagement with the other. In all such cases, active and intentional psychological work on the problematic reactions often can help a great deal.

THE LOWER UNCONSCIOUS

When the higher unconscious energizes or inducts psychological patterns that have roots in the lower unconscious, transpersonal psychosynthesis will involve lower unconscious work. For example, the reactions mentioned above—the feelings of hatred and revenge, or the disrespectful attitude toward the natural world—may stem from an underlying rage that has childhood antecedents. Perhaps there is a history of sexual or emotional abuse that has left strong feelings of abandonment and shame in the lower unconscious, and a layer of rage has been used to protect the wounds from these early events.

Transpersonal psychosynthesis here will involve a psychological exploration of these childhood events in order to uncover and heal the earlier wounding. In this way, the attitudes of hatred and disrespect mentioned above may eventually be ameliorated, and the original experiences of compassion for humanity or closeness with nature gradually may begin to be expressed in our lives. Thus the modes of perception once glimpsed in peak moments do not remain simply ideal qualities of momentary experiences but become attitudes, values, and patterns of behavior by which we can live our entire lives.

INFATUATION WITH THE SUBLIME

While transpersonal growth may involve addressing patterns that appear as obstacles to integrating higher unconscious energies, it also may involve work with patterns of overvaluing these energies. Such overvaluing can occur as we engage the idealized nature of the higher unconscious and begin to feel that our more mundane daily lives are less important or indeed illusory in light of such experiences. In Assagioli's (1973c) words, we may become caught in "the illusion that everything is an illusion!"

If we become caught up in an enthrallment with higher unconscious energies, an obsessive striving for higher experiences or "enlightenment" may commence, and we may attempt a flight from the problematic world of personal relationships, life responsibilities, and authentic human growth. This phenomenon has been recognized as *polarizing mysticism* by Maslow (1971), as *infatuation with the sublime* by Haronian (1983), as *spiritual bypassing* by Welwood (2000), and as *dualistic denial* by Firman (1991).

As such an infatuation organizes our lives, we begin to develop an identification based on this—what in Chapter 5 we called a transpersonal identification, where we, in effect, become addicted to the higher unconscious, and our expressions of transpersonal qualities become dissociated from other aspects of our personality. We may be feeling happy, joyous, and free, but others will be aware of the sadness, pain, and anger hidden beneath these emotions—lower unconscious material.[2]

We mentioned that in personal psychosynthesis we may encounter the existential crisis, a crisis of transformation that orients us toward the transpersonal dimension. Conversely, in transpersonal psychosynthesis, we may encounter a crisis of transformation inviting us to include the personal dimension, called the *crisis of duality* by Vargiu (see Firman and Vargiu 1977; Firman and Gila 1997; Firman and Vargiu 1980).

In this crisis we are faced with an inherent duality, an unbridgeable chasm, in our quest for enlightenment—we find that we "cannot get there from here." That is, we find that our sublime sense of the beauty and joy of life cannot maintain itself in a pure, idealized state, that the pain and suffering of life must be accepted, and that an authentic life will mean actively engaging the brokenness in ourselves and in the world.

Of course, as we work through this crisis, we will find that the energies of the higher unconscious are free to find their natural way into expression. No longer idealized, the transpersonal qualities will become a part of the

> But when they have reached the depth of despondency or desperation there may come a sudden flow of inspiration inaugurating a period of renewed and intense productive activity.
>
> —Roberto Assagioli

mysterious mix of light and dark that characterizes human existence. Again, these energies are not ultimately ideal forms separate from the world but normal, everyday modes of relationship to the world.

THE EXPANSION OF THE MIDDLE UNCONSCIOUS

Let us point out once more that personal psychosynthesis and transpersonal psychosynthesis refer simply to particular points of focus within the larger bridging of the higher and lower unconscious. Personal psychosynthesis begins at the "bottom," so to speak, and tends toward the "top," while transpersonal psychosynthesis implies beginning at the "top" and working toward the "bottom."

So, for example, both personal and transpersonal psychosynthesis may involve working with subpersonalities in the middle unconscious, early trauma in the lower unconscious, and the heights of higher unconscious experience. Even the repression of the sublime is not simply a higher unconscious dynamic, because the resistance here is invariably the resistance to experiencing some early traumatic event—for example, loss of control, being overwhelmed, or loss of identity—that will come to light (i.e., be inducted) if the higher unconscious is contacted. Although each of us will have our own unique path, this path seems to tend toward a healed relationship between the heights and depths of human being.

Taken together, these two dimensions amount to an *expansion of the middle unconscious*. That is, as the experiential range represented by the higher and lower unconscious is freed up in us, we become more open to the heights and depths in ourselves and in the world. Our consciousness opens us up to a wider range of life experience and, thus, by definition, our middle unconscious—those experiences that can easily enter consciousness—can be said to have expanded. We are more apt to sense the beauty and pain around us, to rejoice in the good and grieve the losses, to feel inspired by the Divine and concerned about the suffering in the world. We become increasingly open to being touched by life in all of its diverse mystery.

Having said all of this, of course, it must be remembered that Self-realization should not ipso facto be equated to this deeper sense of personhood represented by an expanded middle unconscious. Since the I-Self relationship is transcendent-immanent, an ongoing relationship can occur with or without the expanded empathic range that we have been describing. Different paths of Self-realization will involve many different patterns of engagement and nonengagement with the higher and lower bandwidths of our experiential range. Again, even the extremes of psychological disturbances outlined in the previous chapter do not necessarily prevent a meaningful I-Self relationship. We may contact and respond to the invitations from Self, no matter what the state of our bodies and souls. It is this contact and response that we call Self-realization.

SELF-REALIZATION

If both "I" and Self are distinct but not separate from all levels of experience, then the I-Self relationship cannot be equated to any specific type of experience. Thus an ongoing relationship between "I" and Self, or Self-realization, is independent of any particular level of experience and can occur whether the content is from the lower, middle, or higher unconscious. *Self-realization is distinct from both personal psychosynthesis and transpersonal psychosynthesis and can occur in either.* Thus if we were to chart someone's path of Self-realization, with transpersonal psychosynthesis represented by a vertical axis and personal psychosynthesis represented by a horizontal one, it might look like Figure 8.1.[3]

In other words, Self-realization can take us anywhere on the chart. There is no yardstick, no map of Self-realization that can tell us whither we are called. We must simply listen to our own unique calling and be prepared to follow it, no matter where it leads. Self-realization is not a matter of the content or quality of experience, nor a structuralization of the personality, nor a particular stage of growth. Rather, Self-realization has to do with whether or not we are responding to the invitations of Self in our lives. Self-realization involves us relating to Self, responding to that fundamental union with Self, in whatever type of experience, state of consciousness, or stage of growth we find ourselves.

Seen in this way, Self-realization is a matter of the moment-to-moment, here-and-now relationship to our deepest sense of truth and meaning in life; in Jung's (1954) words, it revolves around "fidelity to the law of one's own being." And we may betray that deeper truth in one moment and realign with it the next, in other words, we may be Self-realizing one moment and not Self-realizing the next. Self-realization is not the culmination of a journey but the journey itself.

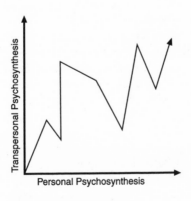

FIGURE 8.1

It follows that we may, for example, *not* be Self-realizing when feeling an ineffable union with the cosmos and may actually *be* Self-realizing when feeling utter isolation and fragmentation. Or we may *not* be Self-realizing when involved in transpersonal psychosynthesis and may actually *be* Self-realizing when working at personal psychosynthesis. Virtually any and all experiences may or may not be Self-realization. The determining factor is not the quality or content of the experience but whether or not we are responding to the deeper source of our being.

CALLED BY SELF

So hearing and responding to the call of Self is a fundamental aspect of Self-realization, a twin phenomena that we have examined also as the contact and response stages of psychosynthesis (Chapter 3). Self is not simply a passive holding of us but acts in our lives as well. Self-realization is an ongoing relationship between "I" and Self, an interplay or a dialogue between *personal will* and *transpersonal will.*

Many stories could be told illustrating call and response. Perhaps immediately we think of famous people who throughout history responded to a powerful call and were led to great tasks. We think of Moses encountering God in the burning bush, called to lead the Israelites out of Egypt; Siddhartha Gautama, led from a sheltered life of wealth and privilege through an arduous journey culminating in his transformation into the Buddha; Jesus of Nazareth saying to God, "Not my will but yours be done," and accepting death on the cross; and Allah speaking to Muhammad in the depths of the cave, sending him as a messenger to the world. Countless others also come to mind, such as Joan of Arc, Mahatma Gandhi, Mother Teresa, and Martin Luther King Jr., who were led and sustained by the voice of a deeper center beyond their limited individuality.

> . . . the establishing of a direct relation to the spiritual will, to the Self, is the goal of psychosynthesis.
>
> —Roberto Assagioli

But many of us less famous can be seen following such a calling, leading us into a fuller sense of ourselves and the world, whether returning to school, discovering a new career, or developing latent artistic gifts. A popular book gives many examples of such calls (Levoy 1997), while the subjects of call, vocation, and dharma have appeared in the psychological literature as well (Bogart 1994, 1995; Bollas 1989; Fleischman 1990; Hillman 1996; Jung 1954; Levoy 1997).[4]

An example of hearing and responding to a transcendent-immanent call was given in Chapter 2 in the case of Ellen. Beginning with the destructuring of her survival personality, she moved through many experiences to discern a rightness in leaving her job for a new life. Along the way, she did much inner work, and she was open to Self through various authentic unifying centers: her prayer group, daily meditation practice, spiritual books, lectures, workshops, nocturnal dreams, and empathic friends. Here was an invitation from Self unfolding in her life.

The story of Jamie in Chapter 6 also illustrates Self-realization. Jamie began with what appeared to be a struggle to find her purpose, a struggle that turned out to be an obsession; here was a driven search for a "Supreme Life's Purpose" that would compensate for her underlying feelings of waste and worthlessness. As she worked with this, it was revealed that her authentic calling was to a healing of her early wounding and thus freedom from her compulsive quest. This led in turn to a deeper, more realistic call to develop her art. Clearly, the path of Self-realization may involve many different types of experience.

Whether in the lives of the famous or the lesser known, it is easiest to see a response to call when it results in a major life change. However, there is a much more immediate dimension of call. Remember, the I-Self relationship is ever present, so hearing and responding to call can occur every moment of every day. This immediacy of Self can be experienced as an invitation to act from our highest values, our most cherished principles, and our deepest sense of truth. Such a call was heard by Sara.

SARA'S CALL TO TRUTH

Sara and Ed, out on a date, were having a wonderfully flowing conversation over a fine meal and a good wine. All was going well until Ed briefly made a comment that involved a racial stereotype. Sara was shocked by this for an instant, but the enjoyable flow of their conversation quickly reestablished itself, and the moment passed.

Inside, however, she was in turmoil. Should she say something about the racism embodied in the stereotype? Ed was a wonderful person in many ways and certainly not consciously racist, but she recently had attended several diversity trainings at school and felt it was right to confront racism and sexism in her personal life. But the comment was now in the distant past—how awkward and offensive it would be to return to it now. Why not just let it slide and mention it if it happened again? Why make a big deal about this right now when it might cause awkwardness or even a break in the relationship? Would it not be better to have a closer relationship with him before approaching such a potentially explosive subject?

> Essentially, it means tuning in and willingly participating in the rhythms of Universal Life.
>
> ——Roberto Assagioli

Like Ellen discerning whether to leave her job or not (Chapter 3), Sara could find no ultimate authority in her rational mind. A rational case could be made on either side: say nothing, get closer, and then gently confront the racism if it emerges, following that political policy known as "constructive engagement"; or, mention it now, even if awkward, because that will show her values clearly and early and will allow the relationship to develop only with these included.

Furthermore, as she realized later, many different feelings were activated in her: a little girl not wanting to displease a father; a lover not wanting to break the romantic mood; a dreamy teenager wondering if Ed were "Mr. Right"; a judge saying that she was a coward if she did not express outrage to him; another feeling bad, small, and immobilized in the face of this judgment; a rebel, angrily refusing the judge's guilt trip, saying that she does not have to do anything that she does not want to do; and, finally, a seemingly spiritual voice saying to let go, that in the larger scheme it does not matter what she does.

SARA'S RESPONSE TO TRUTH

The dinner and evening ended with Sara not voicing her concern after all, but she was left with her turmoil the next day. In a call to authenticity, she refused to ignore the truth of her discomfort and her perception of Ed's behavior. With the knowledge gained from her diversity training and the values gathered over her life experience (unifying centers), her own sense of right and truth called to her—an invitation from Self.

Note that Sara moved through the stages of psychosynthesis in a brief time. She moved out of stage zero, the survival stage, by electing not to go with her old habit of ignoring uncomfortable situations, and then she engaged the remaining stages: (1) in exploration of the personality, she became conscious of the many feelings and thoughts within her by writing in her journal and talking to friends; (2) in the emergence of "I," she became more clear that she was distinct from these many parts, that she was free from them, and that she could choose among them, or not at all; (3) in contact with Self, she began listening more acutely to her heart regarding the right thing to do; and finally, yes, (4) in response to Self, she called Ed on the telephone and discussed the incident, which happily led to a deeper intimacy and respect between them.

> For the Stoics and Spinoza it has been the willing acceptance of one's "destiny."
> —Roberto Assagioli

Later Sara reported a paradox that may occur in a close alignment of "I" and Self. She said that in the end it felt like she had no choice but to call Ed. This can appear to be an odd thought, given the painstaking, conscious journey to her final decision. But this speaks to the ultimate mysterious unity between ourselves and Self. "I had no choice" means here, "It was so right, so true, so obvious, that there was really nothing else I could do." This experience is more in the nature of a discovery, a revelation, than what we usually take for an intentional act. It is a stumbling upon what Martin Buber (1958) called "the deed that intends me." In psychosynthesis terms, this is an alignment of personal will with transpersonal will, so that the two are indistinguishable.

We have described calls that change the course of one's life and a call involving a woman's struggle over twenty-four hours, but calls also happen in the moment and can be responded to in the moment.

CALL IN THE MOMENT: DAVID

David, who received a call that invited an immediate response in the moment, said:

> I am best man at a dear friend's wedding. All afternoon I have been thinking of him, helping him with his nerves, his glee, his fear, his details. Then, it's ten past seven and the cantor has not shown up. She's ten minutes late. All the guests are seated outside by the hoopa waiting for the ceremony. We wait another ten but she still does not show up. I feel sad for my friend now, and for his fiance. We call the cantor and realize that she is ninety minutes away still waiting for the limo (she had no number or address . . . quite strange, but there it was). I am certain things are going to end sadly this day and I feel scared. My friend turns to his father, who says, "Let's go ahead with the ceremony, you can get legally married on Monday." His attitude is light and uncharacteristically supportive. My friend smiles, turns to me, and says, "Dave, marry me." My belly drops and I am swallowed by insecurity and self-doubt—but then something surges through me, something like courage and excitement and a love for my friend all mixing it up together. I rise to the occasion, and I lead the ceremony. To my surprise, everyone is moved—the reception is magical, and my heart grows three times in size.

As in earlier cases, David's path of Self-realization here obviously is not a blissful, unitive state of consciousness. He had to encounter insecurity, self-doubt, and anxiety, as well as courage, love, and excitement. He was held in being, and he thus was able to hold a full range of his experience in responding to call, from the depths to the heights. But the point was, he responded, stood up for his friend, and allowed himself to be in service of something greater than himself.

> The Chinese call this attitude *wu-wei*, or identification with the *tao*.
>
> —Roberto Assagioli

CALL IN THE MOMENT: ANNE

Yet another call in the moment, received by Anne through the comments from a friend and a cup of ginger tea, is described as thus:

I was at a loss to be in touch with my center, with God, with Self. The need was acute, but my usual paths (writing, meditation, breathing, walking at the water, etc.) weren't working. I was sick at the time, and intensely nauseated. A friend whom I called in desperation told me to stop trying so hard to reach this Self, and rather to work to alleviate the nausea and fatigue. What could I think of? I focused some, and considered ginger tea. I prepared some, drank it slowly (because it was hot), and began to feel better. Suddenly, I was aware of feeling centered, in touch with Self, reconnected to God and the Universe. . . . It entered me when I was doing a purely mundane thing, and I felt as touched as I've ever been by satisfying prayer, etc. I had realigned, and it had something to do—for me—with Self.

We can see the thread of this call as it reached Anne through her felt disconnection, her willingness to reach out, her friend's sage advice, her intuition about ginger tea, and the simple, pragmatic act of drinking tea. Like Jamie, she was called out of her desperate search for Self by the very Self she was seeking. And while this call did indeed culminate in a wonderful sense of being held, Self-realization was occurring the whole time—her relationship to Self was present and active through all of these different events and experiences.

Clearly, even when we feel disconnected from Self, we are still in a relationship. Whether we feel union or distance, open or closed, conscious or unconscious, our relationship exists and seems to operate at some level deeper than all of this—a level of transcendence-immanence.

It is as if we are married to Self. Whether we forget this marriage, feel its fullness, or feel estranged from it, this abiding communion remains. Indeed, marriage may be one of the most accurate metaphors for the I-Self relationship. As with any committed relationship, this relationship cannot be limited to any single moment or special event, however wondrous; rather, it is lived out in all life events, for better or worse, in sickness and in health.

CALL AND PSYCHOSYNTHESIS THERAPY

This spiritual marriage—or at least spiritual courtship—between "I" and Self is recognized and facilitated in psychosynthesis therapy as well. The individual client invariably, if implicitly, embodies some desired sense of direction; there is some sense that things can be better than they are now, that there is something more to be revealed. In psychosynthesis therapy, this "something more" or sense of direction will be taken operationally as an invitation from Self and will be recognized in many different guises as the therapist remains empathic.

For example, this direction may be sensed as a feeling that life need not be as painful as it has been; or as a need for better interpersonal relationships; or as a wish to integrate spirituality more fully into one's life. The issue of call also appears clearly in statements such as: "I am afraid that at the end of my life I will discover I missed my true vocation," or, "I feel I have something to accomplish in life, but I don't know what it is." Sometimes we need a guide to help us clarify what it is we are seeking:

Client: Work is a mess, I'm being run ragged by all the pressures. It's just way too much

Therapist: How would you wish to be at work? [Asking for direction.]

C: I don't know, just feeling more peace, more spaciousness.

T: Have you ever felt that type of peace and spaciousness before? [Clarifying direction.]

C: Not for a long time, but I used to feel that way when my wife and I would go camping down in Big Sur.

T: Would you like to explore this more?

C: Sure.

T: Okay, take a moment to imagine you are there now, in Big Sur. How does it feel? Let yourself experience it in your body. [Allowing the state the client is seeking to become energetically present.]

C: [Closing his eyes; long pause.] It feels wonderful. I wish I could feel this way at work.

T: Can you imagine feeling this way at work?

C: Not really. It seems impossible.

T: What happens when you try?

C: I get scared that I won't get anything done, that I'll be irresponsible. [The obstacle to the direction is being triggered or energized, i.e., induction.]

T: Can you get an image for that one who is scared?

C: Yeah, it's a little kid. It's me, at school, scared about the work, feeling overwhelmed and alone. Being scolded by Mr. Rich.

T: What does that little kid need from you?

C: He needs me to listen to him, to hear his story, not let so much work be dumped on him, and yeah, not let him be yelled at.

As we have seen in preceding chapters, this type of work can unfold in many different ways and will mean healing his connection with the wounded aspect of himself. But as this occurs, the client will become more free to feel and express the qualities of peace and spaciousness at work. And, yes, this may mean active engagement with the inner and outer figures who scold him at work (recall the kind of active engagement that we saw in Ellen's case in Chapter 3).

This sense of peace and spaciousness operate here as what Assagioli (1965a, 1973a) called an *ideal model*, something which represents our next attainable step in growth. This burgeoning new way of being—here peace and spaciousness—can be explored by writing about it, visualizing ourselves manifesting it, "acting as if" we are manifesting it, rendering it in creative expressions such as art and music, and seeking unifying centers which represent and support it.

So here is an example of Self-realization in psychosynthesis therapy. The revealed intention to have more peace and spaciousness represents a response to call or vocation, the acceptance of an invitation to a more authentic life. And, quite frequently, the obstacle that is inducted by a contact with call embodies the very aspects of the personality that are needed to respond. For example, this client found that the little kid part of him, as this was included in his life, held much of his ability to feel peaceful and spacious.

Furthermore, helping a client get in touch with his or her deeper direction allows the therapeutic work to be held in a positive context. We are not in therapy simply "working on problems" but attempting to clarify and move toward things that we care most deeply about. Developing this sense of direction in therapy is tremendously motivating and empowering to the client—gone is any need for the therapist to push or pull the client toward some notion of normality or adjustment.

This sense of direction, however inchoate, buried, or even distorted at times, obviously can be present in anyone. It seems that most people have some sense of identity in the present that includes some notion of the past, and some sense of direction toward something new, however ill defined and even unconscious that new possibility may be. Even the most tentative "buds" of call can, held within the empathic concern of the therapist, flower into a more conscious, meaningful direction for the client.

CALL AND AUTHENTIC UNIFYING CENTERS

A more structured way to work with call or direction is to ask the client to imagine a wise, loving person or a symbol of wisdom and love with whom she or he can have a conversation; this can be facilitated much like the dialogue work with subpersonalities, described earlier. Developing a relationship with such an inner figure has long been a technique in psychosynthesis practice (Assagioli 1965a; Brown 1983, 1993; Ferrucci 1982; Miller 1975; Whitmore 1991).

However, remembering our discussion of the various types of possible authentic unifying centers that someone might have, it also can be quite effective to refer to these important figures. For example, knowing that a client had a good, empathic connection with her grandmother, a therapist might ask, "What would your grandmother say to you about that?" Any authentic unifying center can be worked with in this way, from a cherished childhood pet, to a beloved teacher, to a favorite natural setting.

One client received a tremendous amount of inner support and wisdom by renewing her relationship with the mountains and forests where she spent her summers as a child. Developing an ongoing relationship with such authentic unifying centers is a powerful way to facilitate a relationship with Self. This approach is empowering for clients, as they learn to develop and work with their own sense of inner wisdom and direction.

So in speaking of a sense of direction, call, or invitation from Self, we do not mean to imply some ideal vision of how things might be, nor a wish-fulfilling fantasy of the conscious personality. Neither do we mean necessarily to imply some larger perception of meaning in life or the opening to transpersonal qualities. Much more simply and immediately, this direction is the person's best sense of what life might be for her or him, however modest this may seem. And this direction may of course change and clarify as Self-realization becomes more conscious—the I-Self relationship is always a dynamic, changing interplay.

To sum up this discussion of Self-realization, we can say that it is the ongoing dynamic relationship between "I" and Self throughout all life experiences. This relationship may indeed at times involve an experience of profound unity "in which the sense of individual identity is dimmed and may even seem temporarily lost" (Assagioli 1973a, 128), a unity that temporarily obscures any distinction between "I" and Self at all. But the path of Self-realization also may lead through the abyss, through periods of isolation, fragmentation, and pain. In whatever experience, Self is present and available to relationship; in whatever experience, Self-realization is distinct but not separate from the type or content of experience; in whatever experience, the intimate relationship of "I" and Self abides.

> Thus the psychotherapist must have a sense of vocation as well as a technique.
>
> —Roberto Assagioli

IN CONCLUSION

In this book we have attempted to explore the broad outlines of psychosynthesis. Psychosynthesis personality theory has been presented in our discussion of the oval-shaped diagram, subpersonalities, authentic personality, survival personality, psychological disturbances, and "I"; developmental theory has been represented in the stages of psychosynthesis, the phases of personality harmonization, the concentric ring model of the person, personal psychosynthesis, transpersonal psychosynthesis, and Self-realization; and clinical theory has been present throughout, including cases in which various types of work were illustrated.

Note, however, that throughout this discussion there has been little emphasis on specific techniques or methodologies. We have described the terrain of the human journey without exploring the many particular methods of travel, so to speak. One reason for this is that psychosynthesis is fundamentally an orientation, a general approach to the whole human being, and it exists apart from any particular concrete applications. According to Assagioli:

> If we now consider psychosynthesis as a whole, with all its implications and developments, we see that it should not be looked upon as a particular psychological doctrine, nor as a single technical procedure.
>
> It is first and foremost a dynamic, even a dramatic conception of our psychological life. (1965a, 30)

Psychosynthesis provides a broad perspective of the human drama, from personal to transpersonal dimensions, from the individual to the larger world, and it attempts to base this perspective on phenomenological observation. And, as an overall perspective, psychosynthesis may suggest particular techniques and methods, but it nevertheless remains distinct from these.

This fact allows a rich variety of approaches and settings to be informed by psychosynthesis, from guided imagery, dream work, and hypnosis, to art therapy, sand tray, or body work, to cognitive-behavioral techniques, object relations, or family systems, to individual and group psychotherapy, meditation practices, or spiritual direction, to pastoral counseling, teaching, parenting, medicine, or religion, and to ecopsychology, environmental education, and ecological activism. Indeed, it is hard to think of a sphere in which the perspective of psychosynthesis cannot be useful.[5]

But more importantly, the breadth of the psychosynthesis perspective allows us to recognize and validate an extensive range of human experience: the vicissitudes of developmental difficulties and early trauma; the confrontation with existential identity, choice, and responsibility; the heights of inspired creativity, peak performance, and spiritual experience; and the search for purpose and meaning in life. None of these important areas of experience need be reduced to the other, and each can find its right place in the whole. This means that no matter what type of experience is engaged, and no matter what phase of growth is negotiated, the complexity and uniqueness of the individual person may be respected.

> . . . the central, decisive importance of the human factor, of the living interpersonal relation between the therapist and the patient.
>
> —Roberto Assagioli

> It means approaching him or her with sympathy, with respect, even with wonder, as a "thou" and thus establishing a deeper inner relationship.
>
> —Roberto Assagioli

NOTES

INTRODUCTION

1. While this lack of focus on a psychoanalytic or an early childhood perspective was recognized within the field (Firman 1991; Friedman 1984; Haronian 1983; Kramer 1988), it also was noted outside of the field. According to respected transpersonal researcher and thinker Stanislav Grof,

> While I share Assagioli's emphasis on the creative, superconscious, and radiant potential of the psyche, it has been my experience that direct confrontation of its dark side whenever it manifests itself in the process of self-exploration is beneficial. (1985, 194)

It is important to emphasize that these critiques focus on psychosynthesis *as a system* and not necessarily on the work of individual practitioners. Practitioners often understand early childhood dynamics, but in addressing these they have needed to draw upon theories other than psychosynthesis.

2. Of course, an exhaustive exploration of all these topics is beyond the scope of any single volume. For further study, we refer the reader to the writings of Assagioli and to the growing body of psychosynthesis literature.

CHAPTER 1

1. Assagioli's laissez-faire attitude toward the organizational development of psychosynthesis created both benefits and problems. As with anything with no central organization, psychosynthesis was free to take on a wide variety of different forms and applications—a healthy diversity producing some very innovative and creative developments.

On the other hand, the lack of a widely accepted training curriculum and quality control created a diffusion of psychosynthesis that may have hindered its acceptance in both the public and professional communities. Practitioners with widely divergent levels of skills and training could present themselves as psychosynthesists, creating confusion and misunderstandings about the field. Furthermore, no structure—such as an international training school—could emerge to sustain the kind of research, theoretical development, clinical work, and publishing necessary for a coherent, far-reaching impact on the field of psychology.

2. Most of the information in the following section has been drawn from the accounts in Roberto Assagioli (1965a), Eugene Smith (1974), Jean Hardy (1987), and Allesandro Berti (1988).

CHAPTER 2

1. Assagioli (1967) attempted to make a strong distinction between what he considered regressive and progressive elements in the collective unconscious by employing his notions of higher unconscious and lower unconscious. Although he did not ever seem to explicitly use the terms *higher collective unconscious* and *lower collective unconscious*, we consider these useful concepts and thus the horizontal lines in Figure 2.1 move beyond the individual psyche into the collective. This depiction of a higher and lower collective was first rendered by Vargiu (1974a) in the first issue of the journal, *Synthesis*, an issue heartily welcomed by Assagioli not long before his death.

In our view, the higher collective unconscious and lower collective unconscious are the result of past primal wounding and splitting in our collective psyche. Therefore our call to heal as a species, as our call to heal as individuals, could involve an engagement with either realm, and would generally tend toward an integration of both. This integration would occur alongside the natural unfoldment and expression of collective human potential at the level of the *middle collective unconscious*.

2. This active process of inner structuralization or organization implies a self who is doing the organization. Even during these earliest months of life, there is a self (what we shall call *"I"*) who is experiencing this process of emergent organization, or what infant researcher Daniel Stern (1985) has called "a sense of emergent self." According to Stern, modern infant research has demonstrated that the infant is not, as is often understood in psychoanalytic circles, lost in an undifferentiated state of primary narcissism. Rather, the infant is actively engaged in meaningful and reality-based interaction with the environment.

3. Assagioli differentiated between the area of the unconscious that was already structuralized, called the *structured unconscious*, and the area of the unconscious that was still available for structuralization, called the *plastic unconscious* (1965a, 1973a).

4. Laura's story is based on an actual case, but it has been highly disguised in order to guard the identity of the client. All of the cases and examples presented throughout this book are disguised as well: the client's name is not the true name; the gender of the client and therapist may or may not be correct; there are elements of cases that have been borrowed from other cases (again, in disguised forms); and quoted dialogues are paraphrases of the originals. All of these cases represent authentic patterns of psychosynthesis therapy while providing anonymity for therapist and client.

5. Although Assagioli never directly addressed the formation of the higher and lower unconscious, he presented these two sectors within the context of the psychoanalytic understanding of the formation of the unconscious by repression (Assagioli 1965a, 12). He also thought of the higher and lower unconscious as being similar in structure and dynamics, although different in quality of content:

At this point it is necessary to remember that while there is a difference of quality, the superconscious shares some of the other characteristics of the whole unconscious. The superconscious is only a section of the general unconscious, but which has some added qualities that are specific. On the whole it partakes of the nature of the unconscious and the general possible relationships between the unconscious and the personal consciousness. (1965a, 198)

In our work we have gone on to recognize the primal wounding and splitting that underlie the repression involved in the formation of these levels of the unconscious. We have not found useful the earlier psychosynthesis notion that the higher unconscious represents future stages of growth, while the lower unconscious contains past stages (see Note 9 in this chapter).

6. In Jungian terms, we might say that there is always a negative and positive *shadow*—negative and positive material repressed in the formation of the conscious persona. Jung (1959, 8, 266) himself admits the possibility of a positive shadow and not simply a negative one, but psychosynthesis goes further to claim that this polarity of the shadow is the norm.

7. For an overview of "I" as understood in psychology and religion, see the appendices "I in Religion" and "I in Psychology," in Firman 1991.

8. Some earlier theory in psychosynthesis interposed a "Higher Self" or "Transpersonal Self" between "I" and what was called, "Universal Self" (see Assagioli 1973a). Here it was implied that if we could identify with this Higher Self, we could find communion with Universal Self.

This formulation appears to be an attempt to explain that our usual experience of ourselves, masked by identifications, needs to expand beyond those limitations for us to realize our deeper, essential nature in communion with the Divine, Spirit or, in our terms, "Self," who can be experienced as universal (see "Self As Universal" in Chapter 8).

However, the problem with this early formulation of Higher or Transpersonal Self is that there is in fact no "other self" we become: we remain "I" throughout all changes in consciousness, even though the limited experience of ourselves can transform radically as we grow psychologically and spiritually. So to characterize this transformation as "becoming another self," although this poetically captures the profundity of the experience, is finally inaccurate and misleading. What actually has occurred in this transformation is that we have realized who we were all along: "I" in communion with Self, our individuality in communion with universality.

The problem with believing that we must become "another self" in this process makes that "other self" seem like an object that we can pursue, an "other" with whom we can identify, which has the effect of obscuring the truth that we are always and for evermore "I." We may consequently begin looking for "I" in all the wrong places.

So for us there is no "Higher Self" or "Transpersonal Self" understood in this way. Rather, we posit that over the course of Self-realization, human beings can find themselves in communion with Self, often experienced as universal, expressing their unique, essential "I-amness" in the world—the expression we term *authentic personality* (see later discussion). For a more detailed study of this issue of Higher Self, see the appendix "Individuality and Universality" in Firman 1991.

9. Depicting Self at the apex of the higher unconscious also can give the impression that psychospiritual development proceeds from the lower unconscious ("the past") to the higher unconscious ("the future"), when in fact these two areas comprise highly charged structures that have been split off and repressed due to wounding, for example, structures such as the *negative personality* and *negative unifying center* and the *positive personality* and *positive unifying center* (Firman and Gila 1997). (See also Notes 2, 7, and 8 in Chapter 7.) In our view, the higher unconscious and the lower unconscious are not developmental levels but dissociated sectors of the psyche that need to be integrated.

Note that although higher unconscious experience often feels "unitive," *it actually excludes the lower unconscious.* It is not the higher unconscious that includes the wholeness of the person, but rather the middle unconscious as it grows to integrate the material from both the heights and the depths (see Chapter 8).

Beyond this, however, Self-realization also should be distinguished from psychospiritual development itself. Self-realization, as we understand it, is not a developmental achievement but an ongoing relationship with Self throughout all of the day-to-day activities of life—it is not a destination but a journey. True, this journey often will involve the psychospiritual transformation of the person, but this is not so much a goal as it is the by-product of living out a faithfulness to one's deepest callings. We believe that the spiritual leaders of the ages are not so by virtue of their higher consciousness principally but by fidelity to their vocations.

CHAPTER 3

1. Developmental theories that posit an infantile primary fused state from which we individuate (e.g., Mahler, Pine, and Bergman 1975; Wilber 1977), for example, might sound vaguely similar to Assagioli's stages. The problems with such theories have been discussed elsewhere (Firman and Gila 1997; Stern 1985), but in any case, the stages of psychosynthesis are not to be confused with them.

2. Note that the "defense" of defense mechanisms and structures is not primarily against unacceptable desires, fantasies, or wishes, as traditionally held, but more fundamentally against primal wounding—something that *should* be defended against. Thus in psychosynthesis, such defenses might aptly be termed *survival mechanisms* and can be treated with care and respect by the practitioner, recognizing the actual trauma and true danger to which they are a creative response. Without such a sensibility, attempts may be made to "break down defenses" or "break through resistances," tactics that may appear to force new behaviors. However, these new behaviors may, because the primal wounding remains repressed, be simply more sophisticated forms of survival personality.

3. For a description of a workshop based on this approach to addictions, see "An Addiction/Abuse Workshop," in Firman and Gila 1997.

4. Our conception of the collective unconscious here is not the strict concept of species-wide archetypal patterns, but what Jung (1960) termed the *collective consciousness*, which is, in the words of Jungian Jolande Jacobi, "the sum total of traditions, conventions, customs, prejudices, rules, and norms of the environment in which the individual lives, and the spirit of the age by which he is influenced" (1967, 150–51).

We nevertheless consider such influences as a sector of the collective unconscious, because they are collective influences that can and often do affect us unconsciously. However, this is a sector of the collective that is not species wide but comprises patterns that come to us from smaller collectivities or communities (e.g., family of origin, culture, ethnicity, race, nationality, religion). These might be represented as concentric ovals around the oval diagram in Figure 2.1. For example, psychosynthesis thinker Margret Rueffler (1995a, 1995b) recognizes several different subsectors within the collective, including the familial, the ancestral, and the cultural national. One interesting thing about this level of collectivity is that individuals and groups can alter the patterns operating here.

CHAPTER 4

1. Chris Meriam, writing about early work in subpersonality theory, says:

> Somewhere around 1970, Assagioli expressed this concept to psychosynthesis theorist James Vargiu (from a transcribed conversation, courtesy of Ann [Gila] Russell). In the same conversation, Assagioli also said that subpersonality theory could be a potential bridge of his work to that of Freud, Jung, and Reich, via their concepts of "complexes," as well as a point of contact with behaviorism, in that subpersonalities are strongly conditioned by the environment. Vargiu subsequently wrote the first substantial article on subpersonality theory (ibid.), drawing heavily on the work of psychosynthesis theorists Steven Kull and Betsie Carter-Haar at the Psychosynthesis Institute in Palo Alto. (1994, 8–9)

2. This understanding of the creation of subpersonalities differs from earlier formulations in psychosynthesis. For James Vargiu, a subpersonality develops from "an inner drive, or urge, which strives to be expressed, to be realized" (1974b, 60). On the other hand, Piero Ferrucci writes that subpersonalities "are degradations or distortions of timeless qualities existing in the higher levels of the psyche" (1982, 55).

We are positing, rather, that the fundamental developmental axis of a subpersonality is a relationship to what we are calling a unifying center. It is through such a relationship that diverse psyche-soma contents are synthesized into a subpersonality, and these include not only drives and transpersonal qualities but many other elements as well, such as learned skills, inborn gifts, affects, beliefs, attitudes, and values.

3. The influence of the higher and lower unconscious upon subpersonality formation has been explored well by Chris Meriam (1994).

4. This ability to disidentify from one level of organization in order to engage a higher level of organization has been recognized by Robert Kegan (1982) and Ken Wilber (2000) as a key dynamic in negotiating stages of human development.

5. In Arthur Koestler's (1978) terms, a subpersonality is a type of *holon*, an entity that is both a part of a whole and a whole itself. Holons are found at every level of organization: atoms organized as molecules, molecules organized as cells, cells organized as organs, and organs organized as an organism. We might say that subpersonalities are organs that help make up the organism of the personality.

CHAPTER 5

1. Psychologist and meditator Jack Engler, pointing to this absolute subjectivity of "I" as revealed in Theravada meditation says:

> My sense of being an independent observer disappears. The normal sense that I am a fixed, continuous point of observation from which I regard now this object, now that, is dispelled.
>
> In each moment, there is simply a process of knowing (*nama*) and its object (*rupa*). Each arises separately and simultaneously in each moment of awareness. No enduring or substantial entity or observer or experiencer or agent—no self—can be found behind or apart from these moment-to-moment events to which they could be attributed (*an-atta* = no-self). (in Wilber 1977, 41)

One can experience these states of no-self, because "I" is distinct from any "sense of being an independent observer" and, indeed, cannot be found behind the experience, cannot be captured as an object at all (even as a "self-representation").

As we shall see shortly, Assagioli would add this to Engler's account: "I" cannot only be aware in this way but can *will* also. Indeed, meditation is only possible via an act of will, choosing to gently focus awareness and not be caught up in the objects of awareness.

2. In a way, too, it might be said that even Ellen's survival personality is not seen per se, but that she is simply relegated to passive invisibility by the family system. But here "being seen" as this survival personality means that she is invisible within the system, not that she is in any way a focus of attention by the system.

3. Such an identification, arising after a strong transpersonal experience, gnosis, or enlightenment, has been called *positive inflation* by Jung (1966) and has been discussed by R. C. Zaehner (1972) as a phenomenon in a variety of traditions. Here Zaehner quotes the Zen master, Harada Roshi (from Kapleau 1966),

> An ancient Zen saying has it that to become attached to one's own enlightenment is as much a sickness as to exhibit a maddeningly active ego. Indeed, the profounder the enlightenment, the worse the illness.
> *My own sickness lasted almost ten years.* (98, emphasis added)

See also Rosenthal (1987) who maintains that such inflation seems to be a natural stage of spiritual growth through which many people pass.

4. The mysterious nature of "I" has been approached in the experimental laboratory as well. After years of research into human biofeedback, Alyce and Elmer Green wrote:

> What can be said as we work with these levels is: We are not merely what society says we are, as children, as adults, or as old people. That is the first level of field-independence: independence from what we perceive outside the skin. Further, we are not merely what our bodies say we are, not in the voluntary nervous system or in the involuntary nervous system. Not only are we not our emotions . . . , but we are also not our thoughts. The question remains, then: Who are we? (1977, 193)

5. These two stances, one ignoring transcendence and the other ignoring immanence, are examples of what Firman (1974; Firman and Gila 1997) has called, respec-

tively, *morphilia* (or *morphophilia*, i.e., "love of form") and *morphobia* (or *morphophobia*, i.e., "fear of form"). Morphilia involves a reduction of the human being to form, to manifest expression, to the psyche-soma; morphobia involves a reduction of the human being to discarnate spirit or emptiness, whose supposed "true nature" is unmanifest, solely transcendent. These are the two sides of what Wilber calls the "ultimate pathology," or "a failure to integrate the manifest and unmanifest realms" (Wilber, Engler, and Brown 1986, 144). In our terms here, this is a failure to recognize transcendence-immanence.

Assagioli's (1965a) early formulation of a disidentification exercise, "I am not my body, I am not my feelings, I am not my mind," can in some instances support a morphobic position: the belief that human beings are essentially pure spirits to whom the world is unimportant, foreign, or even a prison. This disidentification exercise has been critiqued elsewhere (Firman 1991; O'Regan 1984).

6. This blossoming of freedom that comes with disidentification can be seen clearly in the words of psychiatrist Arthur Deikman:

> By dis-identifying with automatic sequences we lessen their impact and provide free space in which to choose an appropriate response. Thus, we achieve autonomy where previously we were overwhelmed and helpless. (1982, 108)

7. Our ability to engage complete helplessness, to, in effect, "die to self," points to a profound truth about the nature of human spirit—*"I" can experience the complete loss of any sense of existing at all.* "I" is not something we can have, or hold, or experience. "I" is pure subject, never an object. "I" is distinct but not separate from any experience that affirms either "I exist" or "I do not exist."

You are "I" before, during, and after any experiences of no-thingness and some-thingness, of union and disintegration, of self and no-self. You are transcendent-immanent within any and all experiences, no matter what they are; you are not any particular experience, but the one who experiences.

CHAPTER 6

1. Exceptions to this would be developmental models that do not recognize the conscious and volitional selfhood—the "I-amness"—of infants and children. For example, we do not subscribe to the psychoanalytic idea that infancy is characterized by "primary narcissism," "autism," "symbiosis," or "self-other merger"—notions that imply that the infant is lost in some sort of fused, insular, undifferentiated, nonreality-based state. As researcher Daniel Stern reports:

> Infants begin to experience a sense of an emergent self from birth. They are predesigned to be aware of self-organizing processes. They never experience a period of total self/other undifferentiation. There is no confusion between self and other in the beginning or at any point during infancy. They are also predesigned to be selectively responsive to external social events and never experience an autistic-like phase. (10)

This understanding of early development is crucial in connecting empathically not only with infants and children but with those deeper layers within ourselves. Without this empathy, we are prone to the neglect and even abuse of both "outer children" and "inner children."

This notion of self-other fusion in infancy also can lead to a pathologizing of childhood: psychological disorders can be seen as simple fixations at, or regressions to, various supposedly normal stages of development—psychotic at the supposed early stages of self-other fusion, borderline and narcissism at a slightly more differentiated later stage, and neurosis at a still later stage. Thus the clinician is led to ideas of the client as someone who simply has not grown up, as being infantile and immature, rather than as having developed compensating structures to manage the violations of primal wounding. Here the specific woundings of the unique individual can be completely overlooked in a focus on supposed developmental issues.

Margaret Mahler (Mahler, Pine, and Bergman 1975) herself, who posits an infantile, undifferentiated state, recognizes the problem of pathologizing childhood. In a communication with Stern, she suggested that, for example, "normal autism" might be changed to "awakening" (Stern 1985, 234–35). For a further discussion of this topic, see Bowlby (1988) and Firman and Gila (1997).

2. One theory of what we are calling external unifying centers can be found in the work of transpersonal psychologist Dwight Judy (1991) who, following Baker Brownell, outlines these four types: the phyletic community, the nature community, the mystic community, and the neighborhood, political, and geographic communities.

Another scheme of unifying centers was developed within attachment theory which recognized a number of different *affectional bonds* operating in human development: the attachment bond, the parent's complementary caregiving bond, the sexual pair bond, the sibling/kinship bond, and the friendship bond (cited in Cassidy and Shaver 1999, 46). See also Bowlby's (1969) concept of *behavioral systems*.

Also, Robert Kegan (1982) outlined what he called *cultures of embeddedness* operating as holding environments—our unifying centers—for different stages of individual development: the mothering culture, parenting culture, role recognizing culture, culture of mutuality, culture of identity or self-authorship, and culture of intimacy.

Finally, Alice Miller's (2001) *helping witness* and *enlightened witness* are very much what we would call authentic unifying centers, and Heinz Kohut's (1977, 1971, 1984) concept of *selfobject* is quite akin to our notion of a unifying center.

3. What we recognize as the primal wound also can be seen in aspects of Michael Balint's discussion of the *basic fault* (Balint 1968); Erich Neumann's notion of a break in the child's "primal relationship" with the mother/Self, which then causes "a headlong fall into the forsakenness and fear of the bottomless void" (Neumann 1973, 75); Ludwig Binswanger's insight that a break between self and world leads to "the delivery of the existence to nothingness" (in May, Angel, and Ellenberger 1958, 48); John Bowlby's study of disrupted bonds between the child and caregiver (Bowlby 1980); Abraham Maslow's "primal, terrifying danger" created by parents not meeting the child's fundamental needs and causing the growth of a "pseudo-self" (Maslow 1962); Michael Washburn's "wound that exposes the ego to a terrifying 'black hole' at the seat of the soul" (Washburn 1994, 26); Thomas Yeomans' notion of the *soul wound* (Yeomans 1999); Mark Epstein's "gnawing sense of emptiness" caused by parental neglect (Epstein 1995); and John Welwood's "core wound" caused by "the disconnection from our own being" (Welwood 2000). See also our further discussion of the primal wound (Firman and Gila 1997).

4. This type of emotional incest has been addressed by Patricia Love (1990) and Kenneth Adams (1991).

5. Again, Figure 6.9 is a random selection of addictions, as are the particular experiences underlying each addiction. We are not claiming, for example, that abandonment underlies all relationship addiction, nor that powerlessness invariably underlies alcoholism.

6. As well as "hitting bottom," we also may "hit top," as described in Chapter 3, with an emergence of higher unconscious material. However, even when this is the case, the survival personality is de-integrated by the emerging material, revealing the primal wounding holding the survival personality in place. Thus even in hitting top, we engage the earlier primal wounding.

7. This emergence of wounds in intimate relationships is an important dynamic in psychotherapy, affecting both therapist and client. The interplay between *transference* and *countertransference* in psychosynthesis therapy is discussed at some length elsewhere (Firman and Gila 1997).

8. For a psychosynthesis appreciation of the much-needed work in healing our relationship with nature, see *Reflections on Ecopsychosynthesis* (Firman and Klugman 1999).

CHAPTER 7

1. Although this description of splitting sounds like a conscious intellectual process, the actual experience may be quite automatic and may involve no conscious thought or volition at all.

2. This structuralization involves the formation of a *negative personality* (wounded victim, underdog, "bad ego") relating to a *negative unifying center* (shaming critic, inner perpetrator, "bad object") in the lower unconscious and a *positive personality* (idealized, inflated sense of self, "idealized ego") relating to a *positive unifying center* (idealized spiritual source, "idealized object") in the higher unconscious.

In our view, these "split object relations" form the higher and lower sectors of the unconscious. During empathic failure, the child cannot hold both the positive and negative aspects of the relationship, because the nonempathic environment cannot mirror these, and there often is no other unifying center present that can mirror them; the child is thus left with two impossibly contradictory experiences—being and nonbeing—which therefore must be split off and repressed. For a more detailed discussion of splitting, repression, and the structures involved, see Firman and Gila (1997) and Meriam (1994).

3. Of course, phenomenologically personal annihilation cannot in fact be experienced. The reason for this is simply that in a true nonbeing state, there would be no experiencing subject present at all—no one is there to have the experience. By definition, then, such a state in pure form lies forever beyond experience. Personal nonexistence is unimaginable, unthinkable, and terrifying at a level beyond the reach of consciousness. No, this is not the spiritual experience of "no-self" or "self-emptying," described in different religious traditions.

4. Washburn (1994) appreciates the profundity, the experienced cosmic nature, of splitting. He posits a splitting of the archetypal, numinous, and magical Great Mother into a Good Mother and Terrible Mother, even writing that this is ultimately due to

"fear of object loss, anxiety of losing the primary caregiver" (56)—what we would call the threat of nonbeing caused by primal wounding. We differ with Washburn's view, in that he sees this splitting as a result of ambivalence within the child, while we see it as an effect of empathic failure in the environment.

5. Again, see Bowlby (1980) for a further understanding of the unconscious, not only as a repression of past experience but as a brokenness of current experiential range (what is called "perceptual blocking").

6. Of course, much more research is needed into the etiology of psychopathology, although given the often-noted societal propensity to overlook the role of early trauma (see Herman 1992; Miller 2001; Van der Kolk, McFarlane, and Weisaeth 1996), it is important that research should continue to include this area, even within any predominately biological agendas. For example, according to Alice Miller,

> In recent years, neurobiologists have further established that traumatized and neglected children display severe lesions affecting up to 30 percent of those areas of the brain that control emotions. The explanation is that severe traumas inflicted on infants lead to an increase in the release of stress hormones that destroy the newly formed neurons and their interconnections.
>
> In the scientific literature there is still next to no discussion of the implications of these discoveries for our understanding of child development and the delayed consequences of traumas and neglect. But this research confirms what I described almost twenty years ago. (2001, 15)

For research into the effects of trauma (including biological effects), see the work of Van der Kolk (1987) and Van der Kolk et al. (1996); for research into psychopathology from an attachment theory viewpoint, see Cassidy and Shaver (1999); and for clinical views of wounding underlying psychological disturbances, see the work of Miller (1981, 1984a, 1984b, 1991, 2001), Herman (1992), Herman and Hirschman (2000), Higgins (1994), Whitfield (1991, 1995), and Terr (1990, 1994).

7. This type of idealized survival personality is based on what we have called the *positive personality* and the *positive unifying center*, both idealized structures of the higher unconscious (see Note 2 in this chapter).

8. This internalized perpetrator is what we call the *negative unifying center*, and it amounts to the distilled essence of the nonempathic unifying centers in our lives. The depressive survival personality that is based on a relationship to this negative center is called the *negative personality* (see Note 2 in this chapter).

9. The first-person accounts of people with bipolar disorder make it clear that mania involves flights into the higher unconscious. Such accounts often are indistinguishable from accounts of peak and unitive experiences, and they frequently are valued as such by the person involved. Some firsthand accounts of mania follow:

> It [mania] is actually a sense of communion, in the first place with God, and in the second place with all mankind, indeed with all creation.
>
> The ordinary beauties of nature, particularly, I remember, the skies at sunrise and sunset, took on a transcendental loveliness beyond belief. (Kaplan 1964, 47, 51)

At the time, however, not only did everything make perfect sense, but it all began to fit into a marvelous kind of cosmic relatedness.

When you're high it's tremendous. The ideas and feelings are fast and frequent like shooting stars, and you follow them until you find better and brighter ones. (Jamison 1995, 36–37, 67)

10. This type of violent survival personality is based on the lower unconscious structure that we have called the *negative unifying center* and is "a way of basing a sense of self upon the inner perpetrator rather than the inner victim" (Firman and Gila 1997, 166). (See Note 2 in this chapter.)

Similarly, the brilliant criminologist, Lonnie Athens (1992, 1997), who studied violent offenders, empathically posits that the violent person makes violent choices in dialogue with an internal *phantom community* that supports violence as a response to life. Athens' concept of phantom community—an advance from George Herbert Mead's *generalized other*—is quite similar to the notion of unifying center. See Richard Rhodes' (1999) lucid exposition of Athens' work.

11. According to Stolorow, Brandchaft, and Atwood (1987):

In a desperate attempt to maintain psychological integrity, the psychotic person elaborates delusional ideas that symbolically concretize the experience whose subjective reality has begun to crumble. (133)

Psychotic delusion formation thus represents a concretizing effort to substantialize and preserve a reality that has begun to disintegrate, rather than a turning away from reality, as has been traditionally assumed (Freud 1911, 1924). (134)

. . . essential to the psychoanalytic treatment of psychotic patients is that the therapist strive to comprehend the core of the subjective truth symbolically encoded in the patient's delusional ideas, and to communicate this understanding in a form that the patient can use. (134)

12. This perspective can be found in the work of R. D. Laing (1965, 1967) and John Perry (1953, 1974, 1976), who both worked with the psychotic process as a creative renewal, a death and rebirth, and a transformative transition toward a more authentic way of being. More recently, some of such experiences might be viewed as a type of *spiritual emergency* (see Grof and Grof 1989).

13. We therefore agree with Harvard psychologist Gina O'Connell Higgins when she writes: "Because posttraumatic stress disorder accurately—albeit implicitly—emphasizes the hammer blows that create so much psychological disruption, I yearn to see some version of this diagnosis as the overarching rubric under which most other disorders are subordinated" (1994, 13).

Psychiatrist Charles Whitfield is quite in agreement with Higgins. He says that co-dependence, caused by early wounding, can be viewed "as a general and pervasive part of the painful side of the human condition such that it is *itself* a category under which many, if not most, conditions can be subsumed" (1991, 83).

In agreement with these views, we posit that many psychological disorders seem to be attempts to manage and survive primal wounding. Again worthy of research are the genetic and biochemical factors that may be associated with psychological disorders as well.

14. For more on this empathic approach within psychosynthesis, see Meriam (1996) and Firman and Gila (1997), and for a look at empathic work with more serious psychological disturbances, see the intersubjective work of Stolorow, Brandchaft, and Atwood (1992, 1994, 1987). The reader who is interested in the empathic approach also is referred to the fine comprehensive collection of articles, *Empathy Reconsidered* (Bohart and Greenberg 1997).

CHAPTER 8

1. This view argues against a monism that would hold that individuality is an illusion, an illusion that must be dispelled by merging ourselves with universality. Here Assagioli quotes Lama Govinda, with whom he agrees on this point:

> Individuality is not only the necessary and complementary opposite of universality, but the focal point through which alone universality can be experienced. The suppression of individuality, the philosophical or religious denial of its value or importance, can only lead to a state of complete indifference and dissolution, which may be a liberation from suffering but a purely negative one, as it deprives us of the highest experience towards which the process of individuation seems to aim: the experience of perfect enlightenment, of Buddhahood, in which the universality of our true being is realized.
>
> Merely to "merge into the whole" like the "drop into the sea," without having realized that wholeness, is only a poetical way of accepting annihilation and evading the problem that the fact of our individuality poses. Why should the universe evolve individualized forms of life and consciousness if this were not consistent with or inherent in the very spirit or nature of the universe? (1973a, 128)

Assagioli also quotes Radhakrishnan on this same issue:

> The peculiar privilege of the human self is that he [*sic*] can consciously join and work for the whole and embody in his own life the purpose of the whole. . . . The two elements of selfhood: uniqueness (each-ness), and universality (all-ness), grow together until at last the most unique becomes the most universal. (1973a, 128)

2. In some extreme instances this infatuation can lead to what Assagioli called a *confusion of levels:* "The distinction between absolute and relative truths, between the Self and the 'I,' is blurred and the inflowing spiritual energies may have the unfortunate effect of feeding and inflating the personal ego" (1965a, 44). Assagioli continues:

> The fatal error of all who fall victim to these illusions is to attribute to their personal ego or "self" the qualities and powers of the Self. In philosophical terms, it is a case of confusion between an absolute and a relative truth, between the metaphysical and the empirical levels of reality; in religious terms, between God and the "soul."
>
> . . . instances of such confusion, more or less pronounced, are not uncommon among people dazzled by contact with truths which are too powerful for their mental capacities to grasp and assimilate. The reader will doubtless be able to record instances of similar self-deception which are found in a number of fanatical followers of various cults. (45)

The dangers of this type of identification with the higher unconscious have been recognized by many writers. Jung (1966) called this "positive inflation," Miller (1981) wrote of "grandiosity" as a defense against depression, Rosenthal (1987) utilized the phrase "inflated by the spirit," and Bogart (1995) warned against "the shadow of vocation." More recently Lifton (2000) has recognized this type of dynamic in his concept of "functional megalomania" which fuels what he calls "the new global terrorism."

This type of extreme, fanatical identification is based on true higher unconscious energies, but these have been incorporated by the survival personality as a defense against the wounding in the lower unconscious. In psychosynthesis terms this places one deeply into Stage Zero, the survival stage, and a crisis of transformation is needed to lead toward the subsequent stages of exploration, the emergence of "I," and authentic contact with, and response to, Self. Indeed, authentic call here might be to engage just such a crisis.

3. This graph is based on that originated by James Vargiu (see Firman and Vargiu 1977, 1980) and subsequently elaborated on by Firman and Gila (1997).

4. Transpersonal thinker Greg Bogart, writing in the *Journal of Humanistic Psychology*, claims that the study of callings offers a new foundation for transpersonal psychology:

> Eventually, I believe, a new foundation for transpersonal psychology may be found, not in the principle of transcendence (Washburn 1990; Wilber 1990), but in the elucidation of the process by which an individual discerns the image of that dharma or life task through which one may fulfill—in an individually appropriate manner—one's place in the universal order. (1994, 31)

5. For example, see the series edited by Weiser and Yeomans (1984, 1985, 1988), who include psychosynthesis applications in areas such as psychotherapy, self-care, education, health, religion, organizational development, and world order.

BIBLIOGRAPHY

Adams, Kenneth M. 1991. *Silently Seduced: When Parents Make Their Children Partners.* Deerfield Beach, Fla.: Health Communications.

Anonymous. 1976. *Alcoholics Anonymous.* New York: Alcoholics Anonymous World Services, Inc.

———. 1985. *Twelve Steps and Twelve Traditions.* New York: Alcoholics Anonymous World Services.

Ariès, Philippe. 1962. *Centuries of Childhood: A Social History of Family Life.* Translated by R. Baldick. New York: Vintage Books.

Assagioli, Roberto. 1965a. *Psychosynthesis: A Manual of Principles and Techniques.* New York and Buenos Aires: Hobbs, Dorman.

———. 1965b. *Psychosynthesis: Individual and Social.* Vol. 16. New York: Psychosynthesis Research Foundation.

———. 1967. *Jung and Psychosynthesis.* Vol. 19. New York: Psychosynthesis Research Foundation.

———. 1973a. *The Act of Will.* New York: Penguin Books.

———. 1973b. *The Conflict between the Generations and the Psychosynthesis of the Human Ages.* Vol. 31. New York: Psychosynthesis Research Foundation.

———. 1973c. Personal communication, November 28.

———. 1974. "Training." Florence: Istituto di Psicosintesi.

———. 1976. *Transpersonal Inspiration & Psychological Mountain-Climbing.* Vol. 36. New York: Psychosynthesis Research Foundation.

———. 1978. "The Crises of Spiritual Awakening, Part I." *Science of Mind* (June): 14–102.

———. 1978. "The Crises of Spiritual Awakening, Part II." *Science of Mind* (July): 36–102.

————. 1991a. "The Perils of Self-Realization." *Sun* (June): 9–13.

————. 1991b. *Transpersonal Development: The Dimension beyond Psychosynthesis*. London: Crucible.

Athens, Lonnie. 1992. *The Creation of Dangerous Violent Criminals*. Urbana: University of Illinois Press.

————. 1997. *Violent Criminal Acts and Actors Revisited*. Urbana: University of Illinois Press.

Balint, Michael. 1968. *The Basic Fault: Therapeutic Aspects of Regression*. London and New York: Tavistock/Routledge.

Barrington, Jacob. 1988. "Twelve Steps to Freedom." *Yoga Journal* (83): 44–56.

Beebe, B., and F. Lachmann. 1988. "Mother-Infant Mutual Influence and Precursors of Self and Object Representations." Pp. 3–26 in *Frontiers in Self Psychology: Progress in Self Psychology*, ed. A. Goldberg. Hillsdale, N.J.: Analytic Press.

Berne, Eric. 1961. *Transactional Analysis in Psychotherapy*. New York: Grove Press.

Berti, Allesandro. 1988. *Roberto Assagioli 1888–1988*. Firenze, Italia: Centro di Studi di Psicosintesi "R. Assagioli."

Blakney, R., ed. 1941. *Meister Eckhart*. New York: Harper & Row.

Bogart, Greg. 1994. "Finding a Life's Calling." *Journal of Humanistic Psychology* 34:4: 6–37.

————. 1995. *Finding Your Life's Calling: Spiritual Dimensions of Vocational Choice*. Berkeley: Dawn Mountain Press.

Bohart, Arthur C., and Leslie S. Greenberg, eds. 1997. *Empathy Reconsidered: New Directions in Psychotherapy*. Washington, D.C.: American Psychological Association.

Bollas, Christopher. 1989. *Forces of Destiny: Psychoanalysis and Human Idiom*. London: Free Association Books.

Boorstein, Seymour, ed. 1980. *Transpersonal Psychotherapy*. Palo Alto, Calif.: Science and Behavior Books.

Bowlby, John. 1969. *Attachment*. 3 vols. Vol. I, *Attachment and Loss*. New York: Basic Books.

————. 1980. *Loss: Sadness and Depression*. 3 vols. Vol. III, *Attachment and Loss*. New York: Basic Books.

————. 1988. *A Secure Base: Parent-Child Attachment and Healthy Human Development*. New York: Basic Books.

Brooks, Philip. 2000. Personal communication.

Brown, Molly. 1983. *The Unfolding Self*. Los Angeles: Psychosynthesis Press.

Brown, Molly Young. 1993. *Growing Whole: Self-Realization on an Endangered Planet, A Hazelden Book*. New York: HarperCollins.

Buber, Martin. 1958. *I and Thou*. Translated by R. G. Smith. New York: Charles Scribner's.

Bucke, Richard. 1967. *Cosmic Consciousness*. New York: E. P. Dutton.

Carter-Haar, Betsie. 1975. "Identity and Personal Freedom." *Synthesis* 2:1:2: 56–91.

Cassidy, Jude, and Phillip R. Shaver, eds. 1999. *Handbook of Attachment: Theory, Research, and Clinical Applications*. New York and London: Guilford Press.

Cunningham, Tom. 1986. *King Baby*. Center City, Minn.: Hazelden.

Deikman, A. 1982. *The Observing Self*. Boston: Beacon Press.

deMause, Lloyd, ed. 1974. *The History of Childhood: The Untold Story of Child Abuse*. New York: Peter Bedrick Books.

Djukic, Dragana. 1997. "No Need to Change the Egg Diagram." *Psicosintesi* 14:2: 38–40.

Epstein, Mark. 1995. *Thoughts without a Thinker*. New York: BasicBooks.

Fairbairn, W. Ronald D. 1986. *Psychoanalytic Studies of the Personality*. London, Henley, and Boston: Routledge & Kegan Paul.

Ferrucci, Piero. 1982. *What We May Be*. Los Angeles: Jeremy P. Tarcher.

Finley, J. 1988. "The Contemplative Attitude." Paper read at Course in Spiritual Direction, Los Angeles.

Firman, Dorothy, and David Klugman, eds. 1999. *Reflections on Ecopsychosynthesis*. Amherst, Mass.: Association for the Advancement of Psychosynthesis.

Firman, J., and J. Vargiu. 1977. "Dimensions of Growth." *Synthesis* 3/4: 60–120.

Firman, John. 1974. "Morphophobia and Morphophilia." Paper read at Psychosynthesis Professional Training Program, Palo Alto.

————. 1991. *"I" and Self: Re-Visioning Psychosynthesis*. Palo Alto, Calif.: Psychosynthesis Palo Alto.

Firman, John, and Ann Gila. 1997. *The Primal Wound: A Transpersonal View of Trauma, Addiction, and Growth*. Albany: State University of New York Press.

Firman, John, and Ann Russell. 1993. *What Is Psychosynthesis?* 2d ed. Palo Alto, Calif.: Psychosynthesis Palo Alto.

————. 1994. *Opening to the Inner Child: Recovering Authentic Personality*. Palo Alto, Calif.: Psychosynthesis Palo Alto.

Firman, John, and James Vargiu. 1980. "Personal and Transpersonal Growth: The Perspective of Psychosynthesis." Pp. 92–115 in *Transpersonal Psychotherapy*, ed. S. Boorstein. Palo Alto, Calif.: Science and Behavior Books.

First, Michael B., ed. 1994. *Diagnostic and Statistical Manual of Mental Disorders (DSM-IV)*. 4th ed. Washington, D.C.: American Psychiatric Association.

Fleischman, Paul R. 1990. *The Healing Spirit*. New York: Paragon House.

Freud, Anna. 1946. *The Ego and the Mechanisms of Defense*. New York: International Universities Press.

Freud, S. 1960. *The Ego and the Id.* New York and London: W.W. Norton.

Freud, Sigmund. 1965. *New Introductory Lectures on Psychoanalysis.* New York and London: W.W. Norton.

———. 1978. *The Question of Lay Analysis.* New York and London: W.W. Norton.

———. 1981. "Splitting of the Ego in the Process of Defence." Pp. 275–78 in *The Standard Edition of the Complete Psychological Works of Sigmund Freud.* Vol. 23. Edited by J. Strachey. London: The Hogarth Press and the Institute of Psychoanalysis.

Friedman, W. 1984. "Psychosynthesis, Psychoanalysis, and the Emerging Developmental Perspective in Psychotherapy." Pp. 31–46 in *Psychosynthesis in the Helping Professions: Now and for the Future,* ed. J. Weiser and T. Yeomans. Toronto, Canada: Department of Applied Psychology/Ontario Institute for Studies in Education.

Gay, Peter. 1988. *Freud: A Life for Our Time.* New York and London: W.W. Norton.

Goldberg, Carl. 1996. *Speaking with the Devil: Exploring Senseless Acts of Evil.* New York: Penguin Books.

Green, Alyce, and Elmer Green. 1977. *Beyond Biofeedback.* San Francisco: Delacorte Press/Seymour Lawrence.

Grof, Stanislav. 1985. *Beyond the Brain: Birth, Death, and Transcendence in Psychotherapy. SUNY Series in Transpersonal and Humanistic Psychology.* Edited by R. D. Mann and J. B. Mann. Albany: State University of New York Press.

Grof, Stanislav, and Christina Grof, eds. 1989. *Spiritual Emergency: When Personal Transformation Becomes a Crisis.* Los Angeles: Jeremy P. Tarcher.

Hardy, Jean. 1987. *A Psychology with a Soul: Psychosynthesis in Evolutionary Context.* New York: Routledge and Kegan Paul.

Haronian, Frank. 1974. "The Repression of the Sublime." *Synthesis* 1: 125–36.

———. 1983. Interview with Frank Haronian. *Psychosynthesis Digest* 2:1: 17–31.

Herman, Judith Lewis. 1992. *Trauma and Recovery, Basic Books.* New York: HarperCollins.

Herman, Judith Lewis, and Lisa Hirschman. 2000. *Father–Daughter Incest.* Cambridge, Mass., and London: Harvard University Press.

Higgins, Gina O'Connell. 1994. *Resilient Adults: Overcoming a Cruel Past.* San Francisco: Jossey-Bass.

Hillman, James. 1996. *The Soul's Code: In Search of Character and Calling.* New York: Random House.

Jacobi, Jolande. 1967. *The Way of Individuation, Meridian.* New York and Scarborough, Ont.: New American Library.

James, William. 1961. *The Varieties of Religious Experience.* New York: Collier Books.

Jamison, Kay Redfield. 1995. *An Unquiet Mind.* New York: Vintage Books.

Judy, Dwight H. 1991. *Christian Meditation and Inner Healing*. New York: Crossroad.

Jung, C. G. 1954. *The Development of Personality, Bollingen Series XX*. Princeton: Princeton University Press.

———. 1959. *Aion: Researches into the Phenomenology of the Self*. Princeton: Princeton University Press.

———. 1960. *The Structure and Dynamics of the Psyche*. 2d ed. 20 vols. Vol. 8, *Bollingen Series XX*. Edited by J. Read, M. Fordham, G. Adler, and W. McGuire. Princeton: Princeton University Press.

———. 1964. *Civilization in Transition*. Vol. 10, *Bollingen Series XX*. Edited by H. Read, M. Fordham, and G. Adler. New York: Pantheon Books.

———. 1966. *The Practice of Psychotherapy*. 2d ed. Vol. 16, *Bollingen Series XX*. Translated by R. F. C. Hull. Princeton: Princeton University Press.

———. 1969a. *The Archetypes and the Collective Unconscious*. Princeton: Princeton University Press.

———. 1969b. *Psychology and Religion: West and East*. Princeton: Princeton University Press.

———. 1971. *Psychological Types*. 20 vols. Vol. 6, *Bollingen Series XX*. Edited by J. Read, M. Fordham, G. Adler, and W. McGuire. Princeton: Princeton University Press.

Kaplan, Bert, ed. 1964. *The Inner World of Mental Illness: A Series of First-Person Accounts of What It Was Like*. Edited by G. Murphy. New York, Evanston, and London: Harper & Row.

Kapleau, Philip. 1966. *The Three Pillars of Zen*. New York: Harper & Row.

Keen, Sam. 1974. "The Golden Mean of Roberto Assagioli." *Psychology Today*, December.

Kegan, Robert. 1982. *The Evolving Self: Problem and Process in Human Development*. Cambridge, Mass., and London: Harvard University Press.

Kernberg, Otto. 1992. *Borderline Conditions and Pathological Narcissism*. Northvale, N.J., and London: Jason Aronson.

Klein, Melanie. 1975. *Envy and Gratitude and Other Works 1946–1963*. New York: Free Press, Macmillan.

Koestler, Arthur. 1978. *Janus: A Summing Up*. New York: Random House.

Kohut, H. 1977. *The Restoration of the Self*. Madison, Conn.: International Universities Press.

Kohut, Heinz. 1971. *The Analysis of the Self*. Vol. 4. *The Psychoanalytic Study of the Child*. Madison, Conn.: International Universities Press.

———. 1984. *How Does Analysis Cure?* Edited by A. Goldberg. Chicago and London: University of Chicago Press.

Kramer, Sheldon Z. 1988. "Psychosynthesis and Integrative Marital and Family Therapy." *Readings in Psychosynthesis: Theory, Process, & Practice* 2: 98–110.

————. 1995. *Transforming the Inner and Outer Family*. New York and London: Haworth Press.

Laing, R. D. 1965. *The Divided Self*. Baltimore: Penguin Books.

————. 1967. *The Politics of Experience*. New York: Ballantine Books.

Lao-tzu. 1968. *Tao Te Ching*. Translated by D. C. Lau. Baltimore: Penguin Books.

Laski, Marghanita. 1968. *Ecstasy: A Study of Some Secular and Religious Experiences*. New York: Greenwood Press.

Levoy, Gregg. 1997. *Callings: Finding and Following an Authentic Life*. New York: Harmony Books.

Lewis, C. S. 1955. *Surprised by Joy*. New York: Harcourt Brace Jovanovich.

Lifton, Robert Jay. 2000. *Destroying the World to Save It*. New York: Henry Holt.

Love, Patricia, and Jo Robinson. 1990. *The Emotional Incest Syndrome: What to Do When a Parent's Love Rules Your Life*. New York, Toronto, London, Sydney, and Auckland: Bantam Books.

Mahler, Margaret S., Fred Pine, and Anni Bergman. 1975. *The Psychological Birth of the Human Infant*. New York: Basic Books.

Marabini, Enrico, and Sofia Marabini. 1996. "Why Change the Egg Diagram?" *Psicosintesi* 13:1: 41–44.

Maslow, Abraham. 1954. *Motivation and Personality*. New York: Harper & Row.

————. 1962. *Toward a Psychology of Being*. Princeton: D. Van Nostrand.

————. 1971. *The Farther Reaches of Human Nature*. New York: Viking Press.

Masterson, James F. 1981. *The Narcissistic and Borderline Disorders*. New York: Brunner/Mazel.

May, R., E. Angel, and H. Ellenberger, eds. 1958. *Existence: A New Dimension in Psychiatry and Psychology*. New York: Basic Books.

McGuire, William, ed. 1974. *The Freud/Jung Letters*. Vol. XCIV, *Bollingen Series*. Princeton: Princeton University Press.

Meriam, Chris. 1994. *Digging up the Past: Object Relations and Subpersonalities*. Palo Alto, Calif.: Psychosynthesis Palo Alto.

————. 1996. *Empathic "I": Empathy in Psychosynthesis Therapy*. Palo Alto, Calif.: Psychosynthesis Palo Alto.

————. 1999. Personal communication.

Miller, Alice. 1981. *The Drama of the Gifted Child*. New York: Basic Books.

————. 1984a. *For Your Own Good: Hidden Cruelty in Child-Rearing and the Roots of Violence*. Translated by H. a. H. Hannum. New York: Farrar, Straus, Giroux.

————. 1984b. *Thou Shalt Not Be Aware: Society's Betrayal of the Child*. Translated by H. a. H. Hannum. New York and Scarborough, Ont.: New American Library.

———. 1991. *Breaking Down the Wall of Silence*. New York, London, Victoria, Toronto, and Auckland: Dutton.

———. 2001. *The Truth Will Set You Free: Overcoming Emotional Blindness and Finding Your True Adult Self*. New York: Basic Books.

Miller, Stuart. 1975. "Dialogue with the Higher Self." *Synthesis* 2:1:2: 122–39.

Mitchell, Stephen A. 1988. *Relational Concepts in Psychoanalysis*. Cambridge, Mass., and London: Harvard University Press.

Nelson, John E. 1994. *Healing the Split: Integrating Spirit into Our Understanding of the Mentally Ill. SUNY Series in the Philosophy of Psychology*. Edited by M. Washburn. Albany: State University of New York Press.

Nelson, John E., and Andrea Nelson. 1996. *Sacred Sorrows: Embracing and Transforming Depression*. Edited by J. P. Tarcher. New York: G. P. Putnam's Sons.

Neumann, Erich. 1973. *The Child: Structure and Dynamics of the Nascent Personality*. Translated by R. Manheim. London: Maresfield Library.

———. 1989. *The Place of Creation*. Vol. LXI, no. 3, *Bollingen Series*. Translated by H. Nagel, E. Rolfe, J. van Heurck, and K. Winston. Princeton: Princeton University Press.

Ogbonnaya, A. Okechukwu. 1994. "Person As Community: An African Understanding of the Person As an Intrapsychic Community." *Journal of Black Psychology* 20:1: 75–87.

O'Regan, Miceal. 1984. "Reflections on the Art of Disidentification." Pp. 44–49 in *Yearbook*, ed. J. Evans. London: Institute of Psychosynthesis.

Perls, Fritz. 1969. *Gestalt Therapy Verbatim*. Moab, Utah: Real People Press.

Perry, John. 1953. *The Self in Psychotic Process*. Berkeley: University of California Press.

———. 1974. *The Far Side of Madness*. Englewood Cliffs, N. J.: Prentice Hall.

———. 1976. *Roots of Renewal in Myth and Madness*. San Francisco: Jossey-Bass.

Piaget, Jean. 1976. *The Child and Reality*. New York: Penguin Books.

Platts, David Earl, ed. 1994. *International Psychosynthesis Directory 1994–1995*. London: Psychosynthesis & Education Trust.

Polster, Erving. 1995. *A Population of Selves: A Therapeutic Exploration of Personal Diversity*. San Francisco: Jossey-Bass.

Rhodes, Richard. 1999. *Why They Kill: The Discoveries of a Maverick Criminologist*. New York: Knopf.

Rindge, Jeanne Pontius. 1974. "Editorial Comment." *Human Dimensions* 3:4: 2.

Rosenthal, Gary. 1987. "Inflated by the Spirit." Pp. 305–19 in *Spiritual Choices*, ed. D. Anthony, B. Ecker, and K. Wilber. New York: Paragon House.

Rowan, John. 1990. *Subpersonalities: The People Inside Us*. London and New York: Routledge.

Rueffler, Margret. 1995a. *Our Inner Actors: The Theory and Application of Subpersonality Work in Psychosynthesis*. Geherenhof, Switzerland: PsychoPolitical Peace Institute Press.

―――. 1995b. "Transforming a National Unconscious." *Psicosintesi* 12:1: 27–32.

Sanville, Prilly. 1994. "Diversity." Paper read at Concord Institute, Concord.

Schaub, Richard, and Bonney Gulino Schaub. 1996. "Freedom in Jail: Assagioli's Notes." *Psicosintesi* 13:1: 19–22.

Schwartz, Richard C. 1995. *Internal Family Systems Therapy*. New York and London: Guilford Press.

Scotton, Bruce W., Allan B. Chinen, and John R. Battista. 1996. *Textbook of Transpersonal Psychiatry and Psychology*. New York: Basic Books, HarperCollins.

Shapiro, S. B. 1976. *The Selves Inside You*. Berkeley: Explorations Institute.

Simpkinson, Anne A. 1993. "Mindful Living." *Common Boundary* 2:4: 34–40.

Sliker, Gretchen. 1992. *Multiple Mind: Healing the Split in Psyche and World*. Boston and London: Shambhala.

Smith, Eugene. 1974. "Biography of Assagioli." *Human Dimensions* 3:4: 2.

Sterba, Richard. 1934. "The Fate of the Ego in Analytic Therapy." *The International Journal of Psycho-analysis* 15: 116–26.

Stern, D. 1985. *The Interpersonal World of the Infant*. New York: Basic Books.

Stolorow, Robert D., and George E. Atwood. 1992. *Contexts of Being: The Intersubjective Foundations of Psychological Life*. Hillsdale, N.Y., and London: Analytic Press.

Stolorow, Robert D., George E. Atwood, and Bernard Brandchaft, eds. 1994. *The Intersubjective Perspective*. Northvale, N.J., and London: Jason Aronson.

Stolorow, Robert D., Bernard Brandchaft, and George E. Atwood. 1987. *Psychoanalytic Treatment: An Intersubjective Approach*. Hillsdale, N.J., Hove and London: Analytic Press.

Stone, Hal, and Sidra Winkelman. 1985. *Embracing Our Selves*. Marina del Rey, Calif.: Devorss.

Tackett, Victoria. 1988. "Treating Mental and Emotional Abuse." Pp. 15–29 in *Readings in Psychosynthesis: Theory, Process, & Practice*, ed. J. Weiser and T. Yeomans. Toronto: Department of Applied Psychology/Ontario Institute for Studies in Education.

Terr, Lenore. 1990. *Too Scared to Cry*. New York: Harper & Row.

―――. 1994. *Unchained Memories: True Stories of Traumatic Memories, Lost and Found*. New York: Basic Books.

Tuchman, Barbara W. 1978. *A Distant Mirror*. New York: Ballantine Books.

Van der Kolk, Bessel A. 1987. *Psychological Trauma*. Washington, D.C.: American Psychiatric Press.

Van der Kolk, Bessel A., Alexander C. McFarlane, and Lars Weisaeth, eds. 1996. *Traumatic Stress: The Effects of Overwhelming Experience on Mind, Body, and Society*. New York and London: Guilford Press.

Vargiu, J., ed. 1974a. *Synthesis 1, the Realization of the Self*. Redwood City, Calif.: Synthesis Press.

———, ed. 1975. *Synthesis 2, the Realization of the Self*. Redwood City, Calif.: Synthesis Press.

Vargiu, James. 1974b. "Subpersonalities." *Synthesis* 1:1:1: 52–90.

———. 1977. Creativity. *Synthesis* 3/4:17–53.

Vaughan, Frances. 1985. *The Inward Arc, New Science Library*. Boston and London: Shambhala.

Washburn, Michael. 1988. *The Ego and the Dynamic Ground*. Albany: State University of New York Press.

———. 1994. *Transpersonal Psychology in Psychoanalytic Perspective, Philosophy of Psychology*. Albany: State University of New York Press.

Watkins, John G., and Helen H. Watkins. 1997. *Ego States: Theory and Therapy*. New York and London: W.W. Norton.

Weiser, J., and T. Yeomans, eds. 1984. *Psychosynthesis in the Helping Professions: Now and for the Future*. Toronto: Department of Applied Psychology/Ontario Institute for Studies in Education.

———, eds. 1985. *Readings in Psychosynthesis: Theory, Process, & Practice*. Vol. 1. Toronto: Department of Applied Psychology/Ontario Institute for Studies in Education.

———, eds. 1988. *Readings in Psychosynthesis: Theory, Process, & Practice*. Vol. 2. Toronto: Department of Applied Psychology/Ontario Institute for Studies in Education.

Welwood, John. 2000. *Toward a Psychology of Awakening: Buddhism, Psychotherapy, and the Path of Personal and Spiritual Transformation*. Boston and London: Shambhala.

Whitfield, Charles L. 1991. *Co-dependence: Healing the Human Condition*. Deerfield Beach, Fla.: Health Communications.

———. 1995. *Memory and Abuse: Remembering and Healing the Effects of Trauma*. Deerfield Beach, Fla.: Health Communications, Inc.

Whitmore, Diana. 1991. *Psychosynthesis Counselling in Action*. Edited by W. Dryden. *Counselling in Action*. London: Sage.

Wilber, K., J. Engler, and D. Brown. 1986. *Transformations of Consciousness*. Boston: Shambhala.

Wilber, Ken. 1977. *The Spectrum of Consciousness*. Wheaton, Ill.: Theosophical Publishing.

———. 1996. *A Brief History of Everything*. Boston and London: Shambhala.

———. 2000. *Integral Psychology: Consciousness, Spirit, Psychology, Therapy.* Boston and London: Shambhala.

Wilson, Colin. 1972. *New Pathways in Psychology: Maslow and the Post–Freudian Revolution.* New York: Taplinger.

Winnicott, D. W. 1984. *Deprivation and Delinquency.* London and New York: Routledge.

———. 1987. *The Maturational Processes and the Facilitating Environment.* London: Hogarth Press and the Institute of Psycho-analysis.

———. 1988. *Playing and Reality.* London: Penguin Books.

———. 1989. "Fear of Breakdown." Pp. 87–95 in *Psycho-Analytic Explorations*, ed. C. Winnicott, R. Shepherd, and M. Davis. Cambridge: Harvard University Press.

Yeomans, Thomas. 1999. *Soul on Earth: Readings in Spiritual Psychology.* Concord, Mass.: The Concord Institute.

Zaehner, R. C. 1972. *Zen, Drugs and Mysticism.* New York: Pantheon Books, Random House.

INDEX